The Essentials of Contraceptive Technology

Robert A. Hatcher, M.D., M.P.H.
Ward Rinehart
Richard Blackburn
Judith S. Geller
James D. Shelton, M.D., M.P.H.

Population Information Program
Center for Communication Programs
The Johns Hopkins University
School of Public Health

January 2001

This book was planned, written, and edited by:

Robert A. Hatcher, M.D., M.P.H., Professor of Gynecology and Obstetrics, Emory University School of Medicine

Ward Rinehart, Project Director, Population Information Program, Center for Communication Programs, The Johns Hopkins University School of Public Health

Richard Blackburn, Senior Research Analyst, **Population Reports**, Population Information Program, Center for Communication Programs, The Johns Hopkins University School of Public Health

Judith S. Geller, Research Analyst, **Population Reports**, Population Information Program, Center for Communication Programs, The Johns Hopkins University School of Public Health

James D. Shelton, M.D., M.P.H., Senior Medical Scientist, Office of Population, United States Agency for International Development.

©2001 Robert A. Hatcher and the Johns Hopkins Center for Communication Programs

The authors and publisher invite you to reproduce and otherwise use original material in this book to inform health care providers, their clients, and the public and to improve the quality of reproductive health care. There is no charge, and you do not need permission. Please credit the authors and publisher; see suggested citation inside front cover. Also, we would like to receive a copy of any publication based on parts of this handbook. If, however, you want to use materials in this handbook (including illustrations) that are credited to other sources, you must obtain permission from the original sources. We encourage you to allow others to use your materials free of charge as well, so that information about good reproductive health care can reach as many people as possible.

Contents

Forewords from WHO and UNFPA iv
Preface from USAID vi
Introduction and Dedication viii
Acknowledgments xi

Chapter 1. How to Use This Book 1–1
Chapter 2. Family Planning Helps Everyone 2–1
Chapter 3. Counseling 3–1
Chapter 4. Important Information 4–1
    Who Provides Family Planning and Where? 4–3
    How to Tell That a Woman Is Not Pregnant 4–6
    Family Planning for the Breastfeeding Woman 4–8
    Infection Prevention in the Clinic 4–10
    Medical Conditions and Method Choice 4–13
    Effectiveness of Family Planning Methods 4–19
    How Important Are Various Procedures? 4–21
Chapter 5. Low-Dose Combined Oral Contraceptives 5–1
Chapter 6. Progestin-Only Oral Contraceptives 6–1
Chapter 7. DMPA Injectable Contraceptive 7–1
Chapter 8. Norplant Implants 8–1
Chapter 9. Female Sterilization 9–1
Chapter 10. Vasectomy 10–1
Chapter 11. Condoms 11–1
Chapter 12. Intrauterine Devices (IUDs) 12–1
Chapter 13. Vaginal Methods 13–1
Chapter 14. Fertility Awareness-Based Methods 14–1
Chapter 15. Lactational Amenorrhea Method (LAM) 15–1
Chapter 16. Sexually Transmitted Diseases
Including HIV/AIDS 16–1

Table: WHO Medical Eligibility Criteria . . . . Appendix: A–1
Suggested Reading . . . . Appendix: A–9
Glossary . . . . Appendix: A–13
Index . . . . Index: I–1
List of Handbook Distributors . . . . Inside back cover

Foreword from WHO

This handbook, *The Essentials of Contraceptive Technology*, which aims at providing state-of-the-art information on family planning methods to health care providers around the world, is a significant contribution to the reproductive health field. The handbook uses a simple, client-centred approach to the provision of family planning care. It covers a wide range of topics that will help to enable women and men to use the method of their choice effectively and with satisfaction while safeguarding against avoidable negative health effects. It helps health care providers give their clients simple but appropriate information and advice on method use and other reproductive health concerns. Further, it offers guidance for appropriate procedures in offering family planning methods and helping continuing users.

This handbook also provides useful guidance to people concerned with improving family planning standards and practices. It is based on growing international consensus on critical medical, epidemiological and clinical research findings and their meaning for reproductive health care providers and clients. The World Health Organization's latest recommendations for revising medical eligibility criteria for contraceptive use are a major contribution to that consensus and a cornerstone of this handbook. These recommendations can lead to major improvements in the way services are provided.

The World Health Organization, through the Family Planning and Population Unit of the Division of Reproductive Health, is pleased to have collaborated with the authors and the Population Information Program at the Johns Hopkins Center for Communication Programs in the production of this handbook supported by the US Agency for International Development. This work is an expression of the common aims of all three institutions and, indeed, of family planning providers everywhere, namely, to help all men and women achieve one of their most fundamental freedoms and human rights—the ability to plan their families by choosing freely the number and spacing of their children.

Dr. Tomris Türmen
Executive Director
Family and Reproductive Health
World Health Organization
Geneva

Foreword from UNFPA

The International Conference on Population and Development held in Cairo, Egypt, in 1994 was a landmark in that, for the first time, the concept of reproductive health and reproductive rights was clearly defined. For the first time the concerns of gender equity, equality and women's empowerment were recognized as essential components of reproductive rights. For the first time, the linkages between population, sustained economic growth and sustainable development were articulated.

Reproductive health implies that people are able to have a satisfying and safe sex life and that they have the capability to reproduce and the freedom to decide if, when and how often to do so. Implicit in this last condition is the right of men and women to be informed and to have access to safe, effective, affordable and acceptable methods of family planning of their choice. Similarly, reproductive rights rest on the recognition of the basic right of all couples to decide freely and responsibly the number, spacing and timing of their children and to have the information and means to do so, and the right to attain the highest standard of sexual and reproductive health.

Family planning information and services are therefore a critical means for the articulation and attainment of reproductive rights and reproductive health, and a central component of reproductive health programmes.

This handbook will be a valuable resource for clinic-based family planning providers, and will enable them to deliver family planning services from a reproductive health perspective, bearing in mind the differing contraceptive needs of the life cycle. The handbook represents an important tool for the spread of correct and timely information to young people and adults allowing individuals and couples to articulate their reproductive rights and enjoy optimal reproductive health.

Sathuramiah L. N. Rao
Director
Technical and Evaluation Division
United Nations Population Fund
New York

Preface from USAID

In the 1990s the many people around the world who are committed to improving access and quality of family planning and related reproductive health services are working together more closely than ever. Researchers, program managers, policy-makers, educators, and communicators all are cooperating to help providers everywhere do their jobs more successfully. The United States Agency for International Development (USAID) has been pleased to join in this growing international collaboration. As part of this effort, *The Essentials of Contraceptive Technology* handbook is designed to provide accurate and up-do-date information that will help clinic-based providers offer readily accessible, good-quality care. This handbook focuses on the major contraceptive methods and how they are provided in clinics and similar settings. It also addresses preventing and treating sexually transmitted diseases.

Ready access to good-quality care is key to the success of family planning and related reproductive health services. With *ready access,* people can easily obtain safe and effective services that meet their needs, free from unreasonable barriers. *Good-quality care* includes courteous, supportive interactions that help clients express their needs and make informed choices *and* the technical knowledge and skills to provide family planning methods and other reproductive health care effectively and safely. Providers who offer ready access to good-quality care can see their success in terms of healthy, satisfied clients who use family planning longer and more effectively.

For more than 30 years of helping providers, USAID has supported a wide range of efforts to improve access and quality of family planning and related reproductive health services. These efforts have produced new ways to deliver supplies and services conveniently and safely, wider choice of contraceptive methods, providers well-trained in technical and communication skills, more types of providers who offer family planning and other reproductive health care, better communication with clients and the public, accurate and easy-to-use information for providers and policy-makers, and improved program management, research, and evaluation.

The Essentials of Contraceptive Technology has been prepared as a collaborative effort involving Dr. Robert A. Hatcher of the Emory University School of Medicine and members of the staff of the journal **Population Reports**, which is published by the Population Information Program at the Johns Hopkins Center for Communication Programs, a part of the Johns Hopkins University School of Public Health. The handbook draws on the work of several international groups dedicated to updating recommendations for family planning guidelines and practices—particularly the scientific working group on medical eligibility criteria, organized by the World Health Organization, and the Technical Guidance/Competence Working Group, begun by USAID and its Cooperating Agencies and now expanded to include many other experts. The authors also had help from a great many expert reviewers and advisors, who contributed their knowledge, the fruits of their work, and the wisdom of their experience in many areas.

USAID is pleased to support the development and distribution of this handbook. We hope that it will aid clinic-based providers as they help clients make informed choices and will serve as a useful resource to all concerned with helping women and men around the world achieve their reproductive goals.

Elizabeth S. Maguire
Director

Dr. James D. Shelton
Senior Medical Scientist

Office of Population, Center for Population, Health and Nutrition
United States Agency for International Development, Washington, D.C.

Introduction and Dedication

amily planning is making great progress. During the past several decades we have moved ahead in many ways:

- Family planning is now seen as a human right—basic to human dignity. People and governments around the world understand this.

- Nearly everyone now knows about family planning. Most people also know of some family planning methods.

- Family planning has community support. People expect that most others in their community practice family planning, and they approve.

- Most people use family planning. At any one time, more than half of the world's married couples are family planning users.

This handbook covers family planning methods and services. Great progress has been made in these areas, too. As family planning providers, we can offer more choices to more people. People can use family planning more effectively and more safely.

- Couples now can choose from more methods. These include injectables, implants, female and male sterilization, new IUDs, oral contraceptives, condoms, various spermicides, diaphragms, and cervical caps. We have a better understanding of fertility awareness-based methods (modern versions of the rhythm method) and breastfeeding. Now they can be used to prevent pregnancy more effectively.

- We have learned that almost everyone can use modern family planning methods safely. At the same time, we are better able to single out the people who should not use certain methods. We also know that, for most methods, most clients do not require physical examinations or laboratory tests.

- We have discovered important health benefits of some family planning methods, besides preventing unintended pregnancies. For example, combined oral contraceptives help stop anemia, reduce pelvic inflammatory disease, decrease menstrual cramps and pain, and even help prevent several types of cancer.

- Condoms help prevent sexually transmitted diseases (STDs) and other infections, especially when used every time. Spermicides, diaphragms, and cervical caps for women also may help somewhat. Many family planning clients need protection from STDs, including HIV/AIDS. Family planning providers are seeing that, and they are helping more clients prevent STDs.

- Many different types of people now provide family planning supplies, services, and information. For example, many different kinds of health professionals, and not just doctors, provide most methods in clinics and in communities. Shopkeepers sell family planning supplies. Community members distribute supplies and help their neighbors.

- We are doing a better job of telling people about family planning and helping them make reproductive health decisions. We are helping them make informed choices. We do this in face-to-face discussion and counseling, through radio, television, and newspapers, and in community events.

- We are making it easy for people to get family planning and other reproductive health care. We are removing unnecessary barriers of all kinds. These barriers have included lack of information, not enough service points, limited hours, few methods, not enough supplies, restrictions on who can be served, out-of-date medical eligibility criteria ("contraindications"), and required tests or physical exams when these did not help decide on a method or make its use safer, and clients did not want them. To make family planning easy, we are giving people more choices—choices among family planning methods, choices among key reproductive health services, choices among places and times to obtain services and supplies, choices among information sources, and choices among the type of personnel who provide care. The more choices that people have, the better they can find what they need to protect their reproductive health.

- We are learning that quality makes a difference. The quality of family planning services affects whether clients can use methods effectively. Quality affects whether clients continue to use family planning. Quality even affects whether people start family planning at all. This handbook is meant to help providers offer good-quality family planning services.

Not every issue has been settled, however. New scientific findings will keep coming out. Sometimes these findings may cause controversy. They will need to be studied, interpreted, and discussed. Decisions will have to be made about changing family planning services and information. This process will help us to keep improving family planning methods and services.

The information in this handbook reflects the latest and most complete scientific understanding. This book represents the thinking of family planning leaders and experts around the world. Many of them helped prepare this book. Their names are listed on the next page.

Many people can use this book. Trainers can use it to plan and carry out training. Program managers can use it to update procedures and standards. Most of all, however, this book is meant for—and dedicated to—the providers all over the world who, every day, help people choose and use family planning.

The authors

Acknowledgments

The wisdom, commitment, and effort of many people made this handbook possible.

Many people provided valuable comments and contributions: Frank Alvarez, Elliott Austin, Sriani Basnayake, Paul Blumenthal, Patricia Bright, David W. Buchholz, Pierre Buekens, Meena Cabral, Charles S. Carignan, Willard Cates, Jr., Shirley Coly, Anne W. Compton, Joseph deGraft-Johnson, Gina Dallabetta, Grace Ebun Delano, Juan Díaz, Soledad Diaz, Laneta Dorflinger, Gaston Farr, Betty L. Farrell, Paul Feldblum, Monica Gaines, Sally Girvin, Stephen M. Goldstein, Ronald H. Gray, David A. Grimes, Joanne Grossi, Gary S. Grubb, Felicia Guest, Pamela Beyer Harper, Philip D. Harvey, Q.M. Islam, Sarah Keller, Theodore King, Nilgun Kircalioğlu, Deborah Kowal, Miriam Labbok, O.A. Ladipo, Virginia Lamprecht, Robert Lande, Ronnie Lovich, Enriquito Lu, Tapani Luukkainen, Jill Mathis, Margaret McCann, Noel McIntosh, Grace Mtawali, Elaine Murphy, Emma Ottolenghi, Juan Palmore, Susan Palmore, Bonnie Pedersen, Bert Peterson, Manuel Pina, Phyllis Tilson Piotrow, Linda Potter, Malcolm Potts, Lisa Rarick, Elizabeth Robinson, Ron Roddy, Sharon Rudy, Cynthia Salter, Harshad Sanghvi, Lois Schaefer, Pamela Schwingl, Pramilla Senanayake, Willibrord Shasha, Jennifer Smith, Jeff Spieler, Cynthia Steele, Linda Tietjen, James Trussell, Ibrahim Türkmenoğlu, Marcel Vekemans, Cynthia Visness, Nancy Williamson, Anne Wilson, Judith Winkler, and Johanna Zacharias.

The technical consensus on medical eligibility criteria developed by the World Health Organization scientific working group on Improving Access to Quality Care in Family Planning and the consensus on updating practices for providing family planning developed by the Technical Guidance/Competence Working Group, organized by the US Agency for International Development and its Cooperating Agencies, are foundation stones of this handbook. So is the work of many other organizations and agencies that have addressed the needs of family planning professionals for practical technical guidance. Valuable publications from some of these groups are listed in the Suggested Reading at the end of this book. In particular, *Contraceptive Technology*, 16th edition, by Robert A. Hatcher, James Trussell, Felicia Stewart, Gary K. Stewart, Deborah Kowal, Felicia Guest, Willard Cates, Jr., and Michael S. Policar, was the starting point for this handbook.

Throughout the development of the handbook, Marcia Angle, Douglas Huber, Roy Jacobstein, and Roberto Rivera offered helpful guidance and assistance.

Under its Maximizing Access and Quality (MAQ) initiative, the US Agency for International Development is playing a leading role in improving family planning and other reproductive health care services. The MAQ initiative has focused attention on services that both respond to the needs of clients and meet scientifically valid criteria for technical quality. This handbook is both a product of that initiative and a contribution to it.

This handbook was made possible through support provided by G/PHN/POP/CMT, Global, United States Agency for International Development, under the terms of Grant No. HRN–A–00–97–00009–00. The opinions expressed herein are those of the authors and do not necessarily reflect the views of the US Agency for International Development.

Chapter 1
How to Use This Book

This handbook is for family planning and reproductive health care providers who work in clinics and other health care facilities. It contains practical information about family planning methods, how to provide them, and how to help clients use them.

You can use this book:

- To look up information in order to serve your clients,
- For background information and study on your own,
- In training courses,
- When you talk to community groups,
- When you prepare information materials for the public or clients,
- To help develop policies, guidelines, procedures, and training materials.

Carry it with you, and consult it often!

Many different people can learn from this book. Please share it with clients, policy-makers, journalists, and volunteers as well as with other health care providers.

The more people who have this book, the more useful it will be. If you have extra copies, please share them with co-workers. You can order more copies, too. This handbook is free of charge to health care providers and programs in developing countries. See the list of distributors inside the back cover. Also, you are welcome to photocopy pages of this book and give the copies to others.

You can adapt and add to this handbook. The handbook has been written for family planning providers all over the world. The situation in your area or your program may call for special information and guidance.

Please tell us how you are using this handbook. Tell us what is helpful and what causes problems. Tell us what should be clearer, what should be changed, and what should be added. With your help, we will be able to make this handbook better in the future.

How to Find Information in This Book

Finding the right chapter. There are 16 chapters in this book, including one chapter for each major family planning method. These methods are listed on the back cover. You can line up the name of the method on the back cover with the ink on the edge of the pages. That way you can turn quickly to the chapter on that method.

Finding information in the chapter. Most chapters about family planning methods have the same sections in them. There are major sections in each chapter and then some subsections. These sections and subsections are always in the same order.

The standard sections and subsections are listed below, and their contents are described:

Key Points—On page 1 of each chapter, a short list of the most important information about the method.

Table of Contents—On page 2 of each chapter. (Note that page numbers are made up of the chapter number and then a page number. For example, this is page 1–2—that is, Chapter 1, page 2.)

Introduction—Brief description of the method and some of its common names.

Deciding About the Method—Information to help decide if the method suits the specific client.

- **How Does It Work?**—How the method prevents pregnancy.

- **Advantages and Disadvantages**—The client may want to consider these. Lists of disadvantages begin with common side effects, if there are any; these are printed in brown.

- **Medical Eligibility Checklist**—After the client has freely chosen a method, this checklist helps make sure that no medical conditions prevent or restrict use of that method.

Starting the Method—Information on providing a new method and explaining how to use it.

- **When to Start?**—When a client can start using the method. This may depend on her or his situation.

- **Providing the Method**—Procedures for providing the new method.

- **Explaining How to Use the Method**—Instructions for the new user. These instructions often include what to do about side effects and reasons to see a doctor or nurse. These pages have brown borders.

Following Up—Information on what to ask and do during later visits.

- **Helping Clients at Any Routine Return Visit**—Procedures when a returning client has no problems.

- **Managing Any Problems**—Suggestions for helping when a returning client has problems with the method.

Important Information for the User to Remember—Brief information to help the client. This information can be copied or adapted and then given to clients.

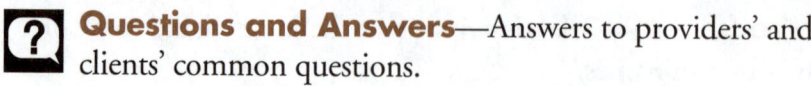 **Questions and Answers**—Answers to providers' and clients' common questions.

In each chapter the main sections are marked with the same small symbols shown above and on page 1–3. The name of the section and method and the symbol for that section are printed at the bottom of each righthand page.

Decision tables appear throughout the chapters. The example below shows how to use these tables:

First look in this column	**Then look in this column**
Find here the client's situation, condition, or problem.	Find here the appropriate information or recommended action that fits the client's situation, condition, or problem.

Besides the chapters on family planning methods (Chapters 5 to 15), this book contains several other chapters. Chapter 2 summarizes benefits of family planning. Chapter 3 briefly describes family planning counseling. Chapter 4 covers various information that applies to many different clients and various family planning methods. Other chapters often refer to information in Chapter 4. Chapter 16 covers sexually transmitted diseases including HIV/AIDS.

A **wall chart** about family planning methods is available from the Johns Hopkins Population Information Program (JHU/PIP). (If you would like copies, write to JHU/PIP at the address on the inside front cover of this book. Please include shipping address and number of copies you require.) You can hang the wall chart in a client waiting area. Clients can look at the chart and see for themselves which methods may suit them best. Then they will be better prepared to talk with a provider. You are welcome to translate this wall chart and any other text into the languages of your area. You also may want to add or change text to suit your clients' needs and situations.

At the back of the book are a table of medical eligibility criteria, a list of suggested reading, a glossary of medical terms, and an index.

Special Notes on Certain Standard Features of Each Chapter

DECIDING ABOUT THE METHOD:
How Effective?

This handbook describes the effectiveness of most family planning methods in terms of *the likelihood of pregnancy in the first year of using the method.* The likelihood of pregnancy is often reported in two ways:

Effectiveness as commonly used. This is the typical, or average likelihood of pregnancy for all users taken together, whether or not they use the method correctly and consistently.

Effectiveness when used correctly and consistently. This is the lowest likelihood of pregnancy reported in reliable studies. This figure is about the best that a client could hope for.

If the user's behavior has little or no effect on the likelihood of pregnancy—as with *Norplant* implants or female sterilization, for example—only one pregnancy rate is reported.

Most estimates of the likelihood of pregnancy in this book were made by James Trussell for publication in Hatcher et al. 1998. They are based on scientific reports. Most of these reports come from developed countries. Estimates for combined oral contraceptives (Chapter 5), various IUDs other than the TCu-380A (Chapter 12), and fertility awareness-based methods (Chapter 14) *as commonly used* come from Moreno and Goldman 1991. They are based on findings of Demographic and Health Surveys in developing countries. Estimates for female sterilization come from a large US study by Peterson et al. published in 1996. Except for fertility awareness-based methods, these estimates are the same or nearly the same as Trussell's. Estimates for progestin-only oral contraceptives (Chapter 6) come from McCann and Potter 1994. Estimates for LAM (Chapter 15) come from Labbok et al. 1994.[1]

DECIDING ABOUT THE METHOD:
Advantages and Disadvantages

Advantages and disadvantages are listed for each family planning method. These lists cover the most important characteristics and effects of the method. Common side effects are printed in brown under "Disadvantages." With the provider's help, the *client* considers how these advantages and disadvantages apply to her or his own situation. Then the *client* can make an informed choice about whether the method meets her or his needs.

Not all advantages and disadvantages apply to every client. Also, a disadvantage to one person may be an advantage to another person. Still, with these lists, a provider can help a client choose whether or not to use that method.

In the Advantages and Disadvantages lists, the word "may" means that the statement is based on theories or on similarity with another family planning method. There is no conclusive evidence from studies of people using this method, however. For example, "progestin-only injectables *may* help prevent ovarian cancer." (They are similar to combined oral contraceptives.) When the word "may" is *not* used, it means that there *is* direct evidence from studies of users. For example, "progestin-only injectables help prevent endometrial cancer."

DECIDING ABOUT THE METHOD:
Medical Eligibility Checklist

Medical Eligibility Checklists appear in most chapters. They list the most important questions for medical screening of clients. These questions are based on recent recommendations from a World Health Organization (WHO) Scientific Working Group.[2] This WHO Scientific Working Group reviewed the latest scientific information and then made its recommendations. The checklist asks clients about characteristics—for example, whether a woman is breastfeeding—and about **known** medical conditions—for example, high blood pressure.

Considering the client's answers, the provider decides whether any medical conditions prevent or restrict the client's use of the method. The Working Group called these characteristics and conditions "medical eligibility criteria." Medical eligibility criteria often have been called "contraindications" when they limit use of a method.

The questions in each medical eligibility checklist are examples. Each program can decide what questions are most important in its own area. Also, the WHO Working Group expects each program to choose the most suitable *means* of screening for these conditions. Information from the client (client history) will often be the best approach, according to the Working Group. Generally, clinical and laboratory tests are not routinely needed for safe use of methods. On occasion, a client's medical history may call for specific tests.

A detailed table covering WHO medical eligibility criteria for major family planning methods appears in the Appendix after Chapter 16.

Information in parts of Chapters 3 through 15, especially in the sections "Deciding About the Method: When to Start" and "Following Up: Managing Any Problems," is based on the work of the Technical Guidance/Competence Working Group. This group, with support from the United States Agency for International Development, has generated expert consensus on updating selected practices in contraceptive use.[3] A condensed version of the Working Group's reports appears in **Population Reports**, *Family Planning Methods: New Guidance*, available from the Johns Hopkins Population Information Program at the address inside the front cover.

1. Trussell, J. Contraceptive efficacy. In: Hatcher et al. Contraceptive technology (17th revised edition). New York, Irvington, 1998. In press.

    Labbok, M., Cooney, K. and Coly, S. Guidelines: Breastfeeding, family planning, and the lactational amenorrhea method—LAM. Washington, D.C., Georgetown University, Institute for Reproductive Health, 1994. 18 p.

    McCann, M.F. and Potter, L.S. Progestin-only oral contraception: A comprehensive review. Contraception 50(6) (Supplement 1): S1–S195. December 1994.

    Moreno, L. and Goldman, N. Contraceptive failure rates in developing countries: Evidence from the Demographic and Health Surveys. International Family Planning Perspectives 17(2): 44-49. June 1991.

    Peterson, H.B., Xia, Z., Hughes, J.M., Wilcox, L.S., Tylor, L.R., and Trussell, J. The risk of pregnancy after tubal sterilization: Findings from the U.S. Collaborative Review of Sterilization. American Journal of Obstetrics and Gynecology 174: 1161-1170. 1996.

2. World Health Organization (WHO). Improving access to quality care in family planning: Medical eligibility criteria for contraceptive use. Geneva, WHO, Family and Reproductive Health, 1996.

3. Technical Guidance/Competence Working Group. Recommendations for updating selected practices in contraceptive use, vols. 1 and 2. Chapel Hill, North Carolina, Program for International Training in Health, University of North Carolina, 1994 and 1997.

The Essentials of Contraceptive Technology
Wall Chart

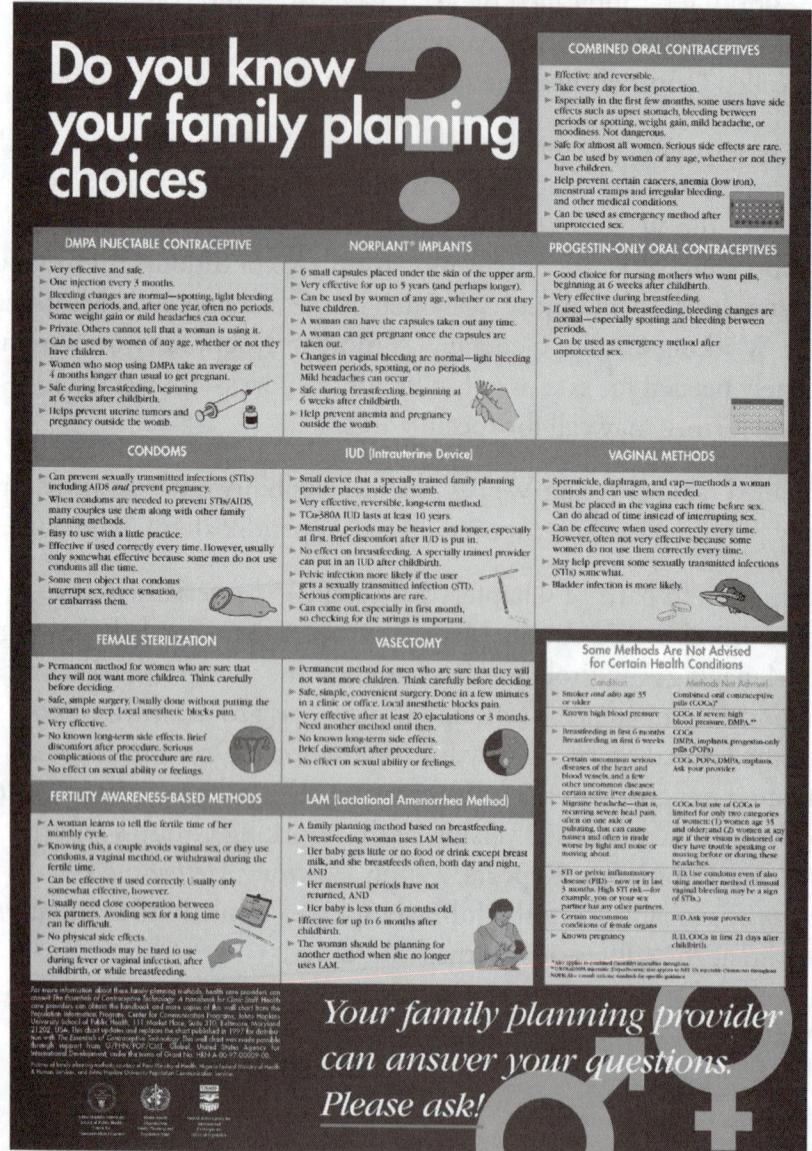

Free for readers in developing countries

To order copies, please remit your complete mailing address, telephone number, fax number, and number of copies required to: Population Information Program, Center for Communication Programs, Johns Hopkins School of Public Health, 111 Market Place, Suite 310, Baltimore, Maryland, 21202, USA; Fax: (410) 659-6266; E-mail: orders@jhuccp.org or order online at http://www.jhuccp.org/wallchart.stm.

Chapter 2
Family Planning Helps Everyone

Family planning providers can be proud of their work because family planning helps everyone. Here are some of the ways:

Women. Family planning helps women protect themselves from unwanted pregnancies. Since the 1960s family planning programs have helped women around the world avoid 400 million unwanted pregnancies. As a result, many women's lives have been saved from high-risk pregnancies or unsafe abortions. If all women could avoid high-risk pregnancies, the number of maternal deaths could fall by one-quarter. Also, many family planning methods have other health benefits. For example, some hormonal methods help prevent certain cancers, and condoms help prevent sexually transmitted diseases, including HIV/AIDS.

Children. Family planning saves the lives of children by helping women space births. Between 13 and 15 million children under age 5 die each year. If all children were born at least 2 years apart, 3 to 4 million of these deaths would be avoided.

Men. Family planning helps men—and women—care for their families. Men around the world say that planning their families helps them to provide a better life for their families.

Families. Family planning improves family well-being. Couples with fewer children are better able to provide them with enough food, clothing, housing, and schooling.

Nations. Family planning helps nations develop. In countries where women are having far fewer children than their mothers did, people's economic situations are improving faster than in most other countries.

The earth. If couples have fewer children in the future, the world's current population of 5.9 billion people will avoid doubling in less than 50 years. Future demands on natural resources such as water and fertile soil will be less. Everyone will have a better opportunity for a good life.

For this free colorful poster illustrating how "Family Planning Helps Everyone," please write to the Population Information Program at the address inside the front cover.

Chapter 3
Counseling

Counseling is crucial. Through counseling, providers help clients make and carry out their own choices about reproductive health and family planning. Good counseling makes clients more satisfied. Good counseling also helps clients use family planning longer and more successfully.

What is needed for good counseling? Particularly for new clients who are choosing a new family planning method, there are *6 principles*, *topics* to cover,* and *steps* in the counseling process. Although these are described separately here, during counseling all are woven together.

Good counseling does not have to take a lot of time, especially if information is tailored to the client's needs. Good counseling does take training and an attitude of caring and respect for clients.

6 Principles

1. **Treat each client well.** The provider is polite, shows respect for every client, and creates a feeling of trust. The provider shows the client that she or he can speak openly, even about sensitive matters. The provider, too, speaks openly and answers questions patiently and fully. Also, the provider assures the client that nothing she or he says will be discussed with others inside or outside the clinic.

2. **Interact.** The provider **listens**, learns, and responds to the client. Each client is a different person. A provider can help best by understanding

---

*The 6 principles and 6 topics are adapted from: Murphy, E.M. and Steele, C. Client-provider interactions in family planning services. In: Technical Guidance/Competence Working Group. Recommendations for updating selected practices in contraceptive use. Vol. 2. Chapel Hill, NC, INTRAH, 1997. p. 187–194.

that person's needs, concerns, and situation. Therefore the provider encourages clients to talk and ask questions.

3. **Tailor information to the client.** Listening to the client, the provider learns what information each client needs. Also, the stage of a person's life suggests what information may be most important. For example, a young, newly married woman may want to know more about temporary methods for birth spacing. An older woman may want to know more about female sterilization and vasectomy. A young, unmarried man or woman may need to know more about avoiding sexually transmitted diseases (STDs). The provider gives the information accurately in language that the client understands.

Also, the provider helps the client understand how information applies to *his or her own* personal situation and daily life. This *personalizing* of information bridges the gap between the provider's knowledge and the client's understanding.

4. **Avoid too much information.** Clients need information to make informed choices (see page 3–3). But no client can use all information about every family planning method. Too much information makes it hard to remember really important information. This has been called "information overload." Also, when the provider spends all the time giving information, little time is left for discussion or for the client's questions, concerns, and opinions.

5. **Provide the method that the client wants.** The provider helps clients make their own informed choices (see page 3–3), and the provider respects those choices—even if a client decides against using family planning or puts off a decision. Most new clients already have a family planning method in mind. Good counseling about method choice starts with that method. Then, in the course of counseling, the provider checks whether the client has conditions that might make use of the method not medically appropriate as well as whether the client understands the method and how it is used. Counseling also addresses advantages and disadvantages, health benefits, risks, and side effects. The provider also may help the client think about other, similar methods and compare them. In this way the provider makes sure that the client is

(Continued on page 3–4.)

What Does "Informed Choice" Mean?

When a person freely makes a thought-out decision based on accurate, useful information, this is an informed choice. One important purpose of family planning counseling is to help the client make informed choices about reproductive health and family planning.

"**Informed**" means that:

- **Clients have the clear, accurate, and specific information that they need** to make their own reproductive choices including a choice among family planning methods. Good-quality family planning programs can explain each family planning method as needed—without information overload—and can help clients use each method effectively and safely.

- **Clients understand their own needs** because they have thought about their own situations. Through person-to-person discussions and counseling and through mass-media messages, good-quality family planning programs help clients match family planning methods with their needs.

"**Choice**" means that:

- **Clients have a range of family planning methods to choose from.** Good-quality family planning services offer different methods to suit people's differing needs—not just 1 or 2 methods. If programs cannot provide a method or service, they refer clients somewhere else for that method.

- **Clients make their own decisions.** Family planning providers help clients think through their decisions, but they do not pressure clients to make a certain choice or to use a certain method.

making an *informed* choice. *If there is no medical reason against it, clients should have the methods that they want.* When clients get the methods they want, they use them longer and more effectively.

6. **Help the client understand and remember.** The provider shows sample family planning materials, encourages the client to handle them, and shows how they are used. Also, the provider shows and explains flip charts, posters, or simple pamphlets or printed pages with pictures. From time to time, the provider checks that the client understands. If the client can be given print materials to take home, they help remind clients what to do. They can be shared with others, too.

6 Topics

Counseling should be tailored to each client. At the same time, most counseling about method choice covers 6 topics. Information on these 6 topics can be found in chapters 5 through 15 of this handbook.

Information on these topics also should reach clients in many other ways—for example, on radio and television, in posters and pamphlets, and in community meetings. When clients have accurate information even *before* they see a provider, the provider's work is easier, and the client can make better decisions. Of course, it is important that information from different sources be as consistent as possible.

1. **Effectiveness.** How well a family planning method prevents pregnancy depends more on the user for some methods than for others (see page 4–18). Pregnancy rates for methods *as commonly used* give clients a rough idea of what they can expect. Still, their own experience may be better or worse—sometimes much better or much worse. Pregnancy rates for methods *used consistently and correctly* give an idea of the best possible effectiveness. Providers can help clients consider whether and how they can use a specific method consistently and correctly.

For some clients, effectiveness is the most important reason for choosing a method. Other clients have other reasons for their choices.

2. **Advantages and disadvantages.** Clients need to understand *both* advantages and disadvantages of a method *for them* (tailored information). It is important to remember that disadvantages for some people are advantages for others. For example, some women prefer injections. Others want to avoid injections.

3. **Side effects and complications.** If methods have side effects, clients need to know about them before they choose and start a method. Clients who learn about side effects ahead of time tend to be more satisfied with their methods and use them longer.

Clients need to know which side effects may be bothersome but are not signs of danger or symptoms of a serious condition. With some methods, such side effects may be fairly common. Also, clients need to know what symptoms, if any, are reasons to see a doctor or nurse or to return to the clinic. These symptoms may point to a rare but serious side effect. Clients need to understand the difference. If a method hardly ever has any side effects or complications, clients need to know that, too. (Side effects and complications are covered under "Disadvantages" in the "Deciding About" sections of chapters 5 through 15.)

4. **How to use.** Clear, practical instructions are important. Instructions should cover what clients can do if they make a mistake with the method (such as forgetting to take a pill) and also what clients and providers can do if problems come up (such as bothersome side effects). Also, clients may need special help on matters such as remembering to take a pill each day or discussing condoms with a sex partner.

5. **STD prevention.** Some STDs, including HIV/AIDS, are spreading in many countries. With sensitivity, family planning providers can help clients understand and measure their risk of getting STDs. Family planning clients should know to use condoms if they might get STDs—even if they are using another family planning method. Providers can explain the ABCs of safe behavior: Abstinence, Being mutually faithful, Condom use. (See Chapter 16.)

6. **When to return.** There are many good reasons to return to the clinic. Some methods require return visits for more supplies. Clients should be told of several places to get more supplies, if possible. In contrast, some methods—for example, IUDs, female sterilization, and vasectomy—require at most one routine return visit. Clients should not be asked to make unnecessary visits. Still, the provider always makes clear that the client is *always welcome back any time for any reason*—for example, if she or he wants information, advice, or another method or wants to stop using an IUD or *Norplant* implants. Providers make clear that changing methods is normal and welcome.

6 Steps in Counseling New Clients

Deciding on a family planning method and using it involve a step-by-step process. The process includes learning, weighing choices, making decisions, and carrying them out. Therefore counseling new clients about family planning usually is a process, too. The process can consist of 6 steps. These steps can be remembered with the word **GATHER**.

Good counseling is flexible, however. It changes to meet the special needs of the client and situation. Not every new client needs all 6 steps. Some clients need more attention to one step than another. Some steps can be carried out in group presentations or group discussions. Other steps usually need one-on-one discussion.

THE GATHER STEPS

G — **Greet clients** in an open, respectful manner. Give them full attention. Talk in a private place if possible. Assure the client of confidentiality. Ask the client how you can help, and explain what the clinic can offer in response.

A — **Ask clients about themselves.** Help clients talk about their family planning and reproductive health experiences, their intentions, concerns, wishes, and current health and family life. Ask if the client has a particular family planning method in mind. Pay attention to what clients express with their words *and* their gestures and expressions. Try to put yourself in the client's place. Express your understanding. Find out the client's knowledge, needs, and concerns so you can respond helpfully.

T — **Tell clients about choices.** Depending on the client's needs, tell the client what reproductive health choices she or he might make, including the choice among family planning methods or to use no method at all. Focus on methods that most interest the client, but also briefly mention other available methods. Also, explain any other available services that the client may want.

H — **Help clients make an informed choice.** Help the client think about what course of action best suits his or her situation and plans. Encourage the client to express opinions and ask questions. Respond fully and openly. Consider medical eligibility criteria for the family planning method or methods that interest the client. Also, ask if the client's sex partner will support the client's decisions. If possible, discuss choices with both partners. In the end, make sure that the client has made a clear decision. The provider can ask, "What have you decided to do?" or perhaps, "What method have you decided to use?"

E — **Explain fully how to use the chosen method.** After a client chooses a family planning method, give her or him the supplies, if appropriate. Explain how the supplies are used or how the procedure will be performed. Again encourage questions, and answer them openly and fully. Give condoms to anyone at risk for sexually transmitted diseases (STDs), and encourage him or her to use condoms along with any other family planning method. Check that clients understand how to use their method.

R — **Return visits should be welcomed.** Discuss and agree when the client will return for follow-up or more supplies, if needed. Also, always invite the client to come back any time for any reason.

Counseling Continuing Clients

Continuing clients are just as important as new clients. They deserve just as much attention as new clients. Counseling continuing clients usually focuses on talking with clients about their experience and needs. Tests and examinations generally are not needed unless a special situation calls for them.

Like counseling new clients, counseling continuing clients can be flexible. It should change to meet the client's needs. For example, returning clients may need more supplies, answers to questions, help with problems, a new method, removal of *Norplant* implants or an IUD, or help with another reproductive health problem such as STDs or unexplained vaginal bleeding.

Usually, counseling the continuing client involves finding out what the client wants and then responding:

- *If the client has problems, resolve them.* This can include offering a new method or referring the client elsewhere if needed.
- *If the client has questions, answer them.*
- *If the client needs more supplies, provide them—generously.*
- Make sure the client is using her or his method correctly, and offer help if not.

See also the "Following Up" sections in chapters 5 through 15.

For a more detailed provider's guide to family planning counseling, see **Population Reports**, *GATHER Guide to Counseling*, available from the Johns Hopkins Population Information Program at the address inside the front cover.

Chapter 4
Important Information for Providing Family Planning

Key Points

- With specific training, many different people in addition to doctors can and do provide family planning information, advice, and methods.
- By asking questions, family planning providers usually can tell when a woman is not pregnant. Pregnancy tests generally are not needed.
- A baby's health often depends on mother's breast milk. It is **important to avoid another pregnancy that cuts off breastfeeding.** Breastfeeding itself helps prevent pregnancy. Some family planning methods are better than others during breastfeeding.
- **Proper infection-prevention procedures are important.**
- **Many people can use most family planning methods.** A few common medical conditions rule out certain methods, however.
- **For effectiveness, some family planning methods depend more on the user than others.**
- **Most family planning methods do not require difficult or expensive physical examinations, tests, or procedures.** Some tests could provide other useful health information.

Chapter 4

Important Information for Providing Family Planning

Note: This chapter contains various information important to family planning providers. The sections in this chapter apply to various family planning methods. They are often referred to in Chapters 5 through 15, each of which covers a specific method.

Contents

Who Provides Family Planning and Where? 4–3

How To Tell That a Woman Is Not Pregnant 4–6

Family Planning for the Breastfeeding Woman 4–8

Infection Prevention in the Clinic 4–10

Medical Conditions and Method Choice 4–13

Effectiveness of Family Planning Methods 4–19

How Important Are Various Procedures? 4–21

Who Provides Family Planning and Where?

Many different people can learn to inform and advise people about family planning. Many different people can provide family planning methods. Countries and programs have various rules about who can offer which methods and where. Still, in countries around the world these people commonly provide family planning:

- Nurses, nurse-midwives, nurse-practitioners,
- Auxiliary nurse-midwives,
- Midwives,
- Physicians, including gynecologists, obstetricians,
- Physicians' assistants, physicians' associates,
- Pharmacists, pharmacists' assistants, chemists,
- Primary health care workers, community health workers,
- Specially trained traditional birth attendants,
- Shopkeepers and vendors,
- Community members serving as community-based distributors,
- Volunteers, experienced users of family planning, peer educators, and community leaders.

Specific training helps all these people do a better job at providing family planning. Training needs to cover skills in informing and counseling clients about choosing and using specific methods and in screening for medical eligibility criteria as well as any specific technical skills such as how to give injections or insert an IUD.

Method	Who Can Provide?	Where?
Combined oral contraceptives	All those listed.	Anywhere.
Progestin-only oral contraceptives	All those listed.	Anywhere.
Injectables	Anyone trained to give injections and to handle needles and syringes properly.	Anywhere sterile needles and syringes can be handled safely.

Method	Who Can Provide?	Where?
Norplant implants	Anyone with training in medical procedures and specific training in insertion of *Norplant* implants, including physicians, nurses, nurse-midwives, nurse-practitioners, midwives, physicians' assistants and associates.	Wherever appropriate infection-prevention procedures can be followed.
Female sterilization	With specific training, general physicians, specialized physicians such as obstetricians, gynecologists, and surgeons, and medical assistants or students under supervision. *Laparoscopy* is best performed by experienced and specifically trained surgeons.	In facilities where surgery can be done. Laparoscopy and certain medical conditions have additional requirements. See page 9–6.
Vasectomy	With specific training, physicians, medical officers, nurse-midwives, nurse-practitioners, midwives, physicians' assistants and associates.	Almost any health facility, including physicians' offices, clinics, hospitals, temporary and mobile clinics. See page 10–7.
Condoms	All those listed.	Anywhere, including shops and vending machines.

Method	Who Can Provide?	Where?
IUDs	Anyone with training in medical procedures and specific training in IUD screening, insertion, and removal, including physicians, nurses, nurse-midwives, midwives, nurse-practitioners, physicians' assistants and associates. In some countries pharmacists sell IUDs; the woman takes the IUD to a health care provider, who inserts it.	Wherever appropriate infection-prevention procedures can be followed, including clinics, hospitals, and physicians' offices.
Spermicides	All those listed.	Anywhere.
Diaphragms and cervical caps	Any provider specifically trained to perform pelvic examinations and to choose the right size diaphragm or cervical cap for each woman.	Anywhere pelvic exam can be done and client has privacy to practice putting in diaphragm or cap.
Fertility awareness-based methods	Anyone specifically trained to teach fertility awareness. Couples experienced with these techniques often make the best teachers.	Anywhere.
Lactational amenorrhea method (LAM)	The breastfeeding woman herself provides the method. Knowledgeable and supportive health care providers can help her use it most effectively.	Anywhere.

How To Tell That a Woman Is Not Pregnant

A woman should not start certain family planning methods while she is pregnant. These methods are combined and progestin-only oral contraceptives, injectables, *Norplant* implants, IUDs, and female sterilization. In contrast, condoms and vaginal methods can and should be used when protection against sexually transmitted diseases is needed during pregnancy.

Although pregnant women should not use some contraceptives, methods other than the IUD probably are not harmful to the mother or the fetus. (See page 12–22.) The best evidence shows that hormonal methods such as oral contraceptives and injectables are not harmful.

A health care provider usually can tell if a woman is not pregnant by asking her questions. Pregnancy tests and physical examinations usually are not needed, they waste resources, and they discourage clients.

▶ It is reasonably certain that a woman is not pregnant if:

- Her **menstrual period started within the last 7 days**, OR
- She **gave birth within the last 4 weeks**, OR
- She **had an abortion or miscarriage within the last 7 days**, OR
- She **gave birth within the last 6 months, is breastfeeding often,** *and* **has not yet had a menstrual period.**

▶ If a woman does not fit any of these categories, it is still reasonably certain that she is not pregnant if:

- She has **not had vaginal sex since her last menstrual period**, OR
- If she has had sex since her last menstrual period, **she used family planning correctly*** *and* **her last menstrual period was** *less than* **5 weeks ago.**

*Note: Appropriate methods include injectables, *Norplant* implants, IUDs, and, *if properly used*, combined or progestin-only oral contraceptives, condoms, Lactational Amenorrhea Method (LAM), spermicide, diaphragm, cervical cap, and fertility awareness-based methods except calendar rhythm.

If she *has* had sex and her last period *was* 5 weeks ago or more, **pregnancy cannot be ruled out**, even if she used effective contraception. Has she noticed early signs of pregnancy? If more than 12 weeks since her last menstrual period, has she noticed later signs of pregnancy?

Signs of Pregnancy

Early signs of pregnancy

- Late menstrual period
- Breast tenderness
- Nausea
- Vomiting
- Weight change
- Always tired
- Mood changes
- Changed eating habits
- Urinating more often

Later signs of pregnancy

- Larger breasts
- Darker nipples
- More vaginal discharge
- Enlarged abdomen
- Movements of a baby

If she has had several of these signs, **she may be pregnant**. Try to confirm by physical examination.

▶ If her answers cannot rule out pregnancy, she should either have a laboratory pregnancy test, if available, or wait until her next menstrual period before starting a method that should not be used during pregnancy. A provider can give her condoms or spermicide to use until then, with instructions and advice on how to use them.

Family Planning For the Breastfeeding Woman

Breastfeeding has **important health benefits:**

- Provides the best nutrition for the child.
- Protects the baby from life-threatening diarrhea that other foods or contaminated water might cause.
- Passes the mother's immunities to the child, which helps protect the baby from life-threatening infectious diseases such as measles.
- Helps develop a close relationship between mother and child.
- May help protect the mother against breast cancer later in life.

Breast milk is the best food for nearly all babies. In some situations the baby's life depends on continuing to breastfeed. Therefore it is very **important to delay another pregnancy.** Delaying pregnancy avoids early weaning and the many health problems that often result.

Breastfeeding itself helps to prevent pregnancy. Breastfeeding alone, without another family planning method, can provide effective protection against pregnancy for the first 6 months after delivery. It does so if:

- The woman has not had her first menstrual period since childbirth (bleeding in the first 56 days—8 weeks—after childbirth is not considered menstrual bleeding), and
- The woman is fully or nearly fully breastfeeding—at least 85% of the baby's feedings are breast milk.

This is called the **Lactational Amenorrhea Method** (LAM). (See Chapter 15.)

By definition, a woman is not using LAM if the baby gets substantial food other than breast milk OR the mother's menstrual periods return OR the baby reaches 6 months of age. **To protect herself from pregnancy, she should then:**

- **Choose another effective family planning method** that does not interfere with breastfeeding (not combined oral contraceptives before her baby is 6 months old).

- **Continue to breastfeed** her baby if possible, even while beginning to give the baby other food. Breast milk is the healthiest food for most babies during the first 2 years of life. She should breastfeed before giving other food, if possible. If the baby's hunger is satisfied first by breast milk, this will help ensure good nutrition and will encourage production of breast milk.

All breastfeeding women, whether or not they are using LAM, should be counseled on:

- When they can and should start particular family planning methods.
- The advantages and disadvantages of each method, including any effects on breastfeeding.

If a breastfeeding woman needs or wants more protection from pregnancy, she should first consider nonhormonal methods (IUDs, condoms, female sterilization, vasectomy, or vaginal methods). She also can consider fertility awareness-based methods, although these may be hard to use. None of these methods affects breastfeeding or poses any danger to the baby.

Women who are breastfeeding can start progestin-only methods—progestin-only oral contraceptives, long-acting injectables, or *Norplant* implants—as early as 6 weeks after childbirth.

The estrogen hormone in combined oral contraceptives may reduce the quantity and quality of breast milk. Therefore the World Health Organization recommends that breastfeeding women wait at least 6 months after childbirth to start using them. Another method, if needed, can be used until then.

Infection Prevention in the Clinic

Infection-prevention procedures protect both clients and providers from the spread of infectious disease. Infection-prevention procedures are simple, easy, effective, and inexpensive.

It is not possible to tell easily which client may have an infectious disease that could be passed in a health clinic. Therefore infection-prevention procedures must be followed with every client. Making infection-prevention procedures a habit—a part of every family planning procedure—will protect both health care providers and clients.

The Principle of Infection Prevention

Infection prevention means *stopping the passage of infectious organisms (germs) between people* by always (1) *making a barrier to body fluids*—for example, by wearing gloves—**and** (2) *removing infectious organisms*—for example, by processing of instruments and by waste disposal.

Blood, semen, vaginal secretions, and body fluids containing blood can carry infectious organisms. These organisms include HIV (the virus that causes AIDS), hepatitis B virus, staphylococcus bacteria ("staph"), and many others. Infections can be passed from one person to another when infection-prevention procedures are not followed and these fluids pass from one person to another.

In the clinic, infectious organisms can be passed between clients and health workers through needle sticks (with used needles) or similar puncture wounds or through broken skin (such as an open cut or scratch). Infectious organisms can be passed from one client to another by surgical instruments, needles, syringes, and other equipment *if it has not been properly decontaminated, cleaned, and high-level disinfected or sterilized* between clients.

For detailed instructions on infection-prevention procedures, see Tietjen et al. Infection prevention for family planning service programs. Baltimore, JHPIEGO, 1992.

Basic Rules of Infection Prevention

- **Wash hands.** *Hand washing may be the single most important infection-prevention procedure.* Wash hands before and after contact with each client. Use soap and clean running water from a tap or bucket. Also wash before putting on gloves and whenever hands get dirty.

- **Wear gloves.** Wear gloves when there is any chance of contact with blood or other body fluids. Before any procedures with each client, put on a new pair of single-use or processed reusable gloves if possible. For surgical procedures, gloves should be sterile.

- **Do vaginal examinations only when needed or requested.** Vaginal or pelvic exams generally are not needed for most contraceptive methods—only for female sterilization and IUDs (see page 4–20). For vaginal exams, wear either a new pair of single-use gloves or reusable, processed high-level disinfected or sterile gloves. Vaginal exams should be done only when there is a reason—such as a Pap smear or suspicion of disease when the exam could help with diagnosis or treatment.

- **Clean the client's skin** appropriately before an injection or insertion of *Norplant* implants. Use a locally available antiseptic.

- **Clean the cervix with antiseptic** as a part of "no touch" technique for IUD insertion.

- For each injection, **use a new, single-use needle and syringe** or a sterilized reusable needle and syringe. (If reusable needle and syringe cannot be sterilized, use high-level disinfection.)

- After use with each client, reusable instruments, equipment, and supplies should be:

    (1) decontaminated (soaked in 0.5% chlorine solution (bleach) or another disinfectant),

    (2) cleaned with soap and water, and

    (3) either high-level disinfected (by boiling or steaming) or sterilized (by steam or dry heat).

- Vaginal specula, uterine sounds, gloves for pelvic exams, and other equipment and instruments that touch *mucous membranes* should be decontaminated, cleaned, and then *either high-level disinfected or sterilized*, as appropriate.
- Needles and syringes, scalpels, trocars for *Norplant* implants, and other equipment and instruments that touch human *tissue beneath the skin* should be decontaminated, cleaned, and then *sterilized*.
- Disinfected or sterilized objects should not be touched with bare hands.
- Wear gloves when cleaning instruments and equipment.
- Wash linens in warm, soapy water and line-dry.
- After each client, exam tables, bench tops, and other surfaces that will come in contact with unbroken skin should be wiped with 0.5% chlorine solution.

- **Dispose of single-use equipment and supplies properly.**
  - Needles and syringes meant for single use must **not** be reused. (See page 7–13.)
  - Used needles should not be broken, bent, or recapped. They should be put at once into a puncture-proof container. The container should be burned or buried when three-quarters full.
  - Dressings and other soiled solid waste should be burned, if possible, or else put in a pit latrine. Do not put dressings in a flush toilet. Liquid wastes should be put in a pit latrine.

Medical Conditions and Method Choice

Some common medical conditions and personal characteristics may affect choice of temporary contraceptive methods. This chart lists common conditions and characteristics, which methods can be used and which should not be used by people with these conditions, and whether these conditions make pregnancy especially dangerous. A woman with a condition that makes pregnancy especially dangerous has a particular need for effective family planning for health reasons.

Note: *Permanent methods—female sterilization and vasectomy—are safe and effective for everyone when performed under the right circumstances.* (See Chapters 9 and 10.)

Methods, Method Categories, and Abbreviations

Low-dose combined oral contraceptives (COCs)
Progestin-only methods *include*:
  Progestin-only oral contraceptives (POPs)
  DMPA and NET EN injectables
  Norplant implants
Copper IUDs

Barrier methods *include*:
  Condoms
  Spermicides
  Diaphragms and cervical caps
Fertility awareness-based methods
Lactational amenorrhea method (LAM)

Condition or Characteristic	Safe and Effective Temporary Methods*	Temporary Methods Not To Be Used**	Pregnancy Especially Dangerous?
Age under 16 (menarche) or over 40	All methods, *but fertility awareness-based methods may be hard to use.*	None	Dangerous
Breastfeeding	*Nonhormonal methods are best:* –LAM –Barrier methods –Copper IUDs		

*Based on WHO medical eligibility criteria categories 1 and 2. See table in appendix for detail.
**Based on WHO medical eligibility criteria categories 3 and 4. See table in appendix for detail.

Condition or Characteristic	Safe and Effective Temporary Methods	Temporary Methods Not To Be Used	Pregnancy Especially Dangerous?
Breastfeeding (continued)	Progestin-only methods *if started at least 6 weeks after childbirth.*		
	Fertility awareness-based *but may be hard to use.*		
	COCs *after 6 months since childbirth.*	COCs *until 6 months or more after childbirth.*	
Smoking	COCs *if under age 35.*	COCs *if age 35 or older.*	
	All other methods		
No children	All methods	None	
High blood pressure (BP)	COCs *if BP less than 140/90.*	COCs *if systolic BP 140 or higher or diastolic BP 90 or higher, or if history of high BP but BP cannot be taken.*	Dangerous especially when BP 160/100 or higher.
	DMPA and NET EN *if BP less than 180/110.*	DMPA and NET EN *if BP 180/110 or higher.*	
	All other methods		

4–14 Essentials of Contraceptive Technology

Condition or Characteristic	Safe and Effective Temporary Methods	Temporary Methods Not To Be Used	Pregnancy Especially Dangerous?
Multiple risk factors for arterial cardiovascular disease (such as smoking, high BP, diabetes)	POPs *Norplant* implants Copper IUDs Barrier methods LAM Fertility awareness-based	COCs DMPA and NET EN	Dangerous
Serious cardiovascular diseases except valvular heart disease	POPs *Norplant* implants Copper IUDs Barrier methods LAM Fertility awareness-based	COCs Progestin-only methods *in cases of current deep vein thrombosis.* DMPA and NET EN *in cases of heart disease caused by blocked arteries, or history of stroke.*	Dangerous *with heart disease due to blocked arteries.*
Valvular heart disease	COCs *in most cases* All other methods	COCs *if with complications.*	Dangerous
Superficial venous thrombosis or varicose veins	All methods	None	

Condition or Characteristic	Safe and Effective Temporary Methods	Temporary Methods Not To Be Used	Pregnancy Especially Dangerous?
Diabetes	COCs, DMPA and NET EN *in most cases.* All other methods	COCs, DMPA and NET EN *if diabetes for 20 years or more or if vascular disease.*	Dangerous *if with vascular disease.*
Ordinary headache (not migraines)	All methods		
Migraine headache (recurring severe head pain, often on one side or pulsating, that can cause nausea and often is made worse by light and noise or moving about)	COCs *if under age 35 and no distortion of vision (aura) or trouble speaking or moving before or during these headaches.* Progestin-only methods Copper IUDs Barrier methods LAM Fertility awareness-based	COCs *if (1) age 35 or older or (2) at any age, vision is distorted (aura) or woman has trouble speaking or moving before or during these headaches.*	

Important Information for Providing Family Planning

Condition or Characteristic	Safe and Effective Temporary Methods	Temporary Methods Not To Be Used	Pregnancy Especially Dangerous?
Suspicious unexplained vaginal bleeding, until evaluated or referred for evaluation	COCs POPs Barrier methods Fertility awareness-based *but may be hard to use.*	DMPA and NET EN *Norplant* implants IUDs	
Breast cancer, current or past	Copper IUDs Barrier methods Fertility awareness-based	COCs Progestin-only methods LAM *if cancer currently treated with drugs.*	Dangerous
Sexually transmitted diseases (STDs) or risk of STDs	Barrier methods *(recommended for STD prevention).* COCs Progestin-only methods LAM Fertility awareness-based *but may be hard to use if current or recent STD.*	IUDs *except for vaginitis without purulent cervicitis.*	Dangerous *(Syphilis and HIV may be transmitted to infant.)*

Medical Conditions and Method Choice 4–17

Condition or Characteristic	Safe and Effective Temporary Methods	Temporary Methods Not To Be Used	Pregnancy Especially Dangerous?
Current viral hepatitis or hepatitis carrier	Copper IUDs COCs and progestin-only methods *if carrier only.* LAM, *but breastfeeding may not be recommended.* Barrier methods Fertility awareness-based	COCs and progestin-only methods *if current disease.*	
Obesity	All methods, *but diaphragm or cap placement may be difficult.*	None	
Tuberculosis (TB)	Copper IUDs *except if pelvic TB.* LAM, *but breastfeeding may not be recommended.* All other methods	IUDs *if pelvic TB.*	

Effectiveness of Family Planning Methods

The table on the next page reports rates of unintended pregnancies among users of various family planning methods in the first 12 months (1 year) of using that method. Two rates are reported for each method. One is the pregnancy rate for the method *as commonly used*. This is a typical, or average rate. A specific couple may be more successful or less successful than this—sometimes much more or much less. The other rate is the pregnancy rate when the method is *used correctly and consistently*. This is about the best rate that a user can expect from the method. The effectiveness of family planning methods can be divided into 3 groups, as shown in the left column of the table.

*LAM is used for no more than 6 months after childbirth. Doubling these rates would give 1-year rates for comparison with other methods.

**When abstinence is used to avoid pregnancy. Effectiveness when used correctly and consistently depends on which fertility signs and abstinence rules are used.

Sources of effectiveness data: Trussell, J. Contraceptive efficacy. In: Hatcher et al. Contraceptive technology (17th revised edition). Except progestin-only oral contraceptives during breastfeeding *as commonly used*, from McCann, M.F. and Potter, L.S. Progestin-only oral contraception: A comprehensive review. Contraception 50(6)(Supplement 1): S1–S195. December 1994; LAM from Labbok, M., Cooney, K., and Coly, S. Guidelines: Breastfeeding, family planning, and the lactational amenorrhea method—LAM. Washington, D.C., Georgetown University, Institute for Reproductive Health, 1994; and combined oral contraceptives and fertility awareness-based methods *as commonly used* from Moreno, L. and Goldman, N. Contraceptive failure rates in developing countries: Evidence from the Demographic and Health Surveys. International Family Planning Perspectives 17(2): 44–49. June 1991. Estimates by Trussell and by Moreno and Goldman are similar for combined oral contraceptives as commonly used.

Table concept developed by Jill Mathis.

			Pregnancies per 100 Women in First 12 Months of Use		
Key to shading in table:	Effectiveness Group	Family Planning Method	As Commonly Used	Used Correctly & Consistently	See Chapter
0–1 Very effective	*Always very effective.*	Norplant implants	0.1	0.1	Ch. 8
		Vasectomy	0.15	0.1	Ch. 10
2–9 Effective		DMPA and NET EN injectables	0.3	0.3	Ch. 7
		Female sterilization	0.5	0.5	Ch. 9
10–30 Somewhat effective		TCu-380A IUD	0.8	0.6	Ch. 12
		Progestin-only oral contraceptives during breastfeeding	1	0.5	Ch. 6
	Effective as commonly used. Very effective when used correctly and consistently.	LAM (for 6 months only*)	2	0.5	Ch. 15
		Combined oral contraceptives	6–8	0.1	Ch. 5
	Only somewhat effective as commonly used. Effective when used correctly and consistently.	Condoms	14	3	Ch. 11
		Diaphragm with spermicide	20	6	Ch. 13
		Fertility awareness-based methods**	20	1–9	Ch. 14
		Female condoms	21	5	Ch. 11
		Spermicides	26	6	Ch. 13
		No method	85	85	—

4–20 Essentials of Contraceptive Technology

How Important Are Various Procedures?

What procedures should family planning providers regularly perform when giving clients a method that is new to them? A group of experts named the Technical Guidance/Competence Working Group has rated the importance of selected procedures to providing family planning methods. For each major family planning method, they put each procedure into 1 of 4 categories, as shown on the next page. This list is not a complete list of all possible procedures. Instead, it is meant to offer examples.

The chart on the next page shows that expensive or difficult procedures are not needed to decide about most methods. Some procedures or tests may provide other useful health information, however. Counseling about family planning methods is important with every method.

Importance of Selected Procedures for Providing Family Planning Methods

Class A = Essential and required or otherwise important for safe use of the family planning method

Class B = Makes medical sense in some cases for safest use of the family planning method but may not be appropriate for all clients in all settings

Class C = May be appropriate for good preventive health care but not materially related to safe use of the family planning method

Class D = Not materially related to either good routine preventive health care or to the safe and effective use of the family planning method

— = Not addressed
NA = Not applicable

*Classification is for both general and local anesthesia.
**Classification is for condoms, spermicides, and diaphragm.
***Specific counseling points: efficacy, common side effects, correct use of method, signs and symptoms for which to see a health care provider, STD protection (when/as appropriate).

1. Class A for diaphragm.
2. STD screening *by history* is Class A, however.
3. Hemoglobin level testing and urine sugar testing are Class B, however.
4. Class A for diaphragm fitting.
5. Including instructions for missed pills.
6. Points to include: permanent method, preoperation and recovery/postoperation instructions.
7. Counseling is a good idea but cannot always be done with over-the-counter sales of condoms and spermicides. Class A for diaphragm, however.
8. Points to include: high-risk behavior; condom use for women who, under certain circumstances, might become at high risk for STDs. NOTE: Women who are currently at high risk for STDs in general should not receive IUDs.
9. Points to include: LAM criteria, best breastfeeding behavior, and when and where to get follow-up method.
10. Point to include: importance of partner's cooperation.

Procedure	Low-Dose Combined Oral Contraceptives	Progestin-Only Pills During Breastfeeding	DMPA & NET EN Injectables	Norplant Implants	Female Sterilization*	Vasectomy	Barrier Methods**	Copper IUDs	Lactational Amenorrhea Method (LAM)	Fertility Awareness-Based Methods
Pelvic exam (speculum and bimanual) for women; genital exam for men	C	C	C	C	A	A	C[1]	A	C	C
Blood pressure reading	B	C	C	C	A	C	C	C	C	C
Breast exam	B	C	C	C	C	NA	C	C	C	C
STD screening by lab tests (for persons without symptoms)	C	C	C	C	C	C	C	B[2]	C	C
Cervical cancer screening	C	C	C	C	C	NA	C	C	C	C
Routine, mandatory lab tests (for example, cholesterol, glucose, liver function tests)	D	D	D	D	C[3]	D	D	D	—	—
Proper infection-prevention procedures	C	C	A	A	A	A	C[4]	A	C	C
Specific counseling points for family planning method***	A[5]	A[5]	A	A	A[6]	A[6]	B[7]	A[8]	A[9]	A[10]
Counseling about change in menses, including irregular or absent menstrual bleeding	A	A	A	A	—	NA	—	A	—	—

4–22 Essentials of Contraceptive Technology

Chapter 5
Low-Dose Combined Oral Contraceptives

Key Points

- Effective, reversible method.
- Should be taken every day to be most effective.
- Side effects—such as irregular vaginal bleeding, missed periods, or upset stomach—sometimes occur, especially during early months of use. Not dangerous but cause discomfort for some women.
- **Safe for almost all women.** Serious side effects are very rare.
- Can be used by women of any age, whether or not they have had children.
- Can be started any time it is reasonably certain a woman is not pregnant—not just during menstruation.
- Protect against certain cancers, anemia, and other conditions.
- Not recommended for breastfeeding women. Can reduce milk supply.
- Can be used for emergency contraception after unprotected sex.

Chapter 5
Low-Dose Combined Oral Contraceptives

Contents

Introduction to Combined Oral Contraceptives 5–3

Deciding About Combined Oral Contraceptives 5–3
    How Do They Work? 5–3
    How Effective? 5–3
    Advantages and Disadvantages 5–4
    Medical Eligibility Checklist 5–6

Starting Low-Dose Combined Oral Contraceptives 5–9
    When to Start 5–9
    Providing Combined Oral Contraceptives 5–10
    Explaining How to Use 5–12

Following Up 5–16
    Helping Clients at Any Routine Return Visit 5–16
    Managing Any Problems 5–17

Important Points for the User to Remember 5–19

Emergency Oral Contraception 5–20

Questions and Answers 5–26

Introduction to Combined Oral Contraceptives

- Women who use oral contraceptives swallow a pill each day to prevent pregnancy. Combined oral contraceptives contain two hormones similar to the natural hormones in a woman's body—an estrogen and a progestin. Also called combined pills, COCs, OCs, the Pill, and birth control pills.

- Present-day combined oral contraceptives contain very low doses of hormones. They are often called low-dose combined oral contraceptives.

- There are two types of pill packets. Some packets have 28 pills. These contain 21 "active" pills, which contain hormones, followed by 7 "reminder" pills of a different color that do not contain hormones. Other packets have only the 21 "active" pills.

See Chapter 6 for information on progestin-only oral contraceptives for breastfeeding women.

Deciding About Combined Oral Contraceptives

How Do They Work?

- Stop ovulation (release of eggs from ovaries).
- Also thicken cervical mucus, making it difficult for sperm to pass through.

They do NOT work by disrupting existing pregnancy.

How Effective?

Effective as commonly used—6 to 8 pregnancies per 100 women in first year of use (1 in every 17 to 1 in every 12).
Very effective when used correctly and consistently—0.1 pregnancies per 100 women in first year of use (1 in every 1,000).

IMPORTANT: Should be taken every day to be most effective. Many women may not take pills correctly and thus risk becoming pregnant. The most common mistakes are starting new packets late and running out of pills.

Advantages and Disadvantages

ADVANTAGES

- Very effective when used correctly.
- No need to do anything at time of sexual intercourse.
- Increased sexual enjoyment because no need to worry about pregnancy.
- Monthly periods are regular; lighter monthly bleeding and fewer days of bleeding; milder and fewer menstrual cramps.
- Can be used as long as a woman wants to prevent pregnancy. No rest period needed.
- Can be used at any age from adolescence to menopause.
- Can be used by women who have children and by women who do not.
- User can stop taking pills at any time.
- Fertility returns soon after stopping.
- Can be used as an emergency contraceptive after unprotected sex (see page 5–20).
- Can prevent or decrease iron deficiency anemia.
- Help prevent:
    - Ectopic pregnancies,
    - Endometrial cancer,
    - Ovarian cancer,
    - Ovarian cysts,
    - Pelvic inflammatory disease,
    - Benign breast disease.

DISADVANTAGES

- Common side effects (*not* signs of sickness):
    - Nausea (most common in first 3 months),
    - Spotting or bleeding between menstrual periods, especially if a woman forgets to take her pills or takes them late (most common in first 3 months),
    - Mild headaches,
    - Breast tenderness,
    - Slight weight gain (some women see weight gain as an advantage),
    - Amenorrhea (some women see amenorrhea as an advantage).

- Not highly effective unless taken every day. Difficult for some women to remember every day.
- New packet of pills must be at hand every 28 days.
- Not recommended for breastfeeding women because they affect quality and quantity of milk.
- In a few women, may cause mood changes including depression, less interest in sex,
- Very rarely can cause stroke, blood clots in deep veins of the legs, or heart attack. Those at highest risk are women with high blood pressure and women who are age 35 or older *and* at the same time smoke more than 15 cigarettes per day.
- Do not protect against sexually transmitted diseases (STDs) including AIDS.

   IMPORTANT: Ask the client if she might have or get a sexually transmitted disease (STD). (Has more than one sex partner? Partner has more than one partner? Could this happen in future?)

   If she has or might get an STD, urge her to use condoms regularly. Give her condoms. She can still use combined oral contraceptives.

Using the Medical Eligibility Checklist

*The list on the next 2 pages checks whether the client has any **known** medical conditions that prevent use of combined oral contraceptives. It is not meant to replace counseling.*

*The questions in the checklist refer to **known conditions**. Generally, you can learn of these conditions by asking the client. You do not usually have to perform laboratory tests or physical examinations.*

IMPORTANT: Low-dose oral contraceptives contain only small amounts of hormone. Many conditions that limited use of oral contraceptives with high doses of estrogen do not apply to low-dose combined oral contraceptives.

DECIDING About Combined Oral Contraceptives

MEDICAL ELIGIBILITY CHECKLIST FOR

Combined Oral Contraceptives (COCs)

Ask the client the questions below. If she answers NO to ALL of the questions, then she CAN use low-dose combined oral contraceptives if she wants. If she answers YES to a question below, follow the instructions.

1.	Do you smoke cigarettes and are you age 35 or older?
☐ No	☐ **Yes** ▶ Urge her to stop smoking. If she is 35 or older and will not stop smoking, do not provide COCs. Help her choose a method without estrogen.
2.	Do you have high blood pressure?
☐ No	☐ **Yes** ▶ If you cannot check blood pressure (BP) and she reports high BP, do not provide COCs. Refer for BP check if feasible or help her choose a method without estrogen. If no report of high BP, okay to provide COCs. Check BP if feasible: *If BP below 140/90,* okay to give COCs without further BP readings. *If systolic BP 140 or higher or diastolic BP 90 or higher,* do not provide COCs. Help her choose another method. (One BP reading in the range of 140–159/90–99 is not enough to diagnose high BP. Offer condoms or spermicide for use until she can return for another BP check, or help her choose another method if she prefers. If BP reading at next check is below 140/90, she can use COCs and further BP readings are not necessary.) If systolic BP 160 or higher or diastolic BP 100 or higher, she also should not use DMPA or NET EN.
3.	Are you breastfeeding a baby less than 6 months old?
☐ No	☐ **Yes** ▶ Can provide COCs now with instruction to start when she stops breastfeeding or 6 months after childbirth—whichever comes first. If she is not fully or almost fully breastfeeding, also give her condoms or spermicide to use until her baby is 6 months old. Other effective methods are better choices than COCs when a woman is breastfeeding, whatever her baby's age.
4.	Do you have serious problems with your heart or blood vessels? Have you ever had such problems? If so, what problems?
☐ No	☐ **Yes** ▶ Do not provide COCs if she reports *heart attack or heart disease due to blocked arteries, stroke, blood clots (except superficial clots), severe chest pain with unusual shortness of breath, diabetes for more than 20 years,* or *damage to vision, kidneys, or nervous system caused by diabetes.* Help her choose another effective method.

MEDICAL ELIGIBILITY CHECKLIST FOR COCs *(continued)*

5. Do you have or have you ever had breast cancer?

   ☐ No   ☐ **Yes** ▶ Do not provide COCs. Help her choose a method without hormones.

6. Do you have jaundice, cirrhosis of the liver, a liver infection or tumor? (Are her eyes or skin unusually yellow?)

   ☐ No   ☐ **Yes** ▶ Perform physical exam or refer. If she has serious active liver disease (*jaundice, painful or enlarged liver, active viral hepatitis, liver tumor*), do not provide COCs. Refer for care as appropriate. Help her choose a method without hormones.

7. Do you often get severe headaches, perhaps on one side or pulsating, that cause nausea and are made worse by light and noise or moving about (migraine headaches)?

   ☐ No   ☐ **Yes** ▶ If she is 35 or older, do not provide COCs. Help her choose another method. If she is under age 35, but her vision is distorted or she has trouble speaking or moving before or during these headaches, do not provide COCs. Help her choose another method. If she is under age 35 and has migraine headaches *without* distortion of vision or trouble speaking or moving, she can use COCs.

8. Are you taking medicine for seizures? Are you taking rifampin (rifampicin) or griseofulvin?

   ☐ No   ☐ **Yes** ▶ If she is taking *phenytoin, carbamezapine, barbiturates,* or *primidone* for seizures or *rifampin* or *griseofulvin*, provide condoms or spermicide to use along with COCs or, if she prefers, help her choose another effective method if she is on long-term treatment.

9. Do you think you are pregnant?

   ☐ No   ☐ **Yes** ▶ Assess whether pregnant (see page 4–6). If she might be pregnant, also give her condoms or spermicide to use until reasonably certain that she is not pregnant. Then she can start COCs.

10. Do you have gallbladder disease? Ever had jaundice while taking COCs? Planning surgery that will keep you from walking for a week or more? Had a baby in the past 21 days?

    ☐ No   ☐ **Yes** ▶ If she has *gallbladder disease* now or takes medicine for gallbladder disease, or if she has had *jaundice while using COCs,* do not provide COCs. Help her choose a method without estrogen. If planning *surgery* or *just had a baby,* can provide COCs with instruction on when to start them later (see pages 5–9 and 5–10).

Be sure to explain the health benefits and risks and the side effects of the method that the client will use. Also, point out any conditions that would make the method inadvisable when relevant to the client.

DECIDING About Combined Oral Contraceptives   5–7

Most Women Can Use Combined Oral Contraceptives

In general, most women CAN use low-dose combined oral contraceptives safely and effectively.* Low-dose combined oral contraceptives can be used in any circumstances by women who:

- Have no children,
- Are fat** or thin,
- Are any age, including adolescents and over 40 (except women who are age 35 or older and who smoke),
- Smoke cigarettes but are under age 35,
- Have just had abortion or miscarriage.

Also, women with these conditions CAN use low-dose combined oral contraceptives in any circumstances:

- Heavy, painful menstrual periods or iron deficiency anemia (condition may improve),
- Irregular menstrual periods,
- Benign breast disease,
- Diabetes without vascular, kidney, eye, or nerve disease,
- Mild headaches,
- Varicose veins,
- Malaria,
- Schistosomiasis,
- Thyroid disease,
- Pelvic inflammatory disease,
- Endometriosis,
- Benign ovarian tumors,
- Uterine fibroids,
- Past ectopic pregnancy,
- Tuberculosis (unless taking rifampin; see checklist question 8 on page 5–7).

IMPORTANT: Nonmedical providers can safely offer low-dose combined oral contraceptives. Nonmedical providers include shopkeepers and community-based distributors. These providers do not need to obtain medical consultation or approval to provide pills to a woman unless she has a condition that requires it.

*Characteristics and conditions listed in this box are in WHO Eligibility Criteria category 1. Women with characteristics and conditions in WHO category 2 also can use this method. See Appendix, page A–1.

**Very fat is WHO category 2.

Starting Low-Dose Combined Oral Contraceptives

When to Start

IMPORTANT: A woman can be given combined oral contraceptives *at any time* and told when to start taking them. The following table shows when to start.

Woman's situation	When to start
Having menstrual cycles	• Any of the first 7 days after her menstrual bleeding starts, if she is cycling normally. The first day of menstrual bleeding may be easiest to remember.
	• Any other time it is reasonably certain that she is not pregnant. (See page 4–6.) If more than 7 days since menstrual bleeding started, she can begin combined oral contraceptives but should avoid sex or also use condoms or spermicide for the next 7 days. Her usual bleeding pattern may change temporarily.
After childbirth if breastfeeding	• After she stops breastfeeding or 6 months after childbirth—*whichever comes first*. (See page 4–8.)
	Note: Can give her pills now. Make sure she knows when to start taking them.
After childbirth if not breastfeeding	• 3 to 6 weeks after childbirth. No need to wait for menstrual periods to return to be certain that she is not pregnant.
	• After 6 weeks, any time it is reasonably certain that she is not pregnant.
	Note: If not reasonably certain, she should avoid sex or use condoms or spermicide until her first period starts, and then begin combined oral contraceptives.

Woman's situation	When to start
After miscarriage or abortion	• In the first 7 days after first- or second-trimester miscarriage or abortion. • Later, any time it is reasonably certain that she is not pregnant.
When stopping another method	• Immediately. No need to wait for a first period after using injectables.

Providing Combined Oral Contraceptives

IMPORTANT: A woman who chooses low-dose combined oral contraceptives benefits from good counseling.

A friendly provider who listens to a woman's concerns, answers her questions, and gives clear, practical information about side effects, especially nausea and vomiting, and about proper use will help the woman use combined oral contraceptives with success and satisfaction.

You can follow these steps to provide combined oral contraceptives:

1. **Give her plenty of pills—a year's supply, if possible.** Running out of pills is a major reason for unintended pregnancies.

2. **Explain how to use** combined oral contraceptives (see page 5–12).

3. If possible, give her **condoms or spermicide** to use:
   - Until she can start taking her pills (if needed) (see page 5–9 and above);
   - If she starts a packet of pills late, if she forgets several pills in a row, or if she stops taking oral contraceptives for any reason;
   - If she thinks she or her partner could get AIDS or any other STD.

   Show her how to use condoms or spermicide.

4. **Plan a return visit** in time to give her more pills before her supply runs out.

5. **Invite the client to come back** any time she has questions, problems, or wants another method.

For clients who use pill packets like the one shown below, this drawing can help explain what to do when they miss pills. Describe the pills by their colors. (See page 5–13 for details.)

Missed pills? Here's what to do.

- *Starting late?* Abstain or use condoms or spermicide until you have taken the first 7 pills.
- *Missed 1 pill?* Take 1 now. Take the rest as usual.
- *Missed 2 or more in a row?* Which ones? (See below.)

Missed 2 or more of these first 14 pills? Take 1 now. Take all the rest as usual. Also can use condoms or spermicide for 7 days.

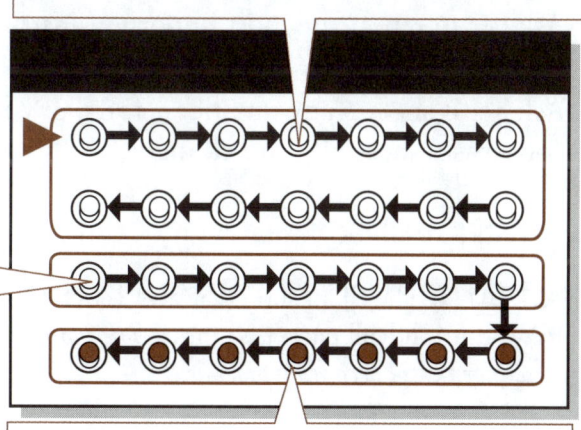

Missed 2 or more of these 7 pills? Take 1 now. Take the rest of this row, 1 each day.

Start a new pack the next day. Throw the last row of this pack away.

Also can use condoms or spermicide for 7 days.

Missed any of these 7 pills? Throw the missed pills away. Take the rest as usual. Do not go more than 7 days between taking hormonal pills.

STARTING Combined Oral Contraceptives 5–11

Explaining How to Use

Follow this procedure

1. Hand her at least one packet of the same pills that she will use, even if she will be getting her pills elsewhere later.
2. Show her:
   - Which kind of pill packet you are giving her—21 pills or 28 pills.

     IMPORTANT: With 28-pill packets, explain that the last 7 pills do not contain hormones. They are "reminder" pills. Point out that they are a different color from the first 21 pills. Explain that, if she forgets to take reminder pills, she is still protected from pregnancy. If she forgets to take active, hormonal pills, however, she risks pregnancy.

   - How to take the first pill out of the packet.
   - How to follow the directions or arrows on the packet to take the rest of the pills, one each day (first the hormonal pills, then any reminder pills).
3. Give her instructions on starting the first packet, starting the next packet, and what to do after missing pills (see below and next page).
4. Ask her to repeat the most important instructions and show how she will take her pills, using the pill packet.
5. Ask her if she has any questions, fears, or concerns, and answer her concerns respectfully and caringly.

Give specific instructions

IMPORTANT: The client should always TAKE ONE PILL EACH DAY—until the pill packet is empty. *The more pills she misses, the greater her risk of becoming pregnant.*

▶ **Starting the first packet:**
   - See pages 5–9 and 5–10 for *when* to start.
   - If she starts beyond day 7 after the start of her menstrual period, she may have irregular menstrual bleeding for a few days.
   - Taking the pill at the same time each day may help her remember them.

▶ **Starting the next packet:**

If you provide:	Give this instruction:
28-pill packets	When she finishes one packet, she should take the first pill from the next packet on the **very next day**.
21-pill packets	After she takes the last pill from one packet, she should **wait 7 days** and then take the first pill from the next packet. **Note:** She **must NOT wait MORE than 7 days** between cycles of 21-pill packets. (Some providers may tell women to wait only 4 or 5 days to reduce the chance of pregnancy.)

▶ **Instructions if a woman forgets to take a pill or pills** (describe the pills by their colors):

Missed only 1 [white] hormonal pill?
1. Take the missed pill at once.
2. Take the next pill at the regular time. This may mean taking 2 pills on the same day or even 2 at the same time.
3. Take the rest of the pills as usual, one each day.

Missed 2 or more [white] hormonal pills in any 7 days?
1. *Most important:* For 7 days use condoms, spermicide or avoid sex.
2. Take a [white] hormonal pill at once.
3. Count how many [white] hormonal pills are left in the packet:

7 or more [white] hormonal pills left?	**OR**	*Fewer than 7 [white] hormonal pills left?*
Take all the rest of the pills as usual, one each day.		• Take the rest of the [white] hormonal pills as usual. • Do *not* take any [brown] reminder pills. Throw them away. • Start a new pack on the next day after the last [white] hormonal pill. You may miss a period. This is okay.

Missed 1 or more of any [brown] reminder pills?
1. Throw the missed pills away.
2. Take the rest of the pills as usual, one each day.
3. Start a new packet as usual on the next day.

GIVE ADVICE ON COMMON PROBLEMS

1. **Mention the most common side effects**—for instance, nausea, mild headaches, tender breasts, spotting between periods, irregular bleeding, moodiness (see page 5–4).
   Explain about these side effects:
   - Not signs of serious sickness.
   - Usually become less or stop within 3 months after starting combined oral contraceptives.
   - Many women never have them.

2. **Explain how she can deal with some common problems.**
   Give these instructions:

If the client experiences:	Then she should:
Common side effects such as nausea, mild headaches, moodiness, tender breasts, spotting between periods, irregular bleeding.	Keep taking her pills. Skipping pills may make these side effects worse. Also, skipping pills risks pregnancy. For spotting or irregular bleeding, she can try taking each pill at the same time of day. Reassure her that these are not signs of more serious problems, and they usually go away.
Vomiting (for any reason) within 1 hour after taking a hormonal pill.	Take another hormonal pill from a separate packet. (Give her extra pills to take if she vomits.)
Severe diarrhea or vomiting for more than 24 hours. (Probably not caused by low-dose combined oral contraceptives.)	Keep taking her pills (if she can) despite her discomfort AND either use condoms or spermicide or else avoid sex until she has taken a pill each day for 7 days in a row after the diarrhea or vomiting has stopped.

3. **Invite the client to come back** if she needs more help with any problems. (See pages 5–17 and 5–18.) Let her know that she can switch to another method any time she wishes.

Explain Specific Reasons to See a Nurse or Doctor

Describe the symptoms of problems that require medical attention. Serious complications of pill use are rare. Still, a woman should see a doctor or nurse or return to the clinic if she has questions or problems or any of these possible symptoms of more serious problems. Combined oral contraceptives may or may not cause these problems:

- Severe, constant pain in belly, chest, or legs.

- Any very bad headaches that start or become worse after she begins to take combined oral contraceptives.

- Brief loss of vision, seeing flashing lights or zigzag lines (with or without bad headache); brief trouble speaking or moving arm or leg.

- Jaundice (skin and eyes look yellow).

Following Up

IMPORTANT: The client can return for more pills at her convenience, any time before her supply runs out. A scheduled return visit is not necessary.

Helping Clients at Any Routine Return Visit

ASK QUESTIONS

At any return visit:

1. Ask if the client has any questions or anything to discuss.

2. Ask the client about her experience with the method, whether she is satisfied, and whether she has any problems. Give her any information or help that she needs and invite her to return again any time she has questions or concerns. If she has problems that cannot be resolved, help her choose another method.

3. Ask if she has had any health problems since her last visit.

   - If she has developed *high blood pressure, heart disease due to blocked arteries, stroke, breast cancer, active liver disease, or gallbladder disease* or she is taking *medicines for seizures, rifampin, or griseofulvin,* see pages 5–6 and 5–7 for instructions. If appropriate, help her choose another method.
   - If she has developed *very bad headaches,* see page 5–18 for instructions.

PLAN FOR HER NEXT VISIT

If she has not developed any condition that means she should not use combined oral contraceptives, provide more supplies if needed. Plan for her next visit before she will need more pills.

Managing Any Problems

If the client reports any of the common side effects of low-dose combined oral contraceptives:

1. Do not dismiss the woman's concerns or take them lightly.
2. If the woman is worried, reassure her that such side effects are not usually dangerous or signs of danger. If she has just started the method, tell her that these side effects usually become less or go away within 3 months.
3. Urge her to keep taking a pill each day *even if she has these side effects*. Skipping pills can risk pregnancy.
4. If she is not satisfied after treatment and counseling, help her choose another method if she wishes.

For this problem:	Try this suggestion:
Nausea	• Suggest taking the pill at night or with food.
Minor headaches	• Suggest taking ibuprofen, aspirin, paracetamol, or other nonsteroidal anti-inflammatory drug (NSAID).
Amenorrhea (no monthly bleeding period). Common. Not usually a sign of pregnancy.	• **Ask if she is having any bleeding at all.** (She may have just a small stain on her underclothing and not recognize it as vaginal bleeding.) If so, reassure her. • **Ask if she is sure she has been taking a pill every day.** If she has, reassure her that she is not likely to be pregnant. She should start the next packet of pills on time. *If she is not sure:* – **Ask if she might have missed the 7-day break between 21-day packets.** This may cause a missed period. Reassure her that she probably is not pregnant. – **Ask if she might have missed 2 or more active, hormonal pills in a row.** If so, assess whether pregnant (see page 4–6). If she

FOLLOWING UP on Combined Oral Contraceptives

For this problem:	Try this suggestion:
Amenorrhea (no monthly bleeding period) *(continued)*	– may be pregnant, tell her. Ask her to stop taking oral contraceptives. Offer her condoms and/or spermicide. She can use them until her next period comes or until it is otherwise clear whether or not she is pregnant. • **Ask if she has recently stopped taking oral contraceptives.** – If she is not pregnant, her periods may take a few months to return. – Ask if she had irregular periods before she took combined oral contraceptives. If so, her periods may be irregular again after she stops the pills.
Spotting or **bleeding** between monthly periods over several months that bothers the client. Common.	• Ask if she has missed any pills. Explain that missing pills can cause bleeding between periods. (Can occur even when taking pills every day, however.) • Ask if she has had vomiting or diarrhea. This may cause the problem. (See page 5–14.) • Ask if she is taking rifampin or medicines for seizures (except valproic acid). These medicines may make oral contraceptives less effective. Encourage her to use condoms and/or spermicide.
Very bad headaches (migraines) — that is, recurring severe head pain, often on one side or pulsating, that can cause nausea and often is made worse by light and noise or moving about	• A woman who develops migraines while using COCs should switch to another method. She should not choose a progestin-only method if she has blurred vision or brief loss of vision, sees flashing lights or zigzag lines, or has brief trouble speaking or moving before or during these headaches. • Refer for care as appropriate.
Minor side effects that last more than 3 months	• If the client prefers pills, consider offering another low-dose combined oral contraceptive or progestin-only oral contraceptives (see Chapter 6).

IMPORTANT POINTS FOR THE USER TO REMEMBER ABOUT

Combined Oral Contraceptives (Pills)

▸ Can be **very effective if taken regularly every day**. If you miss a pill, take it as soon as you can. Then take the next pill at your regular time, even if you take 2 pills at once or on the same day.

▸ **Safe.** Serious problems are very rare.

▸ **Side effects sometimes occur** such as upset stomach (nausea), light bleeding between periods, very light menstrual periods, occasional missed periods, mild headaches, tender breasts, and moodiness. These side effects are **not dangerous and generally become less or stop** in a few months.

▸ You are **welcome back any time** you want help, advice, or another method.

▸ Please **come back for more pills** *before* they run out.

▸ Please **come back or see another health care provider at once** if you have severe, constant pain in the chest, leg, or belly, or very bad headaches, if you see flashing lights or zigzag lines, or if your skin or eyes become unusually yellow (jaundice).

▸ **Pills do not prevent sexually transmitted diseases (STDs) including HIV/AIDS.** If you think you might get an STD, use condoms regularly along with your pills.

IMPORTANT POINTS About Combined Oral Contraceptives 5–19

Emergency Oral Contraception: Oral Contraceptives for Postcoital Contraception

Introduction to Emergency Oral Contraception

What Is Emergency Oral Contraception?

After unprotected sex, emergency oral contraception can prevent pregnancy. Sometimes called postcoital or "morning after" contraception.

Deciding About Emergency Oral Contraception

How Does It Work?

Mainly stops ovulation (release of egg from ovary) but perhaps also works in other ways. Does NOT disrupt existing pregnancy.

How Effective?

Seems to prevent at least three-fourths of pregnancies that would otherwise have occurred. (Average chance of pregnancy due to one act of unprotected intercourse in the second or third week of the menstrual cycle is 8%; after emergency oral contraception, 1–2%.) The sooner emergency oral contraceptives are used, the better they prevent pregnancy.

IMPORTANT: Emergency oral contraception does not prevent sexually transmitted diseases.

Medical Eligibility Criteria for Emergency Oral Contraception

Any woman can use emergency oral contraception if she is not already pregnant.

IMPORTANT: Emergency oral contraception should not be used in place of family planning methods. It should be used only in an emergency—for example:

- A woman has had sex against her will or has been forced to have sex (rape).
- A condom has broken.
- An IUD has come out of place.
- A woman has run out of oral contraceptives, has missed 2 or more progestin-only oral contraceptives, or is more than a few weeks late for a DMPA injection and has had sex without using other family planning.
- Sex took place without contraception, and the woman wants to avoid pregnancy.

Using Emergency Oral Contraception

When to Start

Up to 72 hours after unprotected sex.

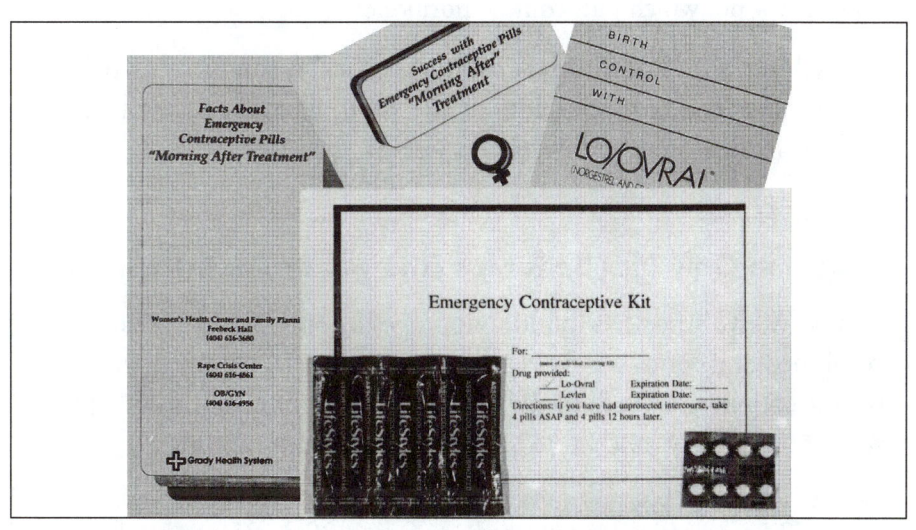

Family planning providers at Grady Memorial Hospital in Atlanta, USA, make up emergency contraceptive kits for clients. Each kit contains 8 low-dose combined oral contraceptive tablets, some condoms, and printed materials about emergency oral contraception and continuing oral contraceptives.

Explaining How to Use Emergency Oral Contraception

FOLLOW THIS PROCEDURE

1. Ask careful questions to determine likelihood of pregnancy. (See page 4–6.) If she is clearly already pregnant, do not provide emergency oral contraceptives.
2. Explain emergency oral contraception, its side effects, and effectiveness. (See advice on page 5–23.)
3. Provide the pills for emergency oral contraception.

GIVE SPECIFIC INSTRUCTIONS

1. Up to 72 hours after unprotected sex, the woman should take 4 low-dose or 2 "standard-dose" combined oral contraceptives, or else take 20 or 25 progestin-only oral contraceptives, and then take another equal dose 12 hours later. (See table on next page.)

IMPORTANT: If she takes pills from a 28-day packet of combined oral contraceptives, she must be sure to take hormone-containing pills. Show her which pills contain hormones.

2. If willing, she should start another method immediately, such as condoms and/or spermicide, or she should avoid sex until she can start her preferred method. (See page 5–24.)

Progestin-Only Pills Better for Emergency Contraception

A large WHO study has found that progestin-only pills are better than combined oral contraceptives (progestin + estrogen) for emergency contraception. Used for emergency contraception, progestin-only pills were more effective and caused less nausea and less vomiting.

Dosage: Either 20 or 25 progestin-only oral contraceptive tablets up to 72 hours after unprotected sex. Then 20 or 25 more tablets 12 hours later. (See table on next page.) *Note:* Special-purpose pills, each containing 0.75 milligrams levonorgestrel, may be available in some places.

The following table tells how many pills to take according to their formulation:

Formulation (examples of brands)	Number of pills to swallow within 72 hours	Number of pills to swallow 12 hours later
Progestin-only oral contraceptives containing 0.075 milligrams (75 micrograms) of norgestrel *(Ovrette, Neogest, Norgeal)*	20	20
Progestin-only oral contraceptives containing 0.03 milligrams (30 micrograms) of levonorgestrel *(Follistrel, Microval, Microlut, Microluton, Mikro-30 Wyeth, Mikro-30, Norgeston, Nortrel)*	25	25
Low-dose COCs containing 0.15 or 0.25 milligrams of levonorgestrel or 0.5 milligrams of norgestrel plus 0.03 milligrams (30 micrograms) of ethinyl estradiol *(Lo-Femenal, Lo-Ovral, Mala-D* (India)*, Nordette, Microgynon-30)*	4	4
"Standard-dose" COCs containing 0.125 or 0.25 milligrams of levonorgestrel or 0.5 milligrams of norgestrel plus 0.05 milligrams (50 micrograms) of ethinyl estradiol *(Eugynon 50, Nordiol, Ovral, Microgynon-50, Nordette 50)*	2	2
Levonorgestrel 0.75 mg *(Postinor-2)*	1	1

IMPORTANT: Other combined oral contraceptive pills may work, too, but their effectiveness for emergency contraception has not been tested. (Note that equal weights of different hormones do *not* mean equal strength.)

GIVE ADVICE ON COMMON PROBLEMS

- **Nausea.** Suggest that she eat something soon after taking the pills to reduce any nausea. Nonprescription anti-nausea medicines such as *Dramamine®* and *Marezine®* can reduce the risk of nausea when taken one half-hour before taking emergency contraceptive pills and every 4 to 6 hours thereafter.
- **Vomiting.** If the woman vomits within 2 hours after taking the pills, she may take another dose. Otherwise, she should NOT take any extra pills. Extra pills will *not* make the method more effective, and they may increase nausea.
- Her next monthly period may start a few days earlier or later than expected. Reassure her that this is not a bad sign.

USING Emergency Oral Contraception

EXPLAIN SPECIFIC REASONS TO RETURN TO THE HEALTH CARE PROVIDER

1. Advise her to return or see another health care provider if her next period is quite different from usual for her, especially if it is:
   - Unusually light (possible pregnancy).
   - Does not start within 4 weeks (possible pregnancy).
   - Unusually painful. (Possible ectopic pregnancy. But emergency oral contraception does not cause ectopic pregnancy.)
2. Describe the symptoms of sexually transmitted diseases—for example, unusual vaginal discharge, pain or burning on urination. Advise her to see a health care provider if any of these symptoms occurs. (See Chapter 16.)

PLAN CONTINUING CONTRACEPTION AND STD PROTECTION

IMPORTANT: Emergency oral contraception is not as effective as most other contraceptive methods. It should not be used regularly in place of another method.

If:	Then:
The woman is likely to have sex again...	Urge her to start using an effective contraceptive. Help her do so or plan to do so.
She does not start any other method immediately...	Give her condoms or spermicide to use at least until she chooses another ongoing method of contraception.

Along with emergency oral contraception, a woman can start any of various ongoing contraceptive methods. These include combined oral contraceptives, condoms, and vaginal methods.

- For example, if she wants low-dose combined oral contraceptives and no medical conditions prevent their use, give her several months' supply of pills and instructions. (See pages 5–12 to 5–15.) She should start these pills on the next day after she finishes the emergency oral contraceptives.

Help the woman decide if she needs ongoing protection from sexually transmitted diseases (STDs): For example, does she have more than one sexual partner? Does her partner have any other partners? Does he have symptoms of STDs? If so, discuss condoms for STD protection. Give her condoms.

Questions and Answers

1. **Do combined oral contraceptives cause cancer?**

   Oral contraceptives have not been proved to cause any common cancer. Oral contraceptives help to *prevent* two kinds of cancer—cancer of the ovaries and cancer of the endometrium (lining of the womb). For breast and cervical cancer: Some studies find that these cancers are more common among certain women who have used oral contraceptives. Other studies do not find this. More research is taking place.

2. **Should a woman take a break from oral contraceptives after a time?**

   No. There is no evidence that "taking a rest" from oral contraceptives is helpful. This practice can lead to unplanned pregnancy.

3. **Does the Pill cause deformed babies? Will the fetus be harmed if a woman takes the Pill while she is pregnant?**

   Good evidence shows that a child conceived after a woman stops taking oral contraceptives will not be deformed because of the Pill. Also, even if a woman takes some pills accidentally while pregnant, they will not make the baby deformed or cause abortion.

4. **Can the Pill make a woman sterile?**

   No. Women who could get pregnant before taking the Pill will be able to get pregnant when they stop taking it. Some Pill users have to wait a few months for normal menstrual periods to return.

5. **Can a woman take the Pill throughout her reproductive years?**

   Yes. There is no minimum or maximum age. Oral contraceptives can be an appropriate method for most women from menarche to menopause. Women age 35 or older who smoke should not use combined oral contraceptives, however, unless they stop smoking.

6. **Can a woman take the Pill if she has not had any babies?**

   Yes. Both women with children and women without children can safely take the Pill.

7. **Must a woman have a pelvic examination before she can start or continue using the Pill?**

   No. Instead, asking the right questions can help to find out whether pregnancy is likely. (See page 4–6.)

   A woman should not be refused oral contraceptives because a pelvic exam cannot be done or because she does not want one. If a woman has symptoms of a gynecological problem, however, a pelvic exam might help find the reason.

8. **Will the Pill make a woman weak?**

   No. The Pill does not cause weakness. In fact, it helps some women feel stronger by preventing anemia (not enough iron in the blood). Women using the Pill lose much less menstrual blood than other women. That is how the Pill prevents anemia.

   A woman may feel different because of the Pill and describe this as weakness, or she may have some other problem that makes her feel weak. She should keep taking her pills. She can go to a doctor or nurse to find out why she feels weak.

9. **If a woman has been using the Pill for a long time, will she still be protected from pregnancy after she stops taking the Pill?**

   No. A woman is protected only as long as she takes her pills regularly.

10. **Can a woman who smokes take the Pill?**

    Women less than age 35 who smoke can be offered low-dose combined oral contraceptives. Older women who smoke should choose another method. Older women who cannot stop smoking can take the progestin-only pill if they prefer pills. *All women who smoke should be urged to stop smoking.*

11. **For emergency contraception, can a woman use combined oral contraceptives from family planning programs, pharmacies, social marketing programs, retail stores, or other outlets?**

    Yes, if necessary. It would be better for her to see a health care provider who can counsel her about emergency contraception and future family planning. If she will not be able to reach a provider within 72 hours after unprotected intercourse, she can obtain combined oral contraceptives herself. (See pages 5–20 to 5–25.)

12. **Can older women who smoke use the Pill for emergency contraception?**

    Yes. Because of the short treatment, even women age 35 or older who are heavy smokers can take emergency oral contraceptives. Preventing pregnancy is important, since pregnancy can be especially dangerous for such women.

Chapter 6
Progestin-Only Oral Contraceptives: How Are They Different?

Key Points

- A good choice for breastfeeding women who want an oral contraceptive.

- Very effective during breastfeeding.

- Very low dose.

- Do not reduce a mother's milk supply.

- No estrogen side effects.

- If used when not breastfeeding, **changes in vaginal bleeding are likely**—especially irregular periods and bleeding between periods. Not dangerous and not a sign of danger.

- Can be used for emergency contraception after unprotected sex.

Chapter 6

Progestin-Only Oral Contraceptives: How Are They Different?

Progestin-only oral contraceptives differ from combined oral contraceptives in some important ways. This chapter describes those differences. Otherwise, see Chapter 5.

Contents

- Introduction to Progestin-Only Oral Contraceptives 6–3
- Deciding About Progestin-Only Oral Contraceptives 6–4
  - How Do They Work? 6–4
  - How Effective? 6–4
  - Advantages and Disadvantages 6–5
  - Medical Eligibility Checklist 6–7
- Starting Progestin-Only Oral Contraceptives 6–9
  - When to Start 6–9
  - Providing Progestin-Only Oral Contraceptives . . . 6–10
  - Explaining How to Use 6–11
- Following Up 6–13
  - Helping Clients at Any Routine Return Visit 6–13
  - Managing Any Problems 6–13
- Important Points for the User to Remember 6–16
- Questions and Answers 6–17

Introduction to Progestin-Only Oral Contraceptives

- Women who use progestin-only oral contraceptives swallow a pill every day to prevent pregnancy. Progestin-only oral contraceptives contain very small amounts of only one kind of hormone, a progestin. Progestin-only oral contraceptives contain one-half to one-tenth as much progestin as combined oral contraceptives. They do not contain estrogen. Also called progestin-only pills (POPs), POCs, and minipills.

- Progestin-only oral contraceptives are the best oral contraceptive for breastfeeding women. They do not seem to reduce milk production. This chapter looks mainly at progestin-only oral contraceptives for breastfeeding women. Women who are not breastfeeding also can use progestin-only oral contraceptives.

Deciding About Progestin-Only Oral Contraceptives

How Do They Work?

- Thicken cervical mucus, making it difficult for sperm to pass through.
- Stops ovulation (release of eggs from ovaries) in about half of menstrual cycles.

(Breastfeeding prevents pregnancy in the same ways.)

Progestin-only oral contraceptives do NOT work by disrupting existing pregnancy.

How Effective?

For breastfeeding women: Very effective as commonly used—About 1 pregnancy per 100 women in first year of use. (More effective than combined oral contraceptives as commonly used because breastfeeding itself provides much protection against pregnancy.)

(Pregnancy rate for progestin-only oral contraceptives as commonly used by women **not** breastfeeding is not available. Mistakes in pill-taking lead to pregnancy more often than with combined oral contraceptives. But pill-taking may be easier because a woman takes the same pill every day without breaks.)

For all women: Very effective when used correctly and consistently— 0.5 pregnancies per 100 women in first year of use (1 in every 200) (not quite as effective as combined oral contraceptives used correctly and consistently).

IMPORTANT: Most effective when taken at about the same time every day.

Advantages and Disadvantages

ADVANTAGES

- Can be used by nursing mothers starting 6 weeks after childbirth. Quantity and quality of breast milk do not seem harmed. (In contrast, combined oral contraceptives can slightly reduce milk production.)

- No estrogen side effects. Do not increase risk of estrogen-related complications such as heart attack or stroke.

- Women take one pill every day with no break. Easier to understand than taking 21-day combined pills.

- Can be very effective during breastfeeding.

- Even less risk of progestin-related side effects, such as acne and weight gain, than with combined oral contraceptives.

- May help prevent:
    - Benign breast disease,
    - Endometrial and ovarian cancer,
    - Pelvic inflammatory disease.

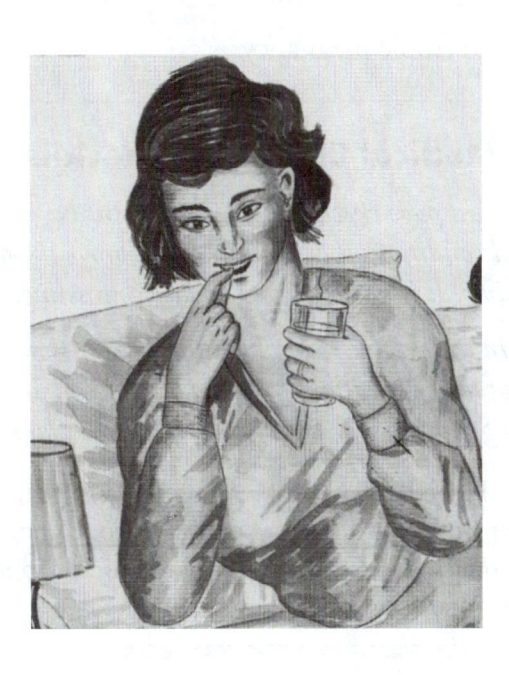

DISADVANTAGES

- For women who are *not breastfeeding*—common side effects (*not* signs of sickness): Changes in menstrual bleeding are normal, including irregular periods, spotting or bleeding between periods (common), and amenorrhea (missed periods), possibly for several months (less common). (Some women see amenorrhea as an advantage.) A few women may have prolonged or heavy menstrual bleeding.

  (Breastfeeding women normally do not have regular periods for some months, whether or not they use progestin-only oral contraceptives. Therefore menstrual changes due to progestin-only oral contraceptives generally are not noticed or bothersome. Progestin-only oral contraceptives may lengthen amenorrhea during breastfeeding.)

- Less common side effects include headaches and breast tenderness.

- Should be taken at about the same time each day to work best. For women who are not breastfeeding, even taking a pill more than a few hours late increases the risk of pregnancy, and missing 2 or more pills increases the risk greatly.

- Do not prevent ectopic pregnancy.

Using the Medical Eligibility Checklist

*The list on the next page checks whether the client has any **known** medical conditions that prevent use of progestin-only oral contraceptives. It is not meant to replace counseling.*

*The questions in the checklist refer to **known conditions**. Generally, you can learn of these conditions by asking the client. You do not usually have to perform laboratory tests or physical examinations.*

IMPORTANT: Progestin-only oral contraceptives contain no estrogen. Many of the criteria that restrict use of combined oral contraceptives, which contain estrogen, do not apply to progestin-only oral contraceptives.

6–6 Essentials of Contraceptive Technology

MEDICAL ELIGIBILITY CHECKLIST FOR

Progestin-Only Oral Contraceptives

Ask the client the questions below. If she answers NO to ALL of the questions, then she CAN use progestin-only oral contraceptives (POCs) if she wants. If she answers YES to a question below, follow the instructions. In some cases she can still use progestin-only oral contraceptives.

1. Do you have or have you ever had breast cancer?

☐ No ☐ **Yes** ▶ Do not provide POCs. Help her choose a method without hormones.

2. Do you have jaundice, severe cirrhosis of the liver, a liver infection or tumor? (Are her eyes or skin unusually yellow?)

☐ No ☐ **Yes** ▶ Perform physical exam or refer. If she has serious active liver disease (*jaundice, painful or enlarged liver, viral hepatitis, liver tumor*), do not provide POCs. Refer for care. Help her choose a method without hormones.

3. Are you breastfeeding a baby less than 6 weeks old?

☐ No ☐ **Yes** ▶ Can give her POCs now with instructions on when to start—when the baby is 6 weeks old (see page 6–9).

4. Do you have serious problems with your blood vessels? If so, what problems?

☐ No ☐ **Yes** ▶ Do not provide POPs if she reports blood clots (except superficial clots). Help her choose another effective method.

5. Are you taking medicine for seizures? Taking rifampin (rifampicin) or griseofulvin?

☐ No ☐ **Yes** ▶ If she is taking *phenytoin, carbamezapine, barbiturates*, or *primidone* for seizures or *rifampin* or *griseofulvin*, provide condoms or spermicide to use along with POCs. If she prefers, or if she is on long-term treatment, help her choose another effective method.

6. Do you think you are pregnant?

☐ No ☐ **Yes** ▶ Assess whether pregnant (see page 4–6). If she might be pregnant, also give her condoms or spermicide to use until reasonably sure that she is not pregnant. Then she can start POCs.

Be sure to explain the health benefits and risks and the side effects of the method that the client will use. Also, point out any conditions that would make the method inadvisable when relevant to the client.

DECIDING About Progestin-Only Oral Contraceptives

Most Women Can Use Progestin-Only Oral Contraceptives

In general, most women CAN use progestin-only oral contraceptives safely and effectively.* Progestin-only oral contraceptives can be used in any circumstances by women who:

- Are breastfeeding (starting as soon as 6 weeks after childbirth),
- Smoke cigarettes,
- Have no children,
- Are any age, including adolescents and over 40,
- Are fat or thin,
- Have just had abortion or miscarriage.

Also, women with these conditions CAN use progestin-only oral contraceptives in any circumstances:

- Benign breast disease,
- Headaches,
- Iron deficiency anemia,
- Varicose veins,
- Valvular heart disease,
- Malaria,
- Sickle cell disease,
- Schistosomiasis,
- Pelvic inflammatory disease,
- Sexually transmitted diseases,
- Heavy, painful menstrual periods,
- Irregular menstrual periods,
- Endometriosis,
- Thyroid disease,
- Benign ovarian tumors,
- Uterine fibroids,
- Epilepsy,
- Tuberculosis (unless taking rifampin; see checklist question 5 on page 6–7).

*Characteristics and conditions listed in this box are in WHO Eligibility Criteria category 1. Women with characteristics and conditions in WHO category 2 also can use this method. See Appendix, page A–1.

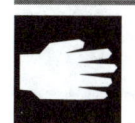

Starting Progestin-Only Oral Contraceptives

When to Start

IMPORTANT: A woman can be *given* progestin-only oral contraceptives *at any time* and told when to start taking them.

Woman's situation	When to start
Breastfeeding	• As early as 6 weeks after childbirth. • *Fully or nearly fully breastfeeding* effectively prevents pregnancy for at least 6 months or until she has a menstrual period, *whichever comes first* (see Chapter 15). Progestin-only oral contraceptives can give her extra protection if she wants it. • If only *partially breastfeeding* and child receives much other food or drink, 6 weeks after childbirth is the best time to start progestin-only pills. If she waits longer, fertility may return. • If *menstrual periods have returned*, she can start progestin-only oral contraceptives any time it is reasonably certain that she is not pregnant (see page 4–6 and "Having menstrual cycles," page 6–10).
After childbirth if not breastfeeding	• Immediately or at any time in the first 4 weeks after childbirth. No need to wait for her menstrual period to return. • After 4 weeks, any time it is reasonably certain that she is not pregnant (see page 4–6). If not reasonably certain, she should avoid sex or use condoms or spermicide until her first period begins and then start progestin-only oral contraceptives.

Woman's situation	When to start
After miscarriage or abortion	• Immediately or in the first 7 days after either first- or second-trimester miscarriage or abortion. • Later, any time it is reasonably certain that she is not pregnant (see page 4–6).
Having menstrual cycles	• Any time it is reasonably certain that she is not pregnant (see page 4–6). • In the first 5 days of menstrual bleeding. The first day of menstrual bleeding may be easiest to remember. No backup method is needed for extra protection. • If not starting in the first 5 days of her menstrual period, she should also use condoms or spermicide or avoid sex for at least the next 48 hours. If possible, give her condoms or spermicide.
When stopping another method	• Immediately. No need to wait for a first period after using injectables.

Providing Progestin-Only Oral Contraceptives

Same as for combined oral contraceptives (see page 5–10).

Also can be used for emergency contraception (see pages 5–22 and 5–23).

Explaining How to Use

Same as for combined oral contraceptives (see pages 5–12 to 5–14) EXCEPT:

GIVE SPECIFIC INSTRUCTIONS

IMPORTANT: The client should always TAKE ONE PILL EVERY DAY. If not breastfeeding, it is best to take the pill at the same time each day if possible; even taking a pill more than a few hours late increases the risk of pregnancy, and missing 2 or more pills in a row greatly increases the risk.

▶ **Starting the next packet:**

When she finishes one packet, she should take the first pill from the next packet **on the very next day.** All pills are active, hormonal pills. There is no wait between packets.

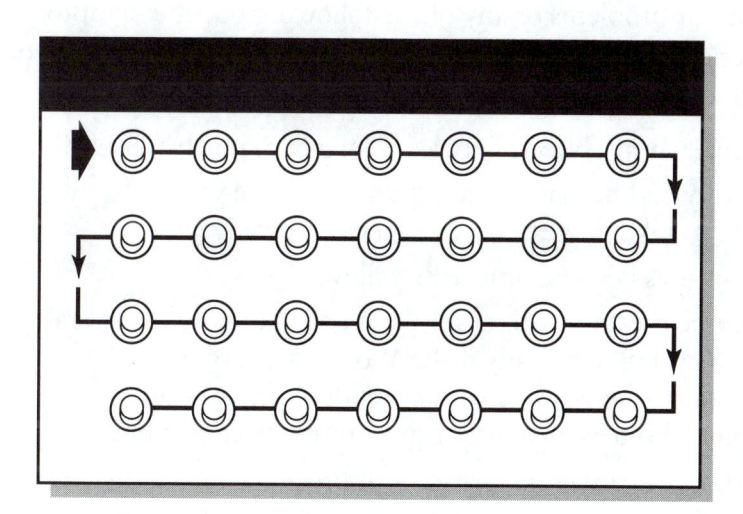

28 or 35 pills of the same color: These are progestin-only oral contraceptives.

▶ If a woman **forgets one or more pills:**

She should take 1 as soon as she remembers and then keep taking 1 pill each day as usual.

- A breastfeeding woman using progestin-only pills for extra protection is still protected if she misses pills.
- If more than 3 hours late taking a pill, a woman who is **not** breastfeeding or who is **breastfeeding but her menses have returned** should also *use condoms or spermicide or else avoid sex for 2 days.* She should take the last missed pill as soon as she can. Then she should keep taking 1 each day as usual.

GIVE ADVICE ON COMMON PROBLEMS

Same as for combined oral contraceptives (see page 5–14) EXCEPT, *for women not breastfeeding*, especially mention spotting or bleeding between periods and mention amenorrhea. These changes are common, normal, and not harmful.

EXPLAIN SPECIFIC REASONS TO SEE A NURSE OR DOCTOR

Describe the symptoms of problems that require medical attention.
Serious complications of progestin-only pill use are rare. Still, a woman should see a doctor or nurse or return to the clinic if she has questions or problems or any of the following possible symptoms of more serious problems. Progestin-only oral contraceptives may or may not cause these problems.

- Extremely heavy bleeding (twice as long or as much as usual for her).
- Any very bad headaches that start or become worse after she begins to take progestin-only oral contraceptives.
- Skin or eyes become unusually yellow.
- Might be pregnant (for example, missed period after several regular cycles), especially if she also has signs of ectopic pregnancy—abdominal pain or tenderness, or faintness. A woman who develops these signs must seek care at once.

Note on ectopic pregnancy: Pregnancies among consistent users of progestin-only oral contraceptives are few, especially during breastfeeding. When pregnancy occurs, however, as many as 1 in every 10 may occur outside the uterus (ectopic pregnancy). Ectopic pregnancy is life-threatening and requires treatment at once.

Following Up

Helping Clients at Any Routine Return Visit

Same as for combined oral contraceptives (see page 5–16) EXCEPT:

If the client has developed *breast cancer or active liver disease* or she is taking *medicine for seizures, rifampin, or griseofulvin*, see page 6–7 for instructions. If appropriate, help her choose another method.

If the client has developed any of the following conditions, see "Managing Any Problems," this page through 6–15.

- *Unexplained abnormal vaginal bleeding* that may suggest pregnancy or an underlying medical condition.
- *Heart disease due to blocked arteries, or stroke.*
- *Very bad headaches.*

Managing Any Problems

Same as for combined oral contraceptives (see page 5–17 and 5–18) EXCEPT the following:

For this problem:	Try this suggestion:
Amenorrhea (no monthly bleeding period) **or** irregular bleeding and spotting in a breastfeeding woman	• **Reassure the woman that this is normal during breastfeeding**, whether or not a woman is using progestin-only oral contraceptives.

FOLLOWING UP on Progestin-Only Oral Contraceptives

For this problem:	Try this suggestion:
Amenorrhea or irregular bleeding and spotting that bothers the client who is *not* breastfeeding	• Ask if she has been having regular monthly periods while taking progestin-only pills and then suddenly had no period. She may have been ovulating (producing eggs). Rule out pregnancy (see page 4–6). • If not likely that she is pregnant, tell the client that **these bleeding patterns are normal** with progestin-only oral contraceptives. They are not harmful. She is losing less blood than she would if she were not using family planning. Explain that this can improve her health. It helps prevent anemia.
Unexplained abnormal vaginal bleeding that suggests pregnancy or underlying medical condition	• **She can continue using progestin-only oral contraceptives** while her condition is being evaluated. • Explain that progestin-only oral contraceptives sometimes change vaginal bleeding patterns. This is not harmful. • Evaluate and treat any underlying medical condition, including ectopic pregnancy, or refer for care.
Heart disease due to blocked arteries (ischemic heart disease) or stroke	• A woman who has this condition can safely start using progestin-only oral contraceptives. If, however, the condition develops after she starts using them, she should switch to a method without hormones. • Refer for care as appropriate.

For this problem:	Try this suggestion:
Very bad headaches (migraines) with blurred vision	• A woman who gets migraine headaches can safely start using progestin-only oral contraceptives. She should switch to a method without hormones, however, if these headaches start or become worse after she begins using progestin-only oral contraceptives *and* these headaches involve blurred vision, temporary loss of vision, seeing flashing lights or zigzag lines, or trouble speaking or moving. • Refer for care as appropriate.

IMPORTANT: If the woman is not satisfied after treatment and counseling, help her choose another method if she wishes.

IMPORTANT POINTS FOR THE USER TO REMEMBER ABOUT

Progestin-Only Oral Contraceptives (Pills) for Breastfeeding Women

▶ Good family planning method for breastfeeding women who want oral contraceptives.

▶ Very effective when used during breastfeeding.

▶ Swallow one pill every day.
  - When a pill packet is empty, take the first pill from another packet on the next day.

▶ Changes in vaginal bleeding are normal when breastfeeding. They are not a sign of danger.

▶ Please **come back to get more pills** *before* they run out.

▶ You are **welcome back any time** you want help, advice, or another method. Keep taking your pills until you come back.

▶ Please **come back at once** if you think you might be pregnant, especially if you also have severe pain or tenderness in the lower belly or you feel faint. Also come back if you have unusually heavy vaginal bleeding or very bad headaches that start or become worse after you begin using progestin-only pills or if your skin or eyes become unusually yellow.

▶ Progestin-only pills do not prevent sexually transmitted diseases (STDs) including HIV/AIDS. If you think you might get an STD, use condoms regularly along with your pills.

❓ Questions and Answers

1. **Can a woman who is breastfeeding a baby take progestin-only pills?**

   Yes. This is a good choice for a breastfeeding mother who wants a hormonal method. Progestin-only pills are safe for both the mother and the baby starting as early as 6 weeks after childbirth.

2. **If a woman does not have her monthly period while taking progestin-only oral contraceptives, does this mean that she is pregnant?**

   Probably not, especially if she is breastfeeding. If she has been taking her pills every day and has no other signs of pregnancy (including ectopic pregnancy), she is very probably not pregnant and can keep taking her pills. If she is still worried about being pregnant after being reassured, she can be offered a pregnancy test, if available, or referred for one. If she is not breastfeeding and not having her period bothers her, she may want to choose another family planning method.

3. **Does it matter what time of day a woman takes her pill?**

   If breastfeeding, no. If not breastfeeding, yes. Because the progestin-only pill contains very little hormone, a woman who is not breastfeeding should try to take her pill at the same time each day. If she is more than 3 hours late taking her pill, she should take the missed pill as soon as she remembers and take the next pill at the usual time of day. Then for added protection, she should either use condoms or spermicide or else avoid sex for the next 2 days. If a woman often misses pills, she may want to consider another family planning method. On a return visit, the provider should ask the client if she has missed pills. If she has missed several pills in a row, the provider may want to assess whether the woman might be pregnant (see page 4–6), especially if she is not breastfeeding.

QUESTIONS & ANSWERS About Progestin-Only Oral Contraceptives

4. **Must the progestin-only pill be taken every day?**

   Yes. All of the pills contain the hormone that prevents pregnancy. If a woman does not take a pill every day, she may become pregnant. (In contrast, the last 7 pills in a 28-pill packet of combined oral contraceptive are not active. They contain no hormones.)

5. **Are ovarian cysts more common with progestin-only pills?**

   Yes. So-called ovarian cysts are more common among women taking progestin-only pills than among women using combined pills or using no contraception at all. What are often called ovarian cysts are really follicles (small fluid-filled structures in the ovary) that continue to grow beyond the usual size in a normal menstrual cycle. They are not very common and usually disappear on their own. They may cause some abdominal pain but rarely require treatment.

6. **Is it hard to get pregnant after using progestin-only pills?**

   No. Women who have used progestin-only pills can become pregnant as quickly as women stopping barrier methods and sooner than women stopping combined pills.

7. **Can progestin-only pills be used for emergency contraception after unprotected sex?**

   Yes. (See pages 5–20 to 5–25.) Up to 72 hours after unprotected sex, the woman should take 20 or 25 progestin-only oral contraceptive tablets containing the progestin levonorgestrel or norgestrel. Then 12 hours later she should take another 20 or 25 progestin-only tablets. Whether she takes 20 + 20 or 25 + 25 depends on the formulation, or brand. Either of these doses will amount to about the same total dose as 4 + 4 low-dose combined oral contraceptives containing levonorgrestrel or norgestrel.

   In some areas a progestin-only formulation may be available especially for emergency use. This formulation may be called *Postinor-2*. Each tablet contains 0.75 milligrams of levonorgestrel. A woman takes one tablet within 72 hours after unprotected sex, and she takes a second tablet 12 hours after the first tablet.

Chapter 7
DMPA Injectable Contraceptive

Key Points

- **Very effective and safe.**

- **Changes in vaginal bleeding are likely** — spotting, light bleeding between periods, or amenorrhea. Weight gain is common. Not dangerous and not a sign of danger. Counseling in advance is important.

- **Private.** Others cannot tell that a woman is using it.

- **Can be used by women of any age, whether or not they have children.**

- **Return of fertility delayed about 4 months longer on average** than if a woman had been using combined oral contraceptives, an IUD, condoms, or a vaginal method.

- **Safe during breastfeeding.** Nursing mothers can start DMPA 6 weeks after childbirth.

Chapter 7
DMPA Injectable Contraceptive

Contents

- Introduction to Injectable Contraceptives 7–3
- Deciding About DMPA 7–3
  - How Does It Work? 7–3
  - How Effective? 7–4
  - Advantages and Disadvantages 7–4
  - Medical Eligibility Checklist 7–6
- Starting DMPA 7–7
  - When to Start 7–7
  - Providing DMPA 7–9
  - Explaining How to Use 7–10
  - Giving the Injection 7–12
  - Proper Handling of Needles and Syringes 7–13
- Following Up 7–14
  - Helping Clients at Routine Return Visits 7–14
  - Managing Any Problems 7–15
- Comparing DMPA and NET EN 7–18
- Important Points for the User to Remember 7–19
- Questions and Answers 7–20

Introduction to Injectable Contraceptives

- Women who use this method receive injections to prevent pregnancy.

- This chapter describes the most common type of injectable contraceptive, DMPA. DMPA is given every 3 months. It contains a progestin, similar to the natural hormone that a woman's body makes. The hormone is released slowly into the bloodstream. Also known as depot-medroxyprogesterone acetate, *Depo-Provera*®, Depo, and *Megestron*®.

- There are other injectable contraceptives. NET EN—also called *Noristerat*®, norethindrone enanthate, and norethisterone enanthate—is given every 2 months. Much of the information that applies to DMPA also applies to NET EN. (For differences between DMPA and NET EN, see page 7–18.) Also, monthly injectable contraceptives are available in some countries. Monthly injectables include *Cyclofem*™, *Cycloprovera*™, and *Mesigyna*®. Monthly injectables contain estrogen and progestin. Therefore they are different from DMPA and NET EN. Monthly injectables are not discussed in this chapter.

Deciding About DMPA

How Does It Work?

- Mainly stops ovulation (release of eggs from ovaries).
- Also thickens cervical mucus, making it difficult for sperm to pass through.

DMPA does NOT work by disrupting existing pregnancy.

How Effective?

Very effective—0.3 pregnancies per 100 women in first year of use (1 in every 333) when injections are regularly spaced 3 months apart. Pregnancy rates may be higher for women who are late for an injection or who miss an injection or if providers run out of supplies.

Advantages and Disadvantages

Advantages
- Very effective.
- Private. No one else can tell that a woman is using it.
- Long-term pregnancy prevention but reversible. One injection prevents pregnancy for at least 3 months.
- Does not interfere with sex.
- Increased sexual enjoyment because no need to worry about pregnancy.
- No daily pill-taking.
- Allows some flexibility in return visits. Client can return as much as 2 to 4 weeks early (although this is not ideal) and 2 weeks and perhaps up to 4 weeks late for next injection.
- Can be used at any age.
- Quantity and quality of breast milk do not seem harmed. Can be used by nursing mothers as soon as 6 weeks after childbirth.
- No estrogen side effects. Does not increase the risk of estrogen-related complications such as heart attack.
- Helps prevent ectopic pregnancies.
- Helps prevent endometrial cancer.
- Helps prevent uterine fibroids.
- May help prevent ovarian cancer.
- Special advantages for some women:
  - May help prevent iron-deficiency anemia.
  - May make seizures less frequent in women with epilepsy.
  - Makes sickle cell crises less frequent and less painful.

DISADVANTAGES

- **Common side effects** (*not* signs of sickness):
  - Changes in menstrual bleeding are likely, including:
    - Light spotting or bleeding. Most common at first.
    - Heavy bleeding. Can occur at first. Rare.
    - Amenorrhea. Normal, especially after first year of use. (Some women see amenorrhea as an advantage.)
  - May cause weight gain (average of 1–2 kilo, or 2–4 lbs., each year). (Changes in diet can help control or prevent weight gain. Some women see weight gain as an advantage.)
- Delayed return of fertility (until DMPA levels in the body drop). About 4 months longer wait before pregnancy than for women who had been using combined oral contraceptives, IUDs, condoms, or a vaginal method.
- Requires another injection every 3 months.
- May cause headaches, breast tenderness, moodiness, nausea, hair loss, less sex drive, and/or acne in some women.
- Does not protect against sexually transmitted diseases including HIV/AIDS.

   IMPORTANT: Ask the client if she might have or get a sexually transmitted disease (STD). (Has more than one sexual partner? Partner has more than one partner? Could this happen in future?)

   If she has or might get an STD, urge her to use condoms regularly. Give her condoms. She can still use DMPA.

Using the Medical Eligibility Checklist

*The list on the next page checks whether the client has any **known** medical conditions that prevent use of DMPA. It is not meant to replace counseling.*

*The questions in the checklist refer to **known conditions**. Generally, you can learn of these conditions by asking the client. You do not usually have to perform laboratory tests or physical examinations.*

IMPORTANT: DMPA contains no estrogen. Many of the criteria that restrict use of combined oral contraceptives, which contain estrogen, do not apply to DMPA.

DECIDING About DMPA

MEDICAL ELIGIBILITY CHECKLIST FOR

DMPA Injectable

Ask the client the questions below. If she answers NO to ALL of the questions, then she CAN use DMPA. If she answers YES to a question below, follow the instructions.

1. Are you breastfeeding a baby less than 6 weeks old?

   ☐ No   ☐ Yes ▶ She can start using DMPA beginning 6 weeks after childbirth. If she is fully or almost fully breastfeeding, however, she is protected from pregnancy for 6 months after childbirth or until her menstrual period returns—*whichever comes first*. Then she must begin contraception at once to avoid pregnancy. Encourage her to continue breastfeeding.

2. Do you have problems with your heart or blood vessels? Have you ever had such problems? If so, what problems?

   ☐ No   ☐ Yes ▶ Do not provide DMPA if she reports *heart attack, heart disease due to blocked arteries, stroke, blood clots (except superficial clots), severe chest pain with unusual shortness of breath, severe high blood pressure, diabetes for more than 20 years, or damage to vision, kidneys, or nervous system caused by diabetes*. Help her choose another effective method.

3. Do you have high blood pressure?

   ☐ No   ☐ Yes ▶ If you cannot check blood pressure (BP) and she reports high BP, can provide DMPA. Refer for BP check.

   Check BP if feasible:

   If systolic BP below 160 and diastolic BP below 100, okay to give DMPA. *If systolic BP over 160 or diastolic BP over 100*, do not provide DMPA. Help her choose another method except not COCs.

4. Do you have or have you ever had breast cancer?

   ☐ No   ☐ Yes ▶ Do not provide DMPA. Help her choose a method without hormones.

5. Do you have severe cirrhosis of the liver, a liver infection or tumor? (Are her eyes or skin unusually yellow?)

   ☐ No   ☐ Yes ▶ Perform physical exam or refer. If she has serious active liver disease (*jaundice, painful or enlarged liver, viral hepatitis, liver tumor*), do not provide DMPA. Refer for care. Help her choose a method without hormones.

6. Do you think you are pregnant?

   ☐ No   ☐ Yes ▶ Assess whether pregnant (see page 4–6). Give her condoms or spermicide to use until reasonably sure that she is not pregnant. Then she can start DMPA.

7. Do you have vaginal bleeding that is unusual for you?

   ☐ No   ☐ Yes ▶ If she is not likely to be pregnant but has unexplained vaginal bleeding that suggests an underlying medical condition, *can* provide DMPA. Assess and treat any underlying condition as appropriate, or refer. Reassess DMPA use based on findings.

Be sure to explain the health benefits and risks and the side effects of the method that the client will use. Also, point out any conditions that would make the method inadvisable when relevant to the client.

Most Women Can Use DMPA

In general, most women CAN use DMPA injectable contraceptive safely and effectively.* DMPA injectable can be used in any circumstances by women who:

- Are breastfeeding (starting as soon as 6 weeks after childbirth),
- Smoke cigarettes,
- Have no children,
- Are any age, including adolescents and over 40,
- Are fat** or thin,
- Have just had abortion or miscarriage.

Also, women with these conditions CAN use DMPA in any circumstances:

- Benign breast disease,
- Mild headaches,
- Mild or moderate high blood pressure,
- Iron deficiency anemia,
- Varicose veins,
- Valvular heart disease,
- Irregular menstrual periods,
- Malaria,
- Schistosomiasis,
- Sickle cell disease
- Thyroid disease,
- Uterine fibroids,
- Epilepsy,
- Tuberculosis.

*Characteristics and conditions listed in this box are in WHO Eligibility Criteria category 1. Women with characteristics and conditions in WHO category 2 also can use this method. See Appendix, page A–1.

**Very fat is WHO category 2.

Starting DMPA

When to Start

Woman's situation	When to start
Having menstrual cycles	• Any time it is reasonably certain that she is not pregnant. (See page 4–6.) **IMPORTANT:** If she is not at risk of pregnancy (for example, has not had sex since last menstrual period), she may start DMPA at any time she wants.

Woman's situation	When to start
Having menstrual cycles *(continued)*	• If starting during the first 7 days after menstrual bleeding starts, no back-up method is needed for extra protection. • If she is starting on or after day 8 of her menstrual period, she should use condoms or spermicide or avoid sex for at least the next 48 hours. If possible, give her condoms or spermicide.
Breastfeeding	• As early as 6 weeks after childbirth. • *Fully or nearly fully breastfeeding* effectively prevents pregnancy for at least 6 months or until she has a menstrual period, whichever comes first (see Chapter 15). DMPA can give her extra protection if she wants it. • If only *partially breastfeeding* and child receives much other food or drink, 6 weeks after childbirth is the best time to start DMPA. If she waits longer, fertility may return. • If *menstrual periods have returned*, she can start DMPA any time it is reasonably certain that she is not pregnant (see page 4–6). See "Having menstrual cycles," above.
After childbirth if not breastfeeding	• Immediately or at any time in the first 6 weeks after childbirth. No need to wait for her menstrual period to return. • After 6 weeks, any time it is reasonably certain that she is not pregnant. (See page 4–6.) If not reasonably certain, she should avoid sex or use condoms or spermicide until her first period begins and then start DMPA.

Woman's situation	When to start
After miscarriage or abortion	• Immediately or in the first 7 days after either first- or second-trimester miscarriage or abortion. • Later, any time it is reasonably certain that she is not pregnant.
When stopping another method	• Immediately.

Providing DMPA

IMPORTANT: A woman who chooses DMPA benefits from good counseling.

A friendly provider who listens to a woman's concerns, answers her questions, and gives clear, practical information about side effects, especially probable bleeding change including amenorrhea (no bleeding at all), will help the woman use DMPA with success and satisfaction.

You can follow these steps to provide DMPA:

1. **Explain how to use DMPA** (see page 7–10).
2. **Give the injection** (see pages 7–12 and 7–13).
3. Plan with the woman for her **return visit in 3 months** for her next injection. Discuss how to remember the date, perhaps tying it to a holiday or change of season.
4. Invite the client to **come back any time** she has questions or problems or wants another method.

Explaining How to Use

Give specific instructions

1. The client should try to **come back on time** for the next injection. She may come as much as 2 to 4 weeks early (although this is not ideal) or 2 weeks and perhaps up to 4 weeks late.

2. If more than 2 weeks late for her next injection, she should use condoms or spermicide or else avoid sex until the next injection.

3. She should come back no matter how late she is. The provider can ask questions to see if she might be pregnant (see page 4–6). She still may be able to get her injection. (See "Managing Any Problems," page 7–15.)

Give advice on common problems

1. **Mention the most common side effects**—in particular, she can expect changes in menstrual bleeding and possibly weight gain.

2. **Explain about these side effects:**
   - At first she probably will have bleeding at unexpected times. The amount of bleeding usually decreases over time. After 6 to 12 months of use, she probably will have little vaginal bleeding or none at all.
   - These changes are common, normal, and not harmful. They do not mean that she is pregnant or sick or that bad blood is building up inside her. Little or no bleeding can make some women healthier. It helps prevent anemia.
   - She may gain weight. This also is common, normal, and not harmful.

3. Invite the client to **come back any time** she needs more help with any problem or wants a different method. (See pages 7–15 through 7–17.)

Explain specific reasons to see a nurse or doctor

Describe the symptoms of problems that require medical attention. Serious complications of DMPA are rare. Still, a woman should see a doctor or nurse or return to the clinic if she has questions or problems or any of the following possible symptoms of more serious problems. DMPA may or may not cause these problems.

- Bothersome extremely heavy bleeding (twice as long or twice as much as usual for her).
- Very bad headaches that start or become worse after she begins DMPA.
- Skin or eyes become unusually yellow.

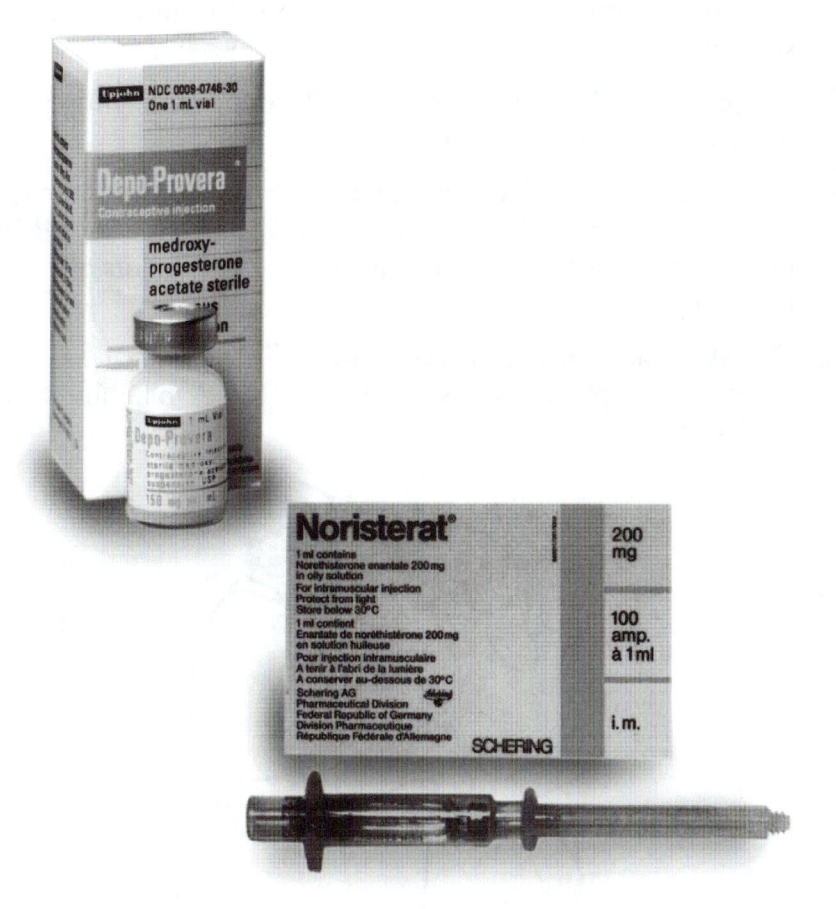

Giving the Injection

Equipment and Supplies Needed:

- One dose of DMPA (150 mg),
- An antiseptic and cotton wool,
- A 2 or 5 ml syringe and a 21- to 23-gauge intramuscular needle. **Syringe and needle should be sterile, or high-level disinfected if sterilization is not possible.**

Steps:

1. Wash hands or else wash hands and wear clean gloves.
2. Wash injection site with soap and water if needed and wipe with antiseptic, if available. Use a circular motion from the injection site outward.
3. Shake vial **gently**, wipe top of vial and stopper with antiseptic, and fill syringe with proper dose.
4. Insert sterile needle deep into the upper arm (deltoid muscle) or into buttocks (gluteal muscle, upper outer portion). For DMPA the upper arm is more convenient. Inject the contents of the syringe.
5. **Do NOT massage the injection site.** Tell client not to massage or rub the site. Explain that this could cause DMPA to be absorbed too fast.

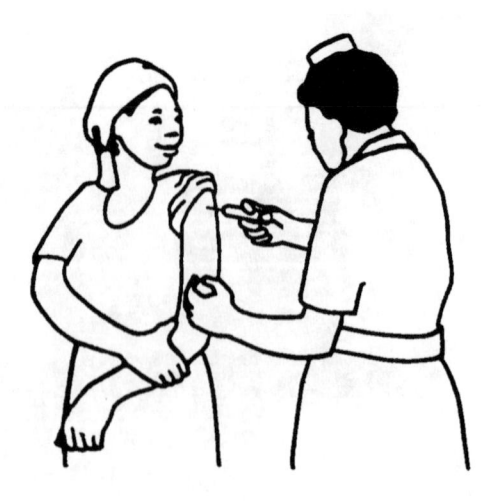

Proper Handling of Needles and Syringes

IMPORTANT: Use DISPOSABLE syringes and needles if available. They do not transmit infections if disposed of properly.

Disposable Needles and Syringes

- Place used disposable syringes and needles in a puncture-proof container.

- Burn or bury the container when three-quarters full.

- Do not put disposable needles in the trash (even if decontaminated). Do not recap them before disposal. Do not bend or break needles before disposal.

- **Do not reuse disposable syringes and needles.** They are meant to be destroyed after one use. Because of their shape, they are very difficult to disinfect. Therefore, they might transmit diseases such as HIV/AIDS.

Reusable Needles and Syringes

- If disposable syringes are not available, use reusable needles and syringes that have been **properly sterilized or high-level disinfected** if sterilization is not possible.

- These needles and syringes must be sterilized or high-level disinfected again after each use. (See page 4–10.)

Following Up

Helping Clients at Routine Return Visits

ASK QUESTIONS

At any return visit:

1. Ask if the client has any questions or anything to discuss.
2. Ask the client about her experience with the method, whether she is satisfied, and whether she has any problems. Give her any information or help that she needs and invite her to return any time she has questions or concerns. If she has problems that cannot be resolved, help her choose another method.
3. Ask about her bleeding patterns.
4. Ask if she has had any health problems since her last visit.

   - If the client has developed *heart disease due to blocked arteries, stroke, blood clots (except superficial clots), breast cancer, severe high blood pressure, or active liver disease*, help her choose a method without hormones (see page 7–6).

   - If the client has developed *very bad headaches*, see "Managing Any Problems" (page 7–17).

PLAN FOR HER NEXT VISIT

If she has not developed any condition that means she should not use DMPA and she wants to continue this method, give her the injection and plan for her next visit in 3 months.

Managing Any Problems

If the client reports any of the common side effects of DMPA:

1. Do not dismiss the woman's concerns or take them lightly.
2. If the woman is worried, reassure her that such side effects are not usually dangerous or signs of danger.
3. If the woman is not satisfied after treatment and counseling, help her choose another method if she wishes.

For this problem:	Try this suggestion:
More than 2 weeks late for her injection and has been sexually active	• If she might be pregnant, assess for pregnancy. (See page 4–6.) Remember that women using DMPA often have no monthly bleeding period (amenorrhea). • If she is not likely to be pregnant, she can continue using DMPA if she prefers it.
Amenorrhea (no monthly bleeding period)	• Reassure her that amenorrhea is normal among DMPA users and not harmful. She is not sterile. She is not pregnant. Menstrual blood is not building up inside her. Instead, her body is not producing blood. Explain that this can improve her health. It helps to prevent anemia. • Reassure her that amenorrhea does not mean she cannot become pregnant after stopping DMPA. It does not mean she has reached menopause early. (If the woman reaches age 50—usual age of menopause—discontinue DMPA for 9 months to see if her period returns. She should use a nonhormonal method during this time.)

FOLLOWING UP on DMPA 7–15

For this problem:	**Try this suggestion:**
Spotting or bleeding between monthly periods that bothers the client	• Reassure her that spotting or bleeding between periods is normal and very common during the first months of DMPA use. It is not harmful. She loses less blood than if she did not use DMPA. • If gynecologic problems are found, treat or refer for care. If irregular bleeding is caused by sexually transmitted disease or pelvic inflammatory disease, she can continue her injections. Treat or refer.

Very heavy or very prolonged bleeding (more than twice as long or twice as much as her usual menstrual period)	• Rare, but requires attention.
	
	Heavy bleeding soon after the injection, but now stopped?
	
	• If the woman wants to continue injections, reassure her and give the next injection.
	
	Heavy bleeding continues?
	
	• If an abnormal condition is causing prolonged or heavy bleeding, treat the condition or refer for care.
	
	• If bleeding is not likely to have some other cause and if no condition rules out estrogen, offer:
	
	  – A low-dose combined oral contraceptive, one a day for 7 to 21 days. May take for 2 or 3 cycles. OR
	
	  – 30 to 50 micrograms of ethinyl estradiol daily for 7 to 21 days. OR
	
	  – Ibuprofen or other nonsteroidal anti-inflammatory drugs, but NOT aspirin.

For this problem:	Try this suggestion:
Very heavy or very prolonged bleeding *(continued)*	• Name foods containing iron, and advise the woman to eat more of them if possible. **Note:** Uterine evacuation is not necessary unless a medical condition that requires it is suspected.
Unexplained abnormal vaginal bleeding that suggests pregnancy or an underlying medical condition	• If her bleeding began after she started using DMPA, she can continue using it while her condition is being evaluated. • Explain that DMPA normally changes vaginal bleeding patterns and that usually these changes are not harmful. • Evaluate and treat any underlying medical condition, or refer for care.
Very bad headaches (migraines) with blurred vision	• A woman who gets migraine headaches can safely start using DMPA. She should switch to a method without hormones, however, if these headaches start or become worse after she begins using DMPA *and* these headaches involve blurred vision, temporary loss of vision, seeing flashing lights or zigzag lines, or trouble speaking or moving. • Refer for care as appropriate.

FOLLOWING UP on DMPA 7–17

Comparing DMPA and NET EN

Characteristic	DMPA	NET EN
Time between injections	3 months	2 months
Latest that client can return for next injection without need to check for pregnancy	2 or perhaps up to 4 weeks	1 to 2 weeks
Injection technique	Deep intramuscular injection into the deltoid (upper arm muscle). Gluteal (buttock) muscle also okay.	Deep intramuscular injection into the deltoid (upper arm) or gluteal (buttock) muscle. May be more painful.
Amenorrhea (no menstrual bleeding)	55% of women by end of first year of use.	30% of women by end of first year of use.
Typical pregnancy rate if on time for injections	About 0.3 women in every 100 in first year (1 in every 333).	About 0.4 women in every 100 in first year (1 in every 250).
Return of fertility (ability to become pregnant again)	Average delay: 4 months longer than for women who had been using combined oral contraceptives, IUDs, condoms, or a vaginal method.	Probably less delay.
Effect on diabetes	Causes some mild glucose (sugar) intolerance but often is used with good results by diabetic women who do not have accompanying vascular disease.	No effect on glucose tolerance.

IMPORTANT POINTS FOR THE USER TO REMEMBER ABOUT

DMPA Injectable

▶ **Very effective and safe.**

▶ **Changes in vaginal bleeding are normal.** They are not a sign of danger. Also, you may gain weight. This also is not harmful and not a sign of danger.

▶ You need an **injection every 3 months**. Try to come back on time. But come back even if you are late.

▶ You are **welcome back any time** you want help, advice, or another method.

▶ Please **come back at once** if you have very heavy bleeding (twice as much or twice as long as your usual menstrual period), you get very bad headaches, your skin or eyes become unusually yellow, or you think you might be pregnant.

▶ **DMPA injections do not prevent sexually transmitted diseases (STDs) including HIV/AIDS.** If you think you might get an STD, use condoms regularly along with DMPA.

IMPORTANT POINTS About DMPA 7–19

Questions and Answers

1. **Can a woman who is breastfeeding use DMPA?**

    Yes. While nonhormonal methods are better, DMPA is a reasonable choice for a breastfeeding mother who wants a hormonal method. It can be started as early as 6 weeks after delivery. She is protected from pregnancy without DMPA for the first 6 *months* after delivery, however, if she is fully or almost fully breastfeeding (at least 85% of the baby's food is breast milk) and her monthly period has not resumed.

2. **Should a woman stop using DMPA because she has no menstrual bleeding for a long time (amenorrhea)?**

    No. This is normal. There is no medical reason to stop because of amenorrhea. Reassure her that this is common and not harmful. Absence of bleeding can make some women healthier because it helps to prevent anemia. If amenorrhea bothers her, she can choose another method, however.

3. **Can young women, older women, and women without children use DMPA?**

    Yes. DMPA is completely reversible. DMPA is safe for women who have not had children as well as for women who have children. Especially younger women and women without children should understand that it may take time for fertility to return, however—an average of 4 months longer than if she had been using combined oral contraceptives, an IUD, condoms, or a vaginal method. DMPA appears to be safe for women of any age. There is theoretical concern that DMPA might affect bone development in women under age 18. The World Health Organization, however, concludes that the advantages of the method generally outweigh this theoretical disadvantage; in general, young women can use DMPA.

4. **Is it dangerous if a pregnant woman uses DMPA?**

   Usually no. It is best avoided, but the higher level of progestin in the body caused by DMPA is not harmful to the mother or the fetus. One study suggests the baby may be born at lower than normal weight, but this is not proven.

5. **Does DMPA cause cancer?**

   No. DMPA has not been shown to cause cancer in humans. Instead, it helps to prevent cancer of the endometrium (lining of the uterus) and perhaps cancer of the ovaries. The World Health Organization (WHO) has declared DMPA safe, but some questions remain about whether DMPA might speed up the development of preexisting breast cancer. Further studies are underway.

6. **Has the US government approved DMPA?**

   Yes. In 1992 the United States Food and Drug Administration (USFDA) approved DMPA for use as a contraceptive. The approval took many years because of concerns about animal studies. High doses of DMPA caused cancer in some laboratory animals. WHO studies of women using DMPA found no overall increase in cancer, however. Therefore the USFDA approved DMPA. Altogether, more than 100 countries throughout Europe, Asia, Africa, the Near East, and Latin America and the Caribbean have approved DMPA.

7. **Does DMPA cause abortion?**

   No. A woman who is already pregnant should not use any contraceptives except, if needed, condoms and/or spermicide to help prevent sexually transmitted disease. Nonetheless, there is no known harm to a fetus if DMPA is used during pregnancy.

QUESTIONS & ANSWERS About DMPA

Chapter 8
Norplant Implants

Key Points

▶ **Very effective for up to 5 years.**

▶ **Convenient.**

▶ **Can be used by women of any age, whether or not they have children.**

▶ **Insertion and removal of *Norplant* capsules require minor surgical procedures by specially trained provider.** Removal of capsules must be convenient and available whenever the client wants.

▶ **No delay in return of fertility after capsules are removed.**

▶ **Changes in vaginal bleeding are likely** — spotting, light bleeding between periods, or amenorrhea. Not dangerous and not a sign of danger. Counseling in advance is important.

▶ **Safe during breastfeeding.** Nursing mothers can start implants 6 weeks after childbirth.

Chapter 8
Norplant Implants

Contents

- Introduction to *Norplant* Implants 8–3
- Deciding About *Norplant* Implants 8–4
    - How Do They Work? 8–4
    - How Effective? 8–4
    - Advantages and Disadvantages 8–4
    - Medical Eligibility Checklist 8–7
- Starting *Norplant* Implants 8–10
    - When to Start 8–10
    - Providing *Norplant* Implants 8–12
    - Explaining How to Use 8–14
- Following Up 8–16
    - Helping Clients at Any Return Visit 8–16
    - Managing Any Problems 8–17
- Important Points for the User to Remember 8–21
- Questions and Answers 8–22

Introduction to Norplant Implants

- The *Norplant** implant system is a set of 6 small, plastic capsules. Each capsule is about the size of a small matchstick. The capsules are placed under the skin of a woman's upper arm.

- *Norplant* capsules contain a progestin, similar to a natural hormone that a woman's body makes. It is released very slowly from all 6 capsules. Thus the capsules supply a steady, very low dose. *Norplant* implants contain no estrogen.

- A set of *Norplant* capsules can prevent pregnancy for at least 5 years. It may prove to be effective longer.

Although other implants may be available, this chapter is limited to *Norplant* implants.

* **Norplant** is the registered trademark of The Population Council for levonorgestrel subdermal implants.

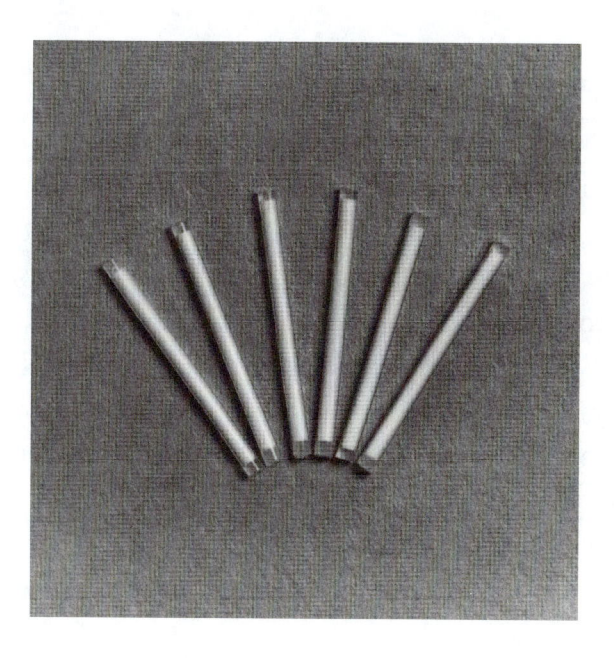

Deciding About Norplant Implants

How Do They Work?

- Thicken cervical mucus, making it difficult for sperm to pass through.
- Stop ovulation (release of eggs from ovaries) in about half of menstrual cycles (after first year of use).

They do NOT work by disrupting existing pregnancy.

How Effective?

Very effective—0.1 pregnancies per 100 women in first year of use (1 in every 1,000). Over 5 years, 1.6 pregnancies per 100 women (1 in every 62).

Note: Pregnancy rates have been slightly higher among women weighing more than about 70 kilograms (about 150 lbs). Over 5 years 2.4 pregnancies per 100 women (1 in every 42) in this heavier group (still a low pregnancy rate).

Advantages and Disadvantages

ADVANTAGES

- Very effective, even in heavier women.
- Long-term pregnancy protection but reversible. A single decision can lead to very effective contraception for up to 5 years.
- No need to do anything at time of sexual intercourse.
- Increased sexual enjoyment because no need to worry about pregnancy.
- Nothing to remember. Requires no daily pill-taking or repeated injections. No repeated clinic visits required.
- Effective within 24 hours after insertion.
- Fertility returns almost immediately after capsules are removed.

- Quantity and quality of breast milk do not seem harmed. Can be used by nursing mothers starting 6 weeks after childbirth.
- No estrogen side effects.
- Help prevent iron deficiency anemia.
- Help prevent ectopic pregnancies.
- May help prevent endometrial cancer.
- May make sickle cell crises less frequent and less painful.
- Insertion involves only minor pain of anesthesia needle. Not painful if anesthetic is given properly.

Disadvantages

- **Common side effects** (*not* signs of sickness):

  Changes in menstrual bleeding are normal, including:
  - Light spotting or bleeding between monthly periods (common),
  - Prolonged bleeding (uncommon, and often decreases after first few months), or
  - Amenorrhea. (Some women see amenorrhea as an advantage.)

  Some women have:
  - Headaches,
  - Enlargement of ovaries or enlargement of ovarian cysts,
  - Dizziness,
  - Breast tenderness and/or discharge,
  - Nervousness,
  - Nausea,
  - Acne or skin rash,
  - Change in appetite,
  - Weight gain (a few women lose weight),
  - Hair loss or more hair growth on the face.

  Most women do not have any of these side effects, and most side effects go away without treatment within the first year.

- Client cannot start or stop use on her own. Capsules must be inserted and removed by a specially trained health care provider.

- Minor surgical procedures required to insert and remove capsules. Some women may not want anything inserted in their arms or may be bothered that implants may be seen or felt under the skin.
- Discomfort for several hours to 1 day after insertion for some women, perhaps for several days for a few. Removal is sometimes painful and often more difficult than insertion.
- In the very rare instances when pregnancy occurs, as many as 1 in every 6 pregnancies is ectopic.
- Do not protect against sexually transmitted diseases including HIV/AIDS.

   IMPORTANT: Ask the client if she thinks she might have or get a sexually transmitted disease (STD). (Has more than one sex partner? Partner has more than one partner? Could this happen in future?)

   If she has or might get an STD, urge her to use condoms regularly. Give her condoms. She can still use *Norplant* implants.

Using the Medical Eligibility Checklist

*The list on the next page checks whether the client has any **known** medical conditions that prevent use of* Norplant *implants. It is not meant to replace counseling.*

*The questions in the checklist refer to **known conditions**. Generally, you can learn of these conditions by asking the client. You do not usually have to perform laboratory tests or physical examinations.*

   IMPORTANT: *Norplant* implants contain no estrogen. Many of the criteria that restrict use of combined oral contraceptives, which contain estrogen, do not apply to *Norplant* implants.

MEDICAL ELIGIBILITY CHECKLIST FOR

Norplant Implants

Ask the client the questions below. If she answers NO to ALL of the questions, then she CAN use *Norplant* implants if she wants. If she answers YES to a question below, follow the instructions. In some cases she can still use *Norplant* implants.

1. Are you breastfeeding a baby less than 6 weeks old?

   ☐ No ☐ **Yes** ▶ She can start using *Norplant* implants beginning 6 weeks after childbirth. If she is fully or almost fully breastfeeding, however, she is protected from pregnancy for 6 months after childbirth or until her menstrual period returns—*whichever comes first*. Then she must begin contraception at once to avoid pregnancy. Encourage her to continue breastfeeding.

2. Do you have serious problems with your blood vessels? If so, what problems?

   ☐ No ☐ **Yes** ▶ Do not provide *Norplant* implants if she reports blood clots (except superficial clots). Help her choose another effective method.

3. Do you have jaundice, severe cirrhosis of the liver, a liver infection or tumor? (Are her eyes or skin unusually yellow?)

   ☐ No ☐ **Yes** ▶ Perform physical exam or refer. If she has serious active liver disease (*jaundice, painful or enlarged liver, viral hepatitis, liver tumor*), do not provide *Norplant* implants. Refer for care. Help her choose a method without hormones.

4. Do you have or have you ever had breast cancer?

   ☐ No ☐ **Yes** ▶ Do not provide *Norplant* implants. Help her choose a method without hormones.

(Continued on next page)

DECIDING About Norplant Implants

MEDICAL ELIGIBILITY CHECKLIST FOR NORPLANT *(continued)*

	✓

5. Do you have vaginal bleeding that is unusual for you?

☐ No   ☐ **Yes** ▶ If she has unexplained vaginal bleeding that suggests pregnancy or an underlying medical condition, do not provide *Norplant* implants. Assess and treat any underlying condition, as appropriate, or refer. Help her choose a method without hormones to use until the problem is assessed. Then she can start using *Norplant* implants.

6. Are you taking medicine for seizures? Are you taking rifampin (rifampicine) or griseofulvin?

☐ No   ☐ **Yes** ▶ If she is taking *phenytoin, carbamezapine, barbiturates,* or *primidone* for seizures or *rifampin* or *griseofulvin,* provide condoms or spermicide to use along with *Norplant* implants. If she prefers, or if she is on long-term treatment, help her choose another effective method.

7. Do you think you are pregnant?

☐ No   ☐ **Yes** ▶ Assess whether pregnant (see page 4–6). If she might be pregnant, give her condoms or spermicide to use until reasonably sure that she is not pregnant. Then she can start *Norplant* implants.

Be sure to explain the health benefits and risks and the side effects of the method that the client will use. Also, point out any conditions that would make the method inadvisable when relevant to the client.

Most Women Can Use Norplant Implants

In general, most women CAN use *Norplant* implants safely and effectively.* *Norplant* implants can be used in any circumstances by women who:

- Are breastfeeding (starting as soon as 6 weeks after childbirth),
- Smoke cigarettes,
- Have no children,
- Are any age, including adolescents and over 40,
- Are fat** or thin,
- Have just had abortion or miscarriage.

Also, women with these conditions CAN use *Norplant* implants in any circumstances:

- Benign breast disease,
- Headaches,
- High blood pressure,
- Iron deficiency anemia,
- Varicose veins,
- Valvular heart disease,
- Diabetes,
- Malaria,
- Sickle cell disease,
- Schistosomiasis,
- Thyroid disease,
- Irregular or painful menstrual periods,
- Pelvic inflammatory disease,
- Benign ovarian tumors or uterine fibroids,
- Endometriosis,
- Sexually transmitted diseases,
- Epilepsy,
- Tuberculosis (unless taking rifampin; see checklist question 6 on page 8–8).

*Characteristics and conditions listed in this box are in WHO Eligibility Criteria category 1. Women with characteristics and conditions in WHO category 2 also can use this method. See Appendix, page A–1.

**Very fat is WHO category 2.

DECIDING About Norplant Implants

Starting Norplant Implants

When to Start

Woman's situation	When to start
Having menstrual cycles	• Any time it is reasonably certain that she is not pregnant. (See page 4–6.) **IMPORTANT:** If she is not at risk of pregnancy (for example, has not had sex since last menstrual period), she may start using *Norplant* at any time she wants. • If starting during the first 7 days after menstrual bleeding starts, no back-up method is needed for extra protection. • If she is starting on or after day 8 of her menstrual period, she should use condoms or spermicide or avoid sex for at least 48 hours after insertion. If possible, give her condoms or spermicide.
Breastfeeding	• As early as 6 weeks after childbirth. • *Fully or nearly fully breastfeeding* effectively prevents pregnancy for at least 6 months or until she has a menstrual period, whichever comes first (see Chapter 15). *Norplant* implants can give her extra protection if she wants it. • If only *partially breastfeeding* and child receives much other food or drink, 6 weeks after childbirth is the best time to start *Norplant* implants. If she waits longer, fertility may return. • If *menstrual periods have returned*, she can start *Norplant* implants any time it is reasonably certain that she is not pregnant. (See page 4–6.) See "Having menstrual cycles," above.

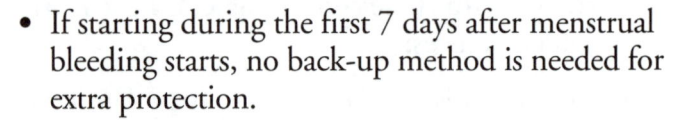

Woman's situation	When to start
After childbirth if not breastfeeding	• Immediately or at any time in the first 6 weeks after childbirth. No need to wait for her menstrual period to return. • After 6 weeks, any time it is reasonably certain that she is not pregnant. (See page 4–6.) If not reasonably certain, she should avoid sex or use condoms or spermicide until her first period begins and then start *Norplant* implants.
After miscarriage or abortion	• Immediately or in the first 7 days after either first- or second-trimester miscarriage or abortion. • Later, any time it is reasonably certain that she is not pregnant.
When stopping another method	• Immediately.

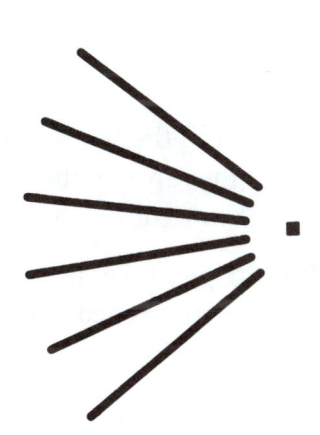

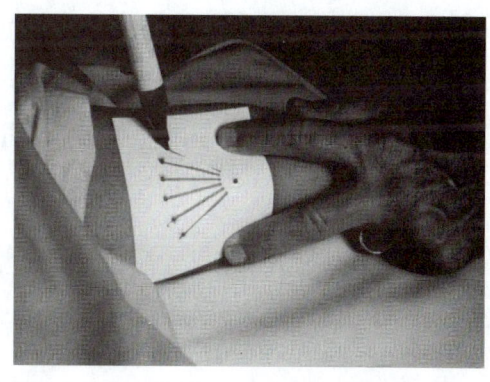

The template (left) can help providers position Norplant *capsules correctly. The provider places the template against a woman's arm and marks the ends of the 6 slots on her skin with a ballpoint pen or similar marker (see photo). When inserting the capsules, the provider lines up each capsule with one of the marks.*

STARTING Norplant Implants

Providing Norplant Implants

IMPORTANT: A woman who chooses *Norplant* implants benefits from good counseling.

A friendly provider who listens to a woman's concerns, answers her questions, and gives clear, practical information about side effects, especially probable bleeding changes, will help the woman use *Norplant* implants with success and satisfaction.

IMPORTANT: All women who choose *Norplant* implants must have convenient access to removal whenever they want it. All family planning programs that offer *Norplant* implants must have qualified staff to remove them, or they must set up referral arrangements for removals.

All staff must understand and agree that any woman can have her implants removed whenever she wants. Women must not be forced or pressured to continue using *Norplant* implants.

INSERTING NORPLANT CAPSULES

Learning Norplant *implant insertion requires training and practice under direct supervision. Therefore the following description is a summary and not detailed instructions. All family planning providers should be able to tell their clients about insertion of* Norplant *implants.*

1. The provider uses proper infection-prevention procedures.

2. The woman receives an injection of local anesthetic under the skin to prevent pain in her arm. She stays fully awake throughout the procedure.

3. The health care provider makes a small incision in the skin on the inside of the upper arm. The provider inserts the capsules just under the skin. This makes the capsules easier to remove later.

4. After all 6 capsules are inserted, the health care provider closes the incision with an adhesive bandage. Stitches are not needed. The incision is covered with a dry cloth and wrapped with gauze.

Insertion takes about 10 minutes. Bruising or slight bleeding at the insertion site is normal and common during the first few days after insertion.

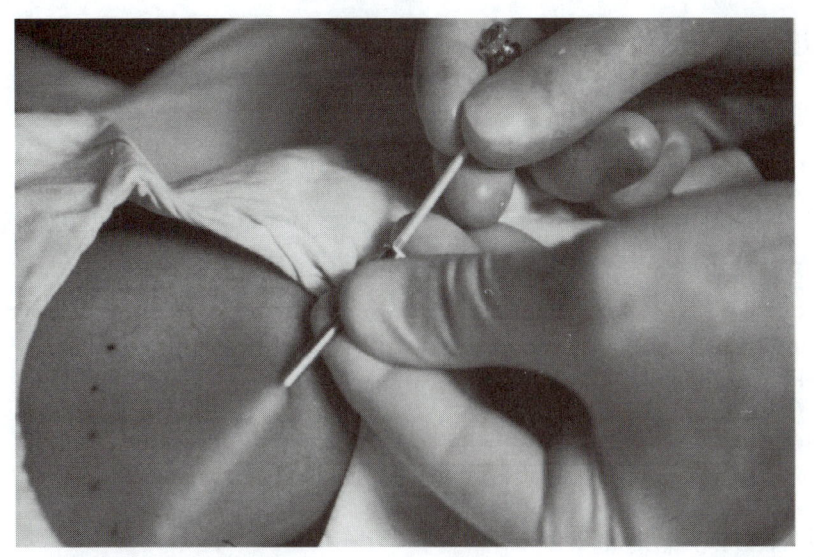

Using proper infection-prevention procedures, the provider inserts each Norplant *capsule just under the skin of a woman's upper arm.*

REMOVING NORPLANT CAPSULES

Learning to remove Norplant *implants requires training and practice under direct supervision. There are several techniques for removing the capsules. The following description is a summary and not detailed instructions. All family planning personnel should be able to tell their clients about removal of* Norplant *implants.*

1. The provider uses proper infection-prevention procedures.
2. The woman is given an injection of local anesthetic to prevent pain in her arm. She stays fully awake throughout the procedure.
3. The health care provider makes a small incision about where the capsules were inserted.
4. There are various ways to remove the capsules from under the skin. The provider may use an instrument to help pull the capsules out.
5. The incision is closed and bandaged. Stitches are not needed.

Removal usually takes about 15 minutes but can take longer. If a woman wants to continue using *Norplant* implants, the new capsules are placed elsewhere in the same arm or in the other arm.

STARTING Norplant Implants

Explaining How to Use

GIVE SPECIFIC INSTRUCTIONS

A woman who has *Norplant* capsules inserted should:

1. Keep the insertion area dry for 4 days. She can take off the gauze after 2 days and the adhesive bandage after 5 days.

2. Remember that, after the anesthetic wears off, her arm may be sore for a few days. She also may have swelling and bruising at the insertion site. This is not cause for alarm.

3. Return to the clinic or see a nurse or doctor if the capsules come out or if soreness in her arm lasts more than a few days.

FOLLOW THIS PROCEDURE

If possible, give each woman a durable card. The card should state:

- Where to go if she has questions or problems.
- Date of *Norplant* implant insertion.
- Date when 5 years of *Norplant* implant use would end. After 5 years she should have the capsules removed.

Whether or not you can give her a card, discuss this information with her. Discuss how to remember the date to return, perhaps tying it to the growth of a child or a child's year in school.

GIVE ADVICE ON COMMON PROBLEMS

1. **Mention the most common side effects**. In particular, she can expect changes in menstrual bleeding, including spotting, bleeding between periods, or amenorrhea. She also may have other side effects. (See page 8–5 for list.)

2. **Explain about these side effects:**
   - Some of these changes are common. None of them are harmful. Bleeding changes are normal. They do not mean that she is pregnant or sick or that bad blood is building up inside her. Little or no bleeding can make some women healthier. It helps prevent anemia.

IMPORTANT: Thorough counseling about bleeding changes and other side effects must come *before* inserting *Norplant* implants. Often, counseling beforehand and repeated reassurance afterward help women deal with bleeding changes. She should be urged to come back if bleeding changes are bothersome. Bleeding problems can be relieved with medication, or the capsules can be removed if she wishes. (See page 8–17.)

EXPLAIN SPECIFIC REASONS TO SEE A NURSE OR DOCTOR

Describe the symptoms of serious problems that require medical attention. Serious complications of *Norplant* implants are rare. Still, a woman should see a doctor or nurse or return to the clinic if she has questions or problems or any of the following possible symptoms of more serious problems. *Norplant* implants may or may not cause these problems.

- Might be pregnant (for example, missed period after several regular cycles), especially if she also has signs of ectopic pregnancy—abdominal pain or tenderness, or faintness. A woman who develops these signs must seek care at once. (See "Note on ectopic pregnancy," below.)
- Severe pain in the lower abdomen,
- Infection at the insertion site (pain, heat and redness), pus or abscess,
- Very heavy menstrual bleeding (twice as much or twice as long as usual for her),
- Very bad headaches that start or become worse after she begins using *Norplant* implants,
- Skin or eyes become unusually yellow.

Other specific reasons to return to the clinic or see a health care provider:

- Any time that she wants the capsules removed for any reason.
- 5 years have passed—time to have the capsules removed. She can get a new set of capsules if she wants.

Note on ectopic pregnancy: Pregnancies among users of *Norplant* implants are very few. *Norplant* implants offer much protection against pregnancy outside the uterus (ectopic pregnancy), but they still sometimes occur. When pregnancy occurs, 1 pregnancy in every 6 is ectopic. Ectopic pregnancy is life-threatening and requires treatment right away. (See page 12–23.)

STARTING Norplant Implants

Following Up

IMPORTANT: No routine return visit is required until it is time for the implants to be removed. The client should be clearly invited to return, however, any time she wants help, advice, information, or to have the implants removed for any reason, whether or not she wants another method.

Helping Clients at Any Return Visit

ASK QUESTIONS

At any return visit:

1. Ask if the client has any questions or anything to discuss.

2. Ask the client about her experience with the method, whether she is satisfied, and whether she has any problems. If she has problems that cannot be resolved, remove the capsules or refer for removal, and help her choose another method. Give her any information or help that she needs and invite her to return any time she has questions or concerns. Remind her how long her implants will keep working.

3. Ask about her bleeding patterns.

4. Ask if she has had any health problems since her last visit.

   - If the client has developed *active liver disease or breast cancer* or she is taking *medicine for seizures, rifampin, or griseofulvin*, see pages 8–7 and 8–8 for instructions. If appropriate, remove the capsules or refer for removal, and help her choose another method.
   - If the client has developed any of the following conditions, see "Managing Any Problems" (pages 8–17 to 8–20):
     - *Unexplained abnormal vaginal bleeding* that suggests pregnancy or an underlying medical condition.
     - *Heart disease due to blocked arteries, stroke, or blood clots (except superficial clots).*
     - *Very bad headaches.*

Managing Any Problems

If the client reports any of the common side effects of *Norplant* implants:

1. Do not dismiss the woman's concerns or take them lightly.
2. If the woman is worried, reassure her that such side effects are not usually dangerous or signs of danger.
3. If the woman is not satisfied after treatment and counseling, ask her if she wants the *Norplant* capsules removed. If so, remove the capsules or refer for removal even if her problems with the *Norplant* implants would not harm her health. If she wants a new method, help her choose one.

For this problem:	Try this suggestion:
Amenorrhea (no monthly bleeding period)	• Reassure her that amenorrhea is normal among *Norplant* implant users and not harmful. She is not sterile. She is almost certainly not pregnant. Menstrual blood is not building up inside her. Instead, her body is not producing menstrual blood. This could help prevent anemia. • If the client still finds amenorrhea unacceptable, remove the implants or refer for removal. Help her choose another method.

Spotting or bleeding between monthly periods over several months that bothers the client	• Reassure her that spotting and bleeding between periods are normal and very common, especially in the first 3 to 6 months. They are not harmful.
	• If the client finds the bleeding unacceptable and no condition rules out estrogen, offer:
	  – 1 cycle of low-dose combined oral contraceptives. A pill containing an estrogen and the progestin levonorgestrel (the same progestin as in *Norplant* implants) is best for controlling bleeding. OR
	  – Ibuprofen or other nonsteroidal anti-inflammatory drugs, but NOT aspirin.

FOLLOWING UP on Norplant Implants

For this problem:	Try this suggestion:

Spotting or bleeding *(continued)*	• If gynecological problems are found, treat or refer for care. Be alert for possible ectopic pregnancy.
	  – If pregnant, remove implants or refer for removal. Advise her not to take aspirin.
	  – If pelvic inflammatory disease or sexually transmitted diseases, implants can remain in place.

Very heavy or prolonged bleeding	• Rare, but requires attention. • If an abnormal condition is causing prolonged or heavy bleeding, treat the condition as appropriate or refer. • If not, treat with combined oral contraceptives or nonsteroidal anti-inflammatory drugs—same as for treatment of spotting (see above). Pills with 50 micrograms of estrogen may be needed. • Check for anemia. If found, treat or refer for care. • Name foods containing iron and suggest that she eat more of them if possible. **Note:** Uterine evacuation is not necessary unless a medical condition requiring it is suspected.
Unexplained abnormal vaginal bleeding that suggests pregnancy or underlying medical condition	• She can continue using *Norplant* implants while her condition is being evaluated. • Explain that *Norplant* implants usually change vaginal bleeding patterns. This is not harmful. • Evaluate and treat any underlying medical problem, or refer for care.
Severe pain in lower abdomen	• Check for ovarian cysts, twisted ovarian follicles, ovarian tumor, pelvic inflammatory disease, appendicitis, ectopic pregnancy, or ruptured liver tumor.

For this problem:	Try this suggestion:
Severe pain in lower abdomen *(continued)*	• If pain is due to **ectopic pregnancy**, treat or refer for care. Remove the implants or refer for removal. Help her choose another method. • If pain is due to **ovarian cysts**, implants can remain in place. Reassure the client that these cysts usually disappear on their own without surgery. To be sure the problem is resolving, see the client again in about 3 weeks if possible. • If pain is due to **other problems**: Implants can remain in place. Treat or refer for care.

Pain after insertion of the capsules	• Advise her to:
	  – Make sure the bandage on her arm is not too tight.
	  – Put a new bandage on the arm.
	  – Avoid pressing on the implants for a few days and never press on the implants if tender.
	• Give aspirin or another nonsteroidal anti-inflammatory drug.

Infection at the insertion site (pain, heat and redness) or abscess (pus present)	*Infection but no abscess?* • Do not remove the implants. • Clean the infected area with soap and water or antiseptic. • Give an oral antibiotic for 7 days and ask the client to return in one week. Then, if no better, remove the implants or refer for removal. *Abscess?* • Prepare the infected area with antiseptic, make an incision, and drain the pus. • Remove the implants or refer for removal. • Treat the wound. • If significant skin infection is involved, give oral antibiotic for 7 days.

FOLLOWING UP on Norplant Implants

For this problem:	Try this suggestion:
Heart disease due to blocked arteries (ischemic heart disease), stroke, or blood clots (except superficial clots)	• A woman who has this condition can safely start using *Norplant* implants. If, however, the condition develops after she starts *Norplant* implants, the capsules should be removed. Help her choose a method without hormones. • Refer for care as appropriate.
Very bad headaches (migraines) with blurred vision	• A woman who gets migraine headaches can safely start using *Norplant* implants. She should switch to a method without hormones, however, if these headaches start or become worse after she begins using *Norplant* implants *and* these headaches involve blurred vision, temporary loss of vision, seeing flashing lights or zigzag lines, or trouble speaking or moving. • Refer for care as appropriate.

IMPORTANT: When a woman seeks help, **make sure you understand what she wants. After counseling and discussion, ask her directly whether she wants to continue *Norplant* or to have the capsules removed.** Help her make her own decision without pressure.

If you do not find out and heed her true wishes, people may say that you forced her to continue using implants or that you refused to remove the capsules. To avoid such rumors, **find out what your client wants, and do it.**

IMPORTANT POINTS FOR THE USER TO REMEMBER ABOUT

Norplant® Implants

▶ **Changes in vaginal bleeding are normal.** They are not a sign of danger.

▶ **You should have the implants removed 5 years after insertion.** This will be in _____ [month] 200___ [year].

▶ You **are welcome back any time** you want help, advice, or another method.

▶ It is **your choice to have the capsules removed** any time you want—for any reason.

▶ Please **come back at once** if your arm is sore for more than a few days, infection occurs (pain, heat and redness), capsules come out, severe headaches start or become worse after you began using implants, or you think you might be pregnant, have unusually heavy vaginal bleeding or severe pain or tenderness in the lower belly, your skin or eyes become unusually yellow, or you feel faint.

▶ *Norplant* implants do not prevent sexually transmitted diseases (STDs) including HIV/AIDS. If you think you might get an STD, use condoms regularly along with the implants.

IMPORTANT POINTS About Norplant Implants 8–21

Questions and Answers

1. **Can young women, women without children, and older women use *Norplant* implants?**

   Yes. Women of any age, with or without children, can use *Norplant* implants.

2. **Is it dangerous to have *Norplant* implants for more than 5 years?**

   Norplant implants themselves are not dangerous if left in for more than 5 years. Leaving them in is not recommended, however, unless the woman wants to avoid removal *and* has either no need for contraception or chooses sterilization. *Norplant* implants become less effective after 5 years, and the risk of pregnancy, including ectopic pregnancy, may rise unless a woman uses another effective method.

3. **If a woman becomes pregnant with *Norplant* implants in place, should she have them removed?**

   This is recommended if she continues the pregnancy, although there are no known risks for the fetus.

4. **Do *Norplant* implants cause cancer?**

   No. The implants do not cause cancer. Instead, they may help to prevent endometrial cancer (cancer of the lining of the uterus).

5. **Can a woman using *Norplant* implants have ovarian cysts?**

   Yes. The great majority of cysts disappear on their own without surgery. If a health care provider finds an ovarian cyst, he or she should reexamine the woman again in about 3 weeks to make sure it is shrinking.

6. **Must a woman have a pelvic examination before she can use *Norplant* implants?**

   No. If a woman has symptoms of reproductive tract conditions, a pelvic exam may help diagnose them. The exam does not help decide about *Norplant* use, however.

7. **Must women using *Norplant* implants return often for follow-up?**

   No. Periodic visits are not necessary. Annual visits may be helpful for other preventive care, but they are not required for a woman to use *Norplant* implants. Of course, a woman is welcome to return whenever she wants to ask questions or has problems.

8. **What if a woman decides she wants to have her capsules removed before 5 years?**

   This is what a woman can expect if she asks to have her capsules removed before 5 years:

   - To be asked courteously why she wants the capsules removed.
   - To have her questions and concerns answered clearly and accurately.
   - To be reassured if her problems are not serious.
   - Never to feel pressured, threatened, or shamed for wanting to stop using *Norplant* implants.
   - After counseling, to be asked clearly, "Do you want to keep the capsules or to have them removed?"
   - If she wants them removed—no matter what her reason—for the health care provider to remove the capsules immediately or to arrange for their prompt removal.

9. **Should heavy women avoid *Norplant* implants?**

   No. Studies found that women weighing more than 70 kilograms were somewhat more likely to get pregnant than women weighing less, but *Norplant* implants were still very effective for these women.

10. **Can implants break or move around within a woman's body?**

    No. The capsules are flexible and cannot break under the woman's skin. They remain where they are inserted until they are removed.

QUESTIONS & ANSWERS About Norplant Implants

11. **Can a woman work immediately after insertion?**

    Yes. She can do her usual work immediately after leaving the clinic as long as she does not bump the insertion site or get it wet. She should keep the insertion site dry and clean for at least 48 hours. After healing (usually 3 to 5 days), the area can be touched and washed with normal pressure.

12. **Isn't there a version of *Norplant* implants with just 2 rods instead of 6 capsules?**

    This version, sometimes called *Norplant II*, is being studied in clinical trials. It is not yet available for general use. A 1-capsule implant system also is being studied. It uses the progestin desogestrel. One- or 2-capsule implants would greatly simplify insertion and removal.

Chapter 9
Female Sterilization

Key Points

▶ **Surgical method of family planning for women who are sure that they will not want more children.**

▶ **Very effective.**

▶ **Convenient.**

▶ **Permanent.**

▶ **Safe, simple procedure.** Preferably done with just local anesthesia and light sedation.

▶ **No known long-term side effects.** The surgery may cause some short-term complications.

▶ **Requires counseling and proper informed consent.**

Chapter 9
Female Sterilization

Contents

- Introduction to Female Sterilization 9–3
- Deciding About Female Sterilization 9–4
    - How Does It Work? 9–4
    - How Effective? 9–4
    - Advantages and Disadvantages 9–4
    - Medical Eligibility Checklist 9–7
- Having a Female Sterilization Procedure 9–12
    - When Can a Woman Undergo Female Sterilization? . . . 9–12
    - Providing Female Sterilization 9–13
    - Explaining Self-Care 9–16
- Following Up 9–18
    - Helping Clients at Any Routine Return Visit 9–18
    - Managing Any Problems 9–18
- Important Points for the User to Remember 9–19
- Questions and Answers 9–20

Introduction to Female Sterilization

- Female sterilization provides permanent contraception for women who will not want more children.
- It is a safe and simple surgical procedure. It can usually be done with just local anesthesia and light sedation. Proper infection-prevention procedures are required (see page 4–10).
- The 2 most common approaches are minilaparotomy and laparoscopy. Both are described in this chapter.
- Female sterilization also is known as voluntary surgical contraception (VSC), tubal ligation (TL), tying the tubes, minilap, and "the operation."

See Chapter 10 for information about vasectomy, the permanent method of family planning for men.

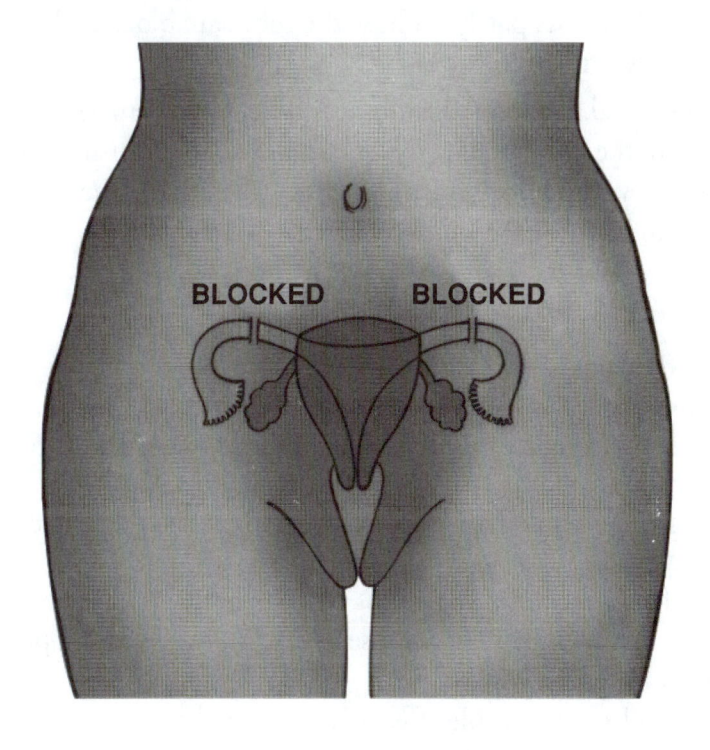

Deciding About Female Sterilization

How Does It Work?

The health care provider makes a small incision in the woman's abdomen and blocks off or cuts the 2 fallopian tubes. These tubes would carry eggs from the ovaries to the uterus. With the tubes blocked, the woman's egg cannot meet the man's sperm. (See drawing, page 9–3.)

The woman continues to have menstrual periods.

How Effective?

Very effective and permanent—
In the first year after the procedure: 0.5 pregnancies per 100 women (1 in every 200 women).

Within 10 years after the procedure: 1.8 pregnancies per 100 women (1 in every 55 women).

Effectiveness depends partly on how the tubes are blocked, but all pregnancy rates are low.

Postpartum tubal ligation is one of the most effective female sterilization techniques. In the first year after the procedure—0.05 pregnancies per 100 women (1 in every 2,000 women). Within 10 years after the procedure—0.75 pregnancies per 100 women (1 in every 133).

Advantages and Disadvantages

ADVANTAGES
- Very effective.
- Permanent. A single procedure leads to lifelong, safe, and very effective family planning.
- Nothing to remember, no supplies needed, and no repeated clinic visits required.
- No interference with sex. Does not affect a woman's ability to have sex.
- Increased sexual enjoyment because no need to worry about pregnancy.
- No effect on breast milk.
- No known long-term side effects or health risks.

- Minilaparotomy can be performed just after a woman gives birth. (Best if the woman has decided before she goes into labor.)
- Helps protect against ovarian cancer.

Disadvantages

- Usually painful at first, but pain starts to go away after a day or two.
- Uncommon complications of surgery:
  - Infection or bleeding at the incision,
  - Internal infection or bleeding,
  - Injury to internal organs.
  - Anesthesia risk:
    - With local anesthesia alone or with sedation, rare risks of allergic reaction or overdose.
    - With general anesthesia, occasional delayed recovery and side effects. Complications are more severe than with local anesthesia. Risk of overdose.
- Very rarely, death due to anesthesia overdose or other complication.
- In rare cases when pregnancy occurs, it is more likely to be ectopic than in a woman who used no contraception.
- Requires physical examination and minor surgery by a specially trained provider.
- Compared with vasectomy, female sterilization is:
  - Slightly more risky.
  - Often more expensive, if there is a fee.
- Reversal surgery is difficult, expensive, and not available in most areas. Successful reversal is not guaranteed. **Women who may want to become pregnant in the future should choose a different method.**
- No protection against sexually transmitted diseases (STDs) including HIV/AIDS.

   IMPORTANT: Ask the client if she might have or get a sexually transmitted disease (STD). (Has more than one sex partner? Partner has more than one partner? Could this happen in future?)

   If she has or might get an STD, urge her to use condoms regularly. Give her condoms. She can still use female sterilization.

DECIDING About Female Sterilization 9–5

Using the Medical Eligibility Checklist

*The list on pages 9–7 to 9–10 checks whether the client has any **known** medical conditions that limit when, where, or how female sterilization should be performed.*

The checklist should be used after your client has decided that she will not want any more children, and she has chosen female sterilization. It is not meant to replace counseling.

*The questions in the checklist refer to **known conditions**. Generally, you can learn of these conditions by asking the client. You do not usually have to perform special laboratory tests to rule out these conditions.*

▶ **No medical condition prevents a woman from using sterilization.** Some conditions and circumstances call for **delay, referral**, or **caution**, however. These conditions are noted in the checklist.

DELAY means delay female sterilization. These conditions must be treated and resolved before female sterilization can be done. Temporary methods should be provided.

REFER means refer client to a center where an experienced surgeon and staff can perform the procedure in a setting equipped for general anesthesia and other medical support. Temporary methods should be provided. (Called "special" conditions by WHO.)

CAUTION means the procedure can be performed in a routine setting but with extra preparation and precautions, depending on the condition.

▶ **If no conditions require delay or referral, female sterilization can be performed in these routine settings:**

Minilaparotomy: In maternity centers and basic health facilities where surgery can be done. These include both permanent and temporary facilities that can refer clients for special care if needed.

Laparoscopy requires a better equipped center, where laparoscopy is performed regularly and an anesthetist can be available.

MEDICAL ELIGIBILITY CHECKLIST FOR

Female Sterilization

Ask the client the questions below. If she answers NO to ALL of the questions, then the female sterilization procedure can be performed in a routine setting without delay. If she answers YES to a question below, follow the instructions.

1. Do you have any gynecologic/obstetric conditions or problems (female conditions), such as pregnancy, infection, cancer? What problems?

   ☐ No   ☐ **Yes** ▶ If she has any of the following, **DELAY** female sterilization and treat if appropriate or refer:

   - Pregnancy,
   - Postpartum or after second-trimester abortion (7–42 days),
   - Serious postpartum or postabortion complications (such as infection or hemorrhage) except uterine rupture or perforation (see below),
   - Unexplained vaginal bleeding that suggests a serious condition,
   - Severe preeclampsia/eclampsia,
   - Pelvic inflammatory disease (PID) within past 3 months,
   - Current sexually transmitted disease (STD),
   - Pelvic cancers (treatment may make her sterile in any case),
   - Malignant trophoblast disease.

   ▶ If she has any of the following, **REFER** her to a center with experienced staff and equipment that can handle potential problems:

   - Fixed uterus due to previous surgery or infection,
   - Endometriosis,
   - Hernia (umbilical or abdominal wall),
   - Postpartum uterine rupture or perforation or postabortion uterine perforation.

   (Continued on next page)

DECIDING About Female Sterilization 9–7

MEDICAL ELIGIBILITY CHECKLIST FOR FEMALE STERILIZATION *(continued)*

▶ If she has any of the following, use **CAUTION**:
- Past PID since last pregnancy,
- Current breast cancer,
- Uterine fibroids.

2. Do you have any cardiovascular conditions, such as heart problems, stroke, high blood pressure, or cardiovascular complications of diabetes? Which ones?

☐ No ☐ **Yes** ▶ If she has the following, **DELAY** female sterilization:
- Acute heart disease due to blocked arteries,
- Deep vein thrombosis or pulmonary embolism.

▶ If she has any of the following, **REFER** her to a center with experienced staff and equipment that can handle potential problems:
- Moderate or severe high blood pressure (160/100 mm or higher),
- Vascular disease, including diabetes-related,
- Complicated valvular heart disease.

▶ If she has any of the following, use **CAUTION**:
- Mild high blood pressure (140/90 mm-159/99 mm),
- History of high blood pressure where blood pressure can be evaluated, or adequately controlled high blood pressure where blood pressure cannot be evaluated,
- Past stroke or heart disease due to blocked arteries,
- Valvular heart disease without complications.

9–8 Essentials of Contraceptive Technology

MEDICAL ELIGIBILITY CHECKLIST FOR FEMALE STERILIZATION *(continued)*

3. Do you have any lingering, chronic diseases or any other conditions? Which ones?

☐ No   ☐ **Yes** ▶ If she has any of the following, **DELAY** female sterilization:

- Gallbladder disease with symptoms,
- Active viral hepatitis,
- Severe iron deficiency anemia (hemoglobin less than 7 g/dl),
- Acute lung disease (bronchitis or pneumonia),
- Systemic infection or significant gastroenteritis,
- Abdominal skin infection,
- Abdominal surgery for emergency or infection at time sterilization is desired, or major surgery with prolonged immobilization,
- Current AIDS-related acute illness.

▶ If she has any of the following, **REFER** her to a center with experienced staff and equipment that can handle potential problems:

- Severe cirrhosis of the liver,
- Diabetes for more than 20 years,
- Hyperthyroid,
- Coagulation disorders (blood does not clot),
- Chronic lung disease,
- Pelvic tuberculosis,
- Schistosomiasis with severe liver fibrosis.

(Continued on next page)

MEDICAL ELIGIBILITY CHECKLIST FOR FEMALE STERILIZATION *(continued)*

▶ If she has any of the following, use **CAUTION:**
- Epilepsy or taking medicine for seizures (phenytoin, carbamezapine, barbiturates, primidone),
- Taking the antibiotics rifampin or griseofulvin,
- Diabetes without vascular disease,
- Hypothyroid,
- Mild cirrhosis of the liver, liver tumors, or schistosomiasis with liver fibrosis (Are her eyes or skin unusually yellow?),
- Moderate iron deficiency anemia (hemoglobin 7-10 g/dl),
- Sickle cell disease,
- Inherited anemia,
- Kidney disease,
- Diaphragmatic hernia,
- Severe lack of nutrition (Is she extremely thin?),
- Obese (Is she extremely overweight?),
- Elective abdominal surgery at time sterilization is desired,
- Young age.

Be sure to explain the health benefits and risks and the side effects of the method that the client will use. Also, point out any conditions that would make the method inadvisable when relevant to the client.

Most Women Can Have Sterilization

In general, most women who want sterilization CAN have safe and effective procedures in routine settings.* With proper counseling and informed consent, sterilization can be used in any circumstances by women who:

- Have no children (with proper counseling and informed consent),
- Just gave birth (within 7 days),
- Are breastfeeding.

Also, women with these conditions CAN have sterilization in a routine setting in any circumstances:

- Mild preeclampsia,
- Past ectopic pregnancy,
- Benign ovarian tumors,
- Irregular or heavy vaginal bleeding patterns, painful menstruation,
- Vaginitis without purulent cervicitis,
- Varicose veins,
- HIV-positive or high risk of HIV or other STD infection,
- Uncomplicated schistosomiasis,
- Malaria,
- Tuberculosis (nonpelvic),
- Cesarean delivery (surgical delivery) at same time.

*Characteristics and conditions listed in this box are in the WHO "Accept" category. See Appendix, page A–1.

Having a Female Sterilization Procedure

IMPORTANT: A woman who is considering female sterilization needs good counseling.

A friendly provider who listens to a woman's concerns, answers her questions, and gives clear, practical information about the procedure, especially its permanence, will help the woman to make an informed choice and to be a successful and satisfied user. Careful counseling can help make sure that she will not be sorry later. (See page 9/10–2.)

In counseling, the provider must cover all 6 points of informed consent (see page 9/10–1). In some programs the client and the provider must sign a written consent form.

The decision about female sterilization belongs to the woman herself. Generally, if a woman is married, it is best if she and her husband agree on sterilization.

Her decision cannot be made for her, however, by her husband, a health care provider, a family member, or anyone else. Family planning providers have a duty to make sure that a woman's decision for or against female sterilization is not pressured or forced by anyone. Providers can and should help a woman think through her decision. If she decides against female sterilization, providers must accept and respect that decision. At the same time, they should not set up hard-and-fast rules that deny sterilization to some women who request it—for example, rules that they must be married or must have a certain number of children or must have reached a certain age.

When Can a Woman Undergo Female Sterilization?

A woman can have a female sterilization procedure almost any time that:
- She decides that she will never want any more children or, if she has none, that she will never want any, and
- It is reasonably certain that she is not pregnant. (See page 4–6.)

These times can include:

- Immediately after childbirth or within 7 days (minilaparotomy procedure only), if she has made a voluntary, informed choice in advance;
- 6 weeks or more after childbirth; or
- Immediately after abortion (within 48 hours), if she has decided voluntarily in advance; and
- Any other time, but NOT between 7 days and 6 weeks postpartum.

Providing Female Sterilization

Learning to perform female sterilization takes training and practice under direct supervision. Therefore this description is a summary and not detailed instructions. All family planning providers should understand these procedures and be able to discuss them with clients, both women and men.

The minilaparotomy procedure

This is a description of the *interval* procedure, used more than 6 weeks after childbirth. The postpartum procedure, used less than 7 days after childbirth, is slightly different.

1. The provider uses proper infection-prevention procedures.
2. The provider asks questions about the woman's past and current health and performs a physical examination and a pelvic examination. This step is to make sure that the surgery is done safely.
3. The woman usually receives light sedation (through pills or intravenous tube) to relax her. Local anesthetic is injected in her abdomen just above the pubic hair line. She stays awake. A small incision (2 cm–5 cm) is made in the anesthetized area. This usually causes little pain.
4. The uterus is raised and turned with an instrument (uterine elevator) to bring each of the 2 fallopian tubes under the incision. This may cause discomfort.

5. Each tube is tied and cut, or else closed with a clip or ring.
6. The incision is closed with stitches and covered with adhesive bandages.
7. The woman receives instructions on what to do after she leaves the clinic or hospital (see page 9–16). She usually can leave in a few hours.

The Laparoscopy Procedure

1. The provider uses proper infection-prevention procedures.
2. The provider asks questions about the woman's past and current health and performs a physical examination and a pelvic examination. This step is to make sure that the surgery is done safely.
3. The woman usually receives light sedation (through pills or intravenous tube) to relax her. Local anesthetic is injected just under the woman's navel. She stays awake. The doctor places a special needle into the woman's abdomen and, through the needle, inflates the abdomen with gas or air. This raises the wall of the abdomen away from the organs inside.
4. The doctor makes a small incision (about 2 cm) just under the woman's navel and inserts a laparoscope. A laparoscope is a special long, thin tube containing lenses. Through the lenses the doctor can see inside the body and find the 2 fallopian tubes.
5. The doctor inserts an instrument through the laparoscope (or, less commonly, through a second incision) to close off the tubes. Each tube is closed with a clip, a ring, or by electrocoagulation (electric current that burns and blocks the tube).
6. After the tubes are closed, the instrument and laparoscope are removed. The gas or air is let out of the woman's abdomen. The incision is closed with stitches and covered with adhesive bandages.
7. The woman receives instructions on what to do after she leaves the clinic or hospital (see page 9–16). She usually can leave in a few hours.

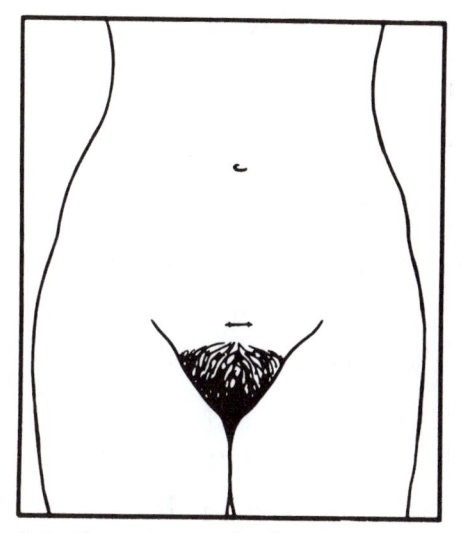

Minilaparotomy for female sterilization involves a small incision just above the pubic hair.

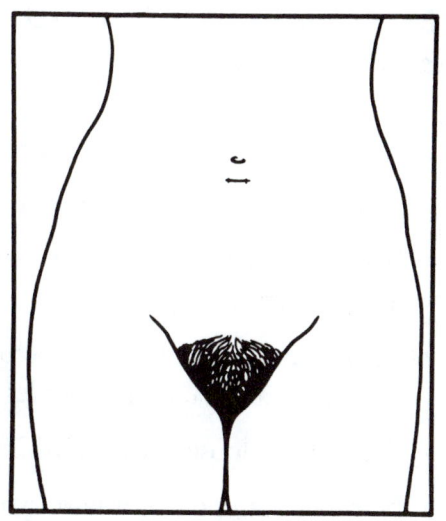

Laparoscopy for female sterilization usually involves 1 small incision just below the navel.

LOCAL ANESTHESIA IS BEST FOR FEMALE STERILIZATION

Local anesthesia, used with or without mild sedation, is best.

- Safer than general, spinal, or epidural anesthesia.
- Lets the woman leave the clinic or hospital sooner.

Health care providers can explain to a woman ahead of time that being awake during the procedure is safer for her. During the procedure providers talk with the woman and help to reassure her if needed.

Many different anesthetics and sedatives are used. Dosage of anesthetic must be adjusted to body weight.

General anesthesia may be needed in some cases. See "Medical Eligibility Checklist," pages 9–7 to 9–10, for medical conditions requiring referral to a center that can provide general anesthesia.

Explaining Self-Care for Minilaparotomy or Laparoscopy

BEFORE THE PROCEDURE THE WOMAN SHOULD:

- Not eat or drink anything for 8 hours before surgery;
- Not take any medication for 24 hours before surgery (unless the doctor performing the procedure tells her to do so);
- Bathe thoroughly the night before the procedure, especially her belly, genital area, and upper legs;
- Wear clean, loose-fitting clothing to the health facility if possible;
- Not wear nail polish or jewelry to the health facility; and
- If possible, bring a friend or relative to help her go home afterwards.

AFTER THE PROCEDURE THE WOMAN SHOULD:

- Rest for 2 or 3 days and avoid heavy lifting for a week;
- Keep the incision clean and dry for 2 or 3 days;
- Be careful not to rub or irritate the incision for 1 week;
- Take paracetamol (*Tylenol*, acetaminophen, *Panadol*) or another safe, locally available pain-relief medicine as needed. Stronger pain reliever is rarely needed. She should **not** take aspirin or ibuprofen, which slow blood clotting.
- Not have sex for at least 1 week. If pain lasts more than 1 week, do not have sex until all pain is gone.

EXPLAIN SPECIFIC REASONS TO SEE A NURSE OR DOCTOR

A woman should return to the clinic **for any of these reasons:**

- For a follow-up visit, if possible, within 7 days or at least within 2 weeks and to have stitches removed, if necessary. Follow-up also can be done at home or at another health center.
- She has questions or problems of any kind.

- Return at once if:
  - High fever (greater than 38°C) in the first 4 weeks and especially in the first week, or
  - Pus or bleeding from the wound, or
  - Pain, heat, swelling, or redness of the wound that becomes worse or does not stop (signs of infection), or
  - Abdominal pain, cramping, or tenderness that becomes worse or does not stop, or
  - Diarrhea, or
  - Fainting or extreme dizziness.

  If the clinic cannot be reached quickly, she should go to another doctor or nurse at once.

- She thinks she might be pregnant. First symptoms of pregnancy are:
  - Missed period,
  - Nausea, and
  - Breast tenderness.

  She should come to the clinic **at once** if she *also* has signs of possible **ectopic** pregnancy:

  - Lower abdominal pain or tenderness on one side,
  - Abnormal or unusual vaginal bleeding, or
  - Faintness (indicating shock).

Note on ectopic pregnancy: Pregnancies among users of voluntary sterilization are few. But when pregnancy occurs, it is more likely to be ectopic than the average pregnancy. Ectopic pregnancy is life-threatening. It requires immediate treatment. (See page 12–23.)

HAVING a Female Sterilization Procedure

Following Up

Helping Clients at Any Routine Return Visit

IMPORTANT: Follow-up within 7 days or at least within 2 weeks is strongly recommended. A health worker checks the site of the incision, looks for any signs of complications, and removes any stitches. This can be done in the clinic, in the client's home (by a specially trained paramedical worker, for example), or at any other health center. No woman should be denied sterilization, however, because follow-up would not be possible.

ASK QUESTIONS

Ask if the client has any questions or anything to discuss and if she is satisfied. Give her any information or help that she needs and invite her to return any time she has questions or problems.

Managing Any Problems

During recovery and healing, if a woman experiences strong pain, heat, swelling, or redness at or around the incision, she should come back to the clinic. If this happens, a health care provider should check for **infection** or **abscess**.

For this problem:	Provide this treatment:
Infection (pus, heat, pain, or redness caused by bacteria or other germs)	1. Clean site with soap and water or antiseptic. 2. Give oral antibiotics for 7 to 10 days.
Abscess (a pocket of pus under the skin caused by infection)	1. Clean site with antiseptic. 2. Incise and drain the abscess. 3. Perform wound care. 4. If significant skin infection involved, give oral antibiotics for 7 to 10 days.

IMPORTANT POINTS FOR THE USER TO REMEMBER ABOUT

Female Sterilization

- **Permanent family planning method.** A woman must think carefully and decide she will never want more children. Then she may choose female sterilization.

- **Very effective.**

- **Involves safe, simple surgery.**

- **After the procedure:**
  - Rest for a few days.
  - Avoid heavy work or lifting heavy objects for a week.
  - You may have some pain for a few days. You may take the pain-killer paracetamol (*Panadol, Tylenol*) but not aspirin or ibuprofen.

- You are **welcome back any time** you want help or advice or have questions or problems.

- Please **come back at once** if you have fever; bleeding or pus in the wound; pain, heat, swelling, or redness of the wound that becomes worse or does not stop.

- Please **come back if you think you might be pregnant.** Come back **at once** if you *also* have pain or tenderness in the lower abdomen, unusual vaginal bleeding, and/or fainting.

- **Sterilization does *not* prevent sexually transmitted diseases (STDs) including HIV/AIDS.** If you think you might have or get an STD, use condoms regularly along with sterilization.

IMPORTANT POINTS About Female Sterilization

❓ Questions and Answers

1. **Will sterilization change a woman's monthly periods or make menstrual bleeding stop?**

   No. Most studies find no major changes in bleeding patterns after female sterilization. A woman's menstrual bleeding pattern may change, however, if she was using a hormonal method or IUD before sterilization. Also, a woman's menstrual period usually becomes less regular as she gets older.

2. **Will sterilization make a woman lose her sexual ability? Will it make her weak and fat?**

   No. After sterilization a woman will look and feel the same as before. She can have sex the same as before. She may find that sex is better since she does not have to worry about getting pregnant. She will be as strong as before.

3. **Will the female sterilization procedure hurt?**

   Women receive local anesthetic to stop pain, and most women remain awake. There is often some minor pain. A woman can feel the health care provider moving her uterus and tubes. This can be uncomfortable. Laparoscopy may hurt less than mini-laparotomy. If a trained anesthetist or anesthesiologist and suitable equipment are available, general anesthesia may be chosen for women who are very frightened of pain.

   Postpartum minilaparotomy (just after delivery) requires less moving of the uterus. Therefore it may hurt less and is quicker than procedures at other times.

   A woman may feel sore and weak for several days or even a few weeks after surgery, but she will soon regain her strength.

4. **Isn't it easier for the woman and the health care provider to use general anesthesia? Why use local anesthesia?**

    Local anesthesia is safer. General anesthesia is more dangerous than the sterilization procedure itself. After general anesthesia, women usually feel nauseous. This does not happen after local anesthesia.

    Proper use of local anesthesia removes the single greatest source of risk in female sterilization procedures. When using local anesthesia, however, providers must take care not to overdose with the sedative. They also must handle the woman gently and talk with her throughout the procedure. This helps her to stay calm. Sedatives can be avoided in many clients, especially with good counseling and a skilled provider.

5. **Will female sterilization stop working after a time? Does a woman who had a sterilization procedure ever have to worry about getting pregnant again?**

    Generally, no. Female sterilization should be considered permanent. Failure rates are probably higher than previously thought, however. A major new US study found that the risk of pregnancy within 10 years after sterilization is about 1.8 per 100 women—about 1 in every 55 women. The risk of sterilization failure is greater for younger women because they are more fertile than older women. Also, some methods of blocking the tubes work better than others. Methods that cut away part of each tube work better than spring clips or bipolar electrocoagulation (electric current). Effectiveness also depends on the skill of the provider.

    The same US study found that 1 of every 3 pregnancies after sterilization was ectopic. If a woman who has had sterilization ever thinks that she is pregnant or has an ectopic pregnancy, she should seek help right away.

QUESTIONS & ANSWERS About Female Sterilization

6. **Pregnancy after female sterilization is rare, but why does it happen at all?**

   The most common reason is that the woman was *already pregnant at the time of sterilization*. Pregnancy also can occur if the provider confused another structure in the body with the fallopian tubes and blocked or cut the wrong place. In other cases pregnancy results because clips on the tubes come open, because the ends of the tubes grow back together, or because abnormal openings develop in the tube, allowing sperm and egg to meet.

7. **Can a woman have her sterilization reversed?**

   Surgery to reverse sterilization is possible only for some women—those who have enough tube left. Even among these women, reversal surgery does not always lead to pregnancy. The procedure is difficult, expensive, and hard to find. When pregnancy occurs, the risk of ectopic pregnancy is increased. Sterilization should be considered **permanent**. People who may want more children should choose a different family planning method.

8. **Is it better for the man to have a vasectomy or for the woman to have female sterilization?**

   Each couple must decide for themselves which method is best for them. Both are very effective, safe, permanent methods for couples who know that they will not want more children. Vasectomy is simpler and safer to perform. It is less expensive and slightly more effective (after the first 20 ejaculations or first 3 months). Ideally, a couple should consider both methods. If both are acceptable to the couple, vasectomy would be preferred for medical reasons.

9. **Should sterilization be offered only to women who have had a certain number of children or who have reached a certain age?**

   No. Health care providers must not limit access to female sterilization because of rigid rules about a woman's age, the number of children she has, or the age of her last child. Each woman must be allowed to decide for herself whether she will want no more children and whether or not to have sterilization.

An important counseling task is to help a woman think through her decision clearly and fully. For example, family planning providers can help her think about possible life changes (such as a change of partner or loss of existing children) and how these changes would affect her decision. (See page 9/10–2.)

10. **How can health care providers help a woman decide about female sterilization?**
    - Provide clear, balanced information about female sterilization and other family planning methods.
    - Discuss thoroughly her feelings about having children and ending her fertility.
    - If possible, arrange for her to talk with women who have already had female sterilization.
    - Review the 6 key points of informed consent to be sure the woman understands the sterilization procedure. (See page 9/10–1.)

11. **How can health care providers who do not perform sterilization procedures help women get them?**
    - Learn where female sterilizations are performed in the area and set up a referral system.
    - Find training to perform female sterilization.
      For more information about training, contact:
        - In-country training institutions.
        - **AVSC International,** 440 Ninth Avenue, New York, New York 10001, USA.
        - **The Johns Hopkins Program for International Education in Reproductive Health (JHPIEGO),** Brown's Wharf, 1615 Thames Street, Suite 200, Baltimore, Maryland 21231, USA.
        - **Pathfinder International,** 9 Galen Street, Suite 217, Watertown, Massachusetts 02172, USA.

The 6 Points of Informed Consent

To make an informed choice about sterilization, the client must understand the following points:

1. **Temporary contraceptives also are available** to the client and her or his partner.
2. Voluntary sterilization is a **surgical procedure**.
3. There are certain **risks** in the procedure as well as **benefits**. (Both risks and benefits must be explained in a way that the client can understand.)
4. If successful, the operation **will prevent the client from having any more children**.
5. The procedure is considered **permanent and probably cannot be reversed**.
6. The **client can decide against the procedure at any time** before it takes place (without losing rights to other medical, health, or other services or benefits).

Because Sterilization Is Permanent

A woman or man considering sterilization should think carefully: "Could I want more children in the future?" Health care providers can help the client think about this question and make an informed choice. If the answer is "Yes, I could want more children," another family planning method would be better.

▶ Questions can help. The provider might ask:
- "Do you want to have any more children in the future?"
- "If not, do you think you could change your mind later? What might change your mind? Suppose one of your children died? Suppose you lost your spouse, and you married again?"
- "Have you discussed sterilization with your spouse?"
- "Does your spouse want more children in the future?"
- "Do you think your spouse might change his or her mind later?"

Clients who cannot answer these questions may need encouragement to think further about their decisions on sterilization.

▶ Take special care:
In general, people most likely to regret sterilization have these characteristics:
- Young,
- Few or no children,
- Have not talked with spouse about sterilization,
- Spouse opposes sterilization,
- Not married,
- Having marriage problems.

Also, for a woman, just after delivery or abortion is a convenient and safe time for voluntary sterilization, but women sterilized at this time are more likely to regret it later. Thorough counseling during pregnancy and the woman's decision *before* labor and delivery help avoid regrets.

▶ The choice belongs to the client.

None of these characteristics rules out sterilization. Sterilization **should not be denied** to people with these characteristics. Rather, health care providers should make especially sure that people with these characteristics make informed, careful choices.

Chapter 10
Vasectomy

Key Points

- **Surgical method of family planning for men who are sure that they will not want more children.**

- **Very effective.**

- **Convenient.**

- **Permanent.**

- **No effect on sexual performance or sensation.**

- **No known long-term side effects.**

- **Safe, simple procedure.** Can be done in a few minutes in a clinic or office.

- **Fully effective only after at least 20 ejaculations or 3 months.** The man should use condoms or his partner should use another method until then.

- **Requires counseling and proper informed consent.**

Chapter 10

Vasectomy

Contents

- Introduction to Vasectomy 10–3
- Deciding About Vasectomy 10–4
  - How Does It Work? 10–4
  - How Effective? 10–4
  - Advantages and Disadvantages 10–4
  - Medical Eligibility Checklist 10–8
- Having a Vasectomy 10–10
  - When Can a Man Have a Vasectomy? 10–11
  - Providing Vasectomy 10–11
  - Explaining Self-Care 10–12
- Following Up 10–14
  - Helping Clients at Any Routine Return Visit . . . 10–14
  - Managing Any Problems 10–14
- Important Points for the User to Remember 10–16
- Questions and Answers 10–17

Introduction to Vasectomy

- Vasectomy provides permanent contraception for men who decide they will not want more children.

- It is a safe, simple, and quick surgical procedure. It can be done in a clinic or office with proper infection-prevention procedures (see page 4–10).

- It is **not** castration, it does **not** affect the testes, and it does **not** affect sexual ability.

- Also called male sterilization and male surgical contraception.

See Chapter 9 for information about female sterilization, the permanent method of family planning for women.

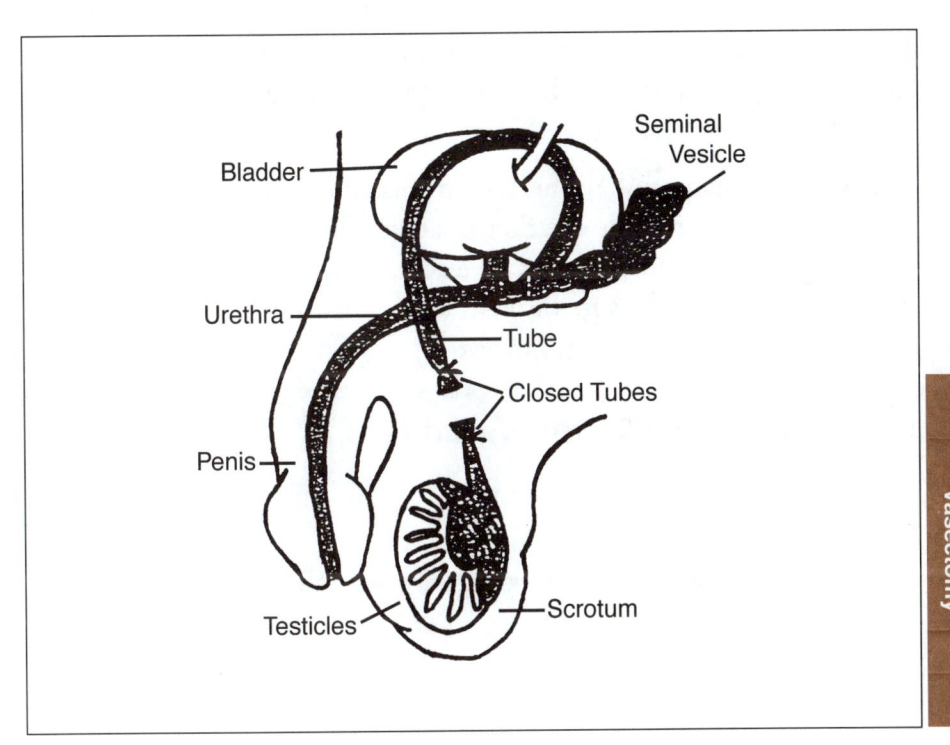

Deciding About Vasectomy

How Does It Work?

The health care provider makes a small opening in the man's scrotum (the sac of skin that holds his testicles) and closes off both tubes that carry sperm from his testicles. (See drawing, page 10–3.) This keeps sperm out of his semen. The man still can have erections and ejaculate semen. His semen no longer makes a woman pregnant, however, because it has no sperm in it.

How Effective?

Very effective and permanent as commonly used—0.15 pregnancies per 100 men in the first year after the procedure (about 1 in every 700).

Even a bit more effective when used correctly. Correct use means using condoms or another effective family planning method consistently for at least the first 20 ejaculations or for 3 months after the procedure—whichever comes first.

If he wants, a man can have his semen checked to be sure that the vasectomy is effective. He can do this at any time after 3 months following the procedure or after 20 ejaculations. If no sperm are found in his semen, he can be sure his vasectomy is working. A semen examination is not necessary, however.

Advantages and Disadvantages

Advantages
- Very effective.
- Permanent. A single, quick procedure leads to lifelong, safe, and very effective family planning.

- Nothing to remember except to use condoms or another effective method for at least the first 20 ejaculations or the first 3 months, whichever comes first.
- No interference with sex. Does not affect a man's ability to have sex.
- Increased sexual enjoyment because no need to worry about pregnancy.
- No supplies to get, and no repeated clinic visits required.
- No apparent long-term health risks.
- Compared with voluntary female sterilization, vasectomy is:
  - Probably slightly more effective,
  - Slightly safer,
  - Easier to perform,
  - If there is a charge, often less expensive,
  - Able to be tested for effectiveness at any time,
  - If pregnancy occurs in the man's partner, less likely to be ectopic than a pregnancy in a woman who has been sterilized.

Disadvantages

- Common minor short-term complications of surgery:
  - Usually uncomfortable for 2 or 3 days,
  - Pain in the scrotum, swelling and bruising,
  - Brief feeling of faintness after the procedure.
- Uncommon complications of surgery:
  - Bleeding or infection at the incision site or inside the incision,
  - Blood clots in the scrotum.
- Requires minor surgery by a specially trained provider.
- Not immediately effective. At least the first 20 ejaculations after vasectomy may contain sperm. The couple must use another contraceptive method for at least the first 20 ejaculations or the first 3 months—whichever comes first.

- Reversal surgery is difficult, expensive, and not available in most areas of the world. Success cannot be guaranteed. **Men who may want to have more children in the future should choose a different method.**

- No protection against sexually transmitted diseases (STDs) including HIV/AIDS.

   IMPORTANT: Ask the client if he might have or get a sexually transmitted disease (STD). (Has more than one sex partner? Partner has more than one partner? Could this happen in future?)

   If he has or might get an STD, urge him to use condoms regularly. Give him condoms. He can still use vasectomy.

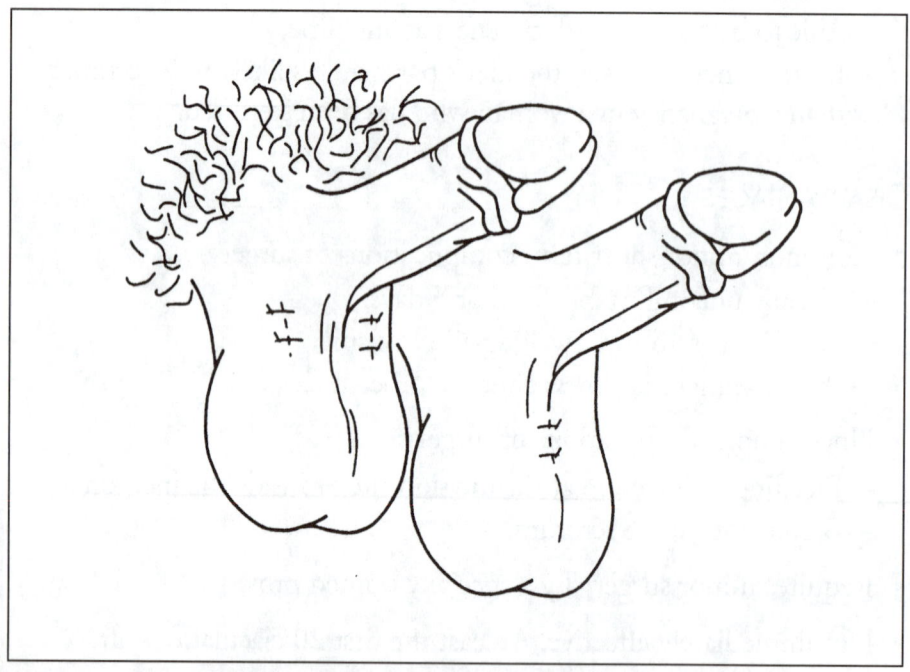

In a vasectomy procedure the provider makes either 1 or 2 small incisions in the scrotum. After the sperm-carrying tubes, or vasa, are cut and tied, the incisions are closed with a few stitches, as shown here, or just with a bandage. The new no-scalpel technique involves a tiny puncture instead of any incisions. (See pages 10–10 and 10–11.)

Using the Medical Eligibility Checklist

*The list on pages 10–8 and 10–9 checks whether the client has any **known** medical conditions that limit when, where, or how vasectomy should be performed.*

The checklist should be used after your client has decided that he will not want more children, and he has chosen vasectomy. It is not meant to replace counseling.

*The questions in the checklist refer to **known conditions**. Generally, you can learn of these conditions by asking the client. You do not usually have to perform special laboratory tests to rule out these conditions.*

▶ **No medical condition prevents a man from using vasectomy.** Some conditions and circumstances call for **delay, referral**, or **caution,** however. The conditions are noted in the checklist.

DELAY means delay vasectomy. These conditions must be treated and resolved before vasectomy can be performed. Temporary methods should be provided.

REFER means refer client to a center where an experienced surgeon and staff can perform the procedure in a setting equipped for general anesthesia and other medical support. Temporary methods should be provided. (Called "special" conditions by WHO.)

CAUTION means the procedure can be performed in a routine setting but with extra preparation and precautions, depending on the condition.

▶ **If no conditions require delay or referral, vasectomy can be performed in these routine settings:** Almost any health facility, including health care centers, family planning clinics, and the treatment rooms of private doctors. Where other vasectomy services are not available, mobile teams can perform vasectomies and any follow-up examinations in nonmedical facilities or in specially equipped vehicles where basic medications, supplies, instruments, and equipment are readily available.

DECIDING About Vasectomy

MEDICAL ELIGIBILITY CHECKLIST FOR

Vasectomy

Ask the client the questions below. If he answers NO to ALL of the questions, then the vasectomy procedure can be performed in a routine setting without delay. If he answers YES to a question below, follow the instructions.

1. Do you have any problems with your genitals, such as infections, swelling, injuries, or lumps in your penis or scrotum? What problems?

☐ **No**   ☐ **Yes** ▶ If he has any of the following, **DELAY** vasectomy and refer for treatment:

- Active sexually transmitted disease (STD),
- Inflamed (swollen, tender) tip of the penis, sperm ducts, or testicles,
- Scrotal skin infection or a mass in the scrotum.

▶ If he has any of the following, **REFER** him to a center with experienced staff and equipment that can handle potential problems:

- Hernia in the groin. (The provider, if able, can perform vasectomy at the same time as repairing the hernia. If this is not possible, the hernia should be repaired first.)
- Undescended testicles—both sides.

▶ If he has any of the following, use **CAUTION**:

- Previous scrotal surgery or injury,
- Large varicocele or hydrocele (swollen veins or membranes in the spermatic cord or testes, causing swollen scrotum),
- Undescended testicle—one side only. (Vasectomy is performed only on the normal side. Then if any semen is present in a semen sample after 3 months, the other side must be done, too.)

MEDICAL ELIGIBILITY CHECKLIST FOR VASECTOMY (continued)

2. Do you have any other conditions or infections? Which ones?

☐ No ☐ **Yes** ▶ If he has any of the following, **DELAY** vasectomy and refer for treatment:

- Acute systemic infection or significant gastroenteritis.
- Filariasis or elephantiasis.

▶ If he has any of the following, **REFER** him to a center with experienced staff and equipment that can handle potential problems:

- Current AIDS-related illness.
- Coagulation disorders (blood fails to clot).

▶ If he has the following, use **CAUTION**:

- Diabetes.

Be sure to explain the health benefits and risks and the side effects of the method that the client will use. Also, point out any conditions that would make the method inadvisable when relevant to the client.

Most Men Can Have Vasectomy

Most men who want vasectomy CAN have safe and effective procedures in routine settings. This includes men of any age; who have no children; who have sickle cell disease or hereditary anemia; or who are HIV-positive or at high risk of HIV or other STD infection. (Vasectomy does not prevent a man from passing HIV and other STDs, however.)

Having a Vasectomy

IMPORTANT: A man considering vasectomy needs good counseling.

A friendly provider who listens to a man's concerns, answers his questions, and gives clear, practical information about the procedure, especially its permanence, will help the man make an informed choice and be a successful and satisfied user. Careful counseling can help make sure that he will not be sorry later. (See page 9/10–2.)

In counseling, the provider must cover all 6 points of informed consent (see page 9/10–1). In some programs the client and the provider must sign a written informed consent form.

Any man should be able to choose vasectomy regardless of his age, whether or not he has children, how many children he has, or whether or not he is married. Generally, if a man is married, it is best if he and his wife agree on sterilization. A man's request for vasectomy should not be rejected, however, just because his wife is against it or because he does not have a partner.

New—No-Scalpel Vasectomy

The no-scalpel vasectomy is a newer procedure now used in many programs.

Differences from conventional procedure:

- Uses a small puncture instead of 1 or 2 incisions in the scrotum.
- Special anesthesia technique needs only 1 needle puncture instead of 2 or more.

Advantages:

- Less pain and bruising and shorter recovery time.
- May reduce operating time.

Both no-scalpel and conventional procedures are quick, safe, and effective.

When Can a Man Have a Vasectomy?

Any time he decides that he will never want any more children.

Providing Vasectomy

Learning to perform vasectomy takes training and practice under direct supervision. Therefore this description is a summary and not detailed instructions. All family planning providers should understand this procedure and be able to discuss it with clients, both men and women.

THE VASECTOMY PROCEDURE

1. The provider uses proper infection-prevention procedures at all times (see page 4–10).

2. The man receives injection of local anesthetic in his scrotum to prevent pain. He stays awake throughout the procedure.

3. The health care provider feels the skin of the scrotum to find each tube (vas deferens) inside. The provider makes a tiny incision in the skin with a scalpel or else uses a special sharp surgical instrument to make a puncture (the "no-scalpel" vasectomy technique).

4. The provider lifts each tube out of the incision. Most providers cut each tube and then tie one or both cut ends closed with thread. Some close off the tubes with heat or clips. The incision may be sewn shut or just covered with an adhesive bandage. The procedure is over.

5. The man may feel faint briefly after the procedure. If possible, he should rest for 15 to 30 minutes.

6. The man receives instructions on how to care for the wound (see page 10–12). If his wife is not using an effective contraceptive, he receives at least 20 condoms to use until sperm are cleared from his system. He leaves the clinic within a few hours, often in less than 1 hour.

Explaining Self-Care

BEFORE THE PROCEDURE THE MAN SHOULD:

- Bathe thoroughly, especially the genital area and upper inner thighs,

- Wear clean, loose-fitting clothing to the health facility,

- Not take any medication for 24 hours before the procedure (unless the health care provider performing the vasectomy tells him to do so).

AFTER THE PROCEDURE THE MAN SHOULD:

- If possible, put cold compresses on the scrotum for 4 hours to lessen swelling. He will have some discomfort, swelling, and bruising. These should stop in 2 to 3 days.

- Rest for 2 days. He should not do any heavy work or vigorous exercise for a few days.

- Keep the incision clean and dry for 2 to 3 days. He can use a towel to wipe his body clean but should not soak in water.

- Wear snug underwear or pants for 2 to 3 days to help support the scrotum. This will lessen swelling, bleeding, and pain.

- Take paracetamol (*Tylenol*, acetaminophen, *Panadol*) or another safe, locally available pain-relief medication as needed. He should **not** take aspirin or ibuprofen, which slow blood clotting.

- **Use condoms or another effective family planning method for at least his next 20 ejaculations or 3 months after the procedure—whichever comes first.**

He can have sex within 2 or 3 days after the procedure if it is not uncomfortable. He can expect his sexual performance to be unchanged. Vasectomy does not affect a man's ability to have sex. (See page 10–17, question 1.)

EXPLAIN SPECIFIC REASONS TO SEE A NURSE OR DOCTOR

A man should return to the clinic **for any of these reasons:**

- For a follow-up, if possible, within 7 days or at least within 2 weeks and to have stitches removed, if necessary. Follow-up also can be done at home or at another health center.
- His wife misses her menstrual period or thinks that she is pregnant.
- He has questions or problems of any kind.
- Return **at once** if he has:
  - High fever (greater than 38°C) in the first 4 weeks and especially in the first week, or
  - Bleeding or pus from the wound, or
  - Pain, heat, swelling, or redness at an incision that becomes worse or does not stop (signs of infection).

If the clinic cannot be reached quickly, he should go to another doctor or nurse at once.

HAVING a Vasectomy

Following Up

Helping Clients at Any Routine Return Visit

IMPORTANT: Follow-up within 7 days or at least within 2 weeks is strongly recommended. A health worker checks the site of the incision, looks for any signs of complications, and removes any stitches. This can be done in the clinic, in the client's home (by a specially trained paramedical worker, for example), or at any other health center. No man should be denied vasectomy, however, because follow-up would not be possible.

A man may want to come back to have his semen examined, if feasible, at least 3 months after the vasectomy. This microscopic examination can make sure his semen contains no sperm, and his vasectomy is working.

Ask Questions

At any return visit:

1. Ask if the client has any questions or anything to discuss.

2. Ask the client about his experience with vasectomy, whether he is satisfied, and whether he has any problems. Give him any information or help that he needs, and invite him to return any time he has questions or problems.

Managing Any Problems

During recovery and healing, if a man experiences strong pain, heat, swelling or redness at or around the incision, he should come back to the clinic. If this happens, a health care provider should check for clots, pus, **infection**, or **abscess**.

For this problem:	Provide this treatment:
Pain	Check for blood clots in the scrotum: • Small, uninfected blood clots require rest and pain-relief medication such as paracetamol. • Large blood clots may need to be surgically drained. • Infected blood clots require antibiotics and hospitalization.
Infection (pus, heat, pain or redness caused by bacteria or other germs)	1. Clean site with soap and water or antiseptic. 2. Give 7- to 10-day course of oral antibiotics.
Abscess (a pocket of pus under the skin caused by infection)	1. Clean site with antiseptic. 2. Incise and drain the abscess. 3. Perform wound care. 4. If significant skin infection involved, give 7- to 10-day course of oral antibiotics.
Fear of impotence	In counseling before the procedure, the health care provider should assure the client that vasectomy does **not** physically change sexual desire, functioning, or pleasure. This information can be repeated at any follow-up visit.

FOLLOWING UP on Vasectomy

IMPORTANT POINTS FOR THE USER TO REMEMBER ABOUT

Vasectomy

▶ **Permanent family planning method.** A man must think carefully and decide that he will never want more children. Then he may choose vasectomy.

▶ **Very effective** after 20 ejaculations or 3 months—whichever comes first.

▶ **Involves safe, simple surgery.**

▶ **After the procedure:**
  - Rest for 2 days.
  - Avoid heavy work or vigorous exercise for a few days.
  - You may have some pain, swelling, or slight bleeding for a few days. You may take paracetamol (*Panadol, Tylenol*) but not aspirin or ibuprofen.

▶ You are **welcome back any time** you want help or advice or have questions or problems.

▶ Please **come back at once** if you have fever, bleeding or pus in the wound, or pain or swelling that becomes worse or does not stop.

▶ **Also use condoms at first.** Use condoms or some other effective family planning method for at least the first 20 ejaculations after the procedure. Vasectomy starts to work after about 20 ejaculations or 3 months after the procedure—whichever comes first.

▶ **Vasectomy does not prevent sexually transmitted diseases (STDs) including HIV/AIDS.** If you think you might have or get an STD, use condoms regularly along with vasectomy.

Questions and Answers

1. **Will vasectomy make a man lose his sexual ability? Will it make him weak or fat?**

   No. After vasectomy, a man will look and feel the same as before. He can have sex the same as before. He may find that sex is better since he is free from worry about making his partner pregnant. He can work as hard as before. His erections and ejaculations of semen will be the same. His beard will still grow. His voice will not change. Vasectomy is not castration. Vasectomy does not harm the testicles, which are the organs that produce male hormones.

2. **Will the vasectomy stop working after a time?**

   Generally, no. Vasectomy is permanent. In rare cases the tubes grow back together, but this is very unlikely.

3. **Can a man have his vasectomy reversed if he decides that he wants another child?**

   Surgery to reverse vasectomy is possible. It does not always lead to pregnancy, however. The procedure is difficult, expensive, and hard to find. Vasectomy should be considered **permanent**. People who may want more children should choose another method.

4. **Is it better for the man to have a vasectomy or for the woman to have female sterilization?**

   Each couple must decide for themselves which method is best for them. Both are very effective, safe, permanent methods for couples who know they will not want more children. Vasectomy is simpler and safer to perform. It is less expensive and slightly more effective (after at least the first 20 ejaculations or the first 3 months). Ideally, a couple should consider both methods. If both are acceptable to the couple, vasectomy would be preferred for medical reasons.

QUESTIONS & ANSWERS About Vasectomy   10–17

5. **Does vasectomy increase a man's risk of prostate cancer or heart disease later in life?**

   No. The best evidence is that vasectomy does not increase risks of prostate cancer or heart disease.

6. **Should vasectomy be offered only to men who have reached a certain age or have a certain number of children?**

   No. Health care providers must not limit access to vasectomy because of rigid rules about a man's age, the number of children he has, or the age of his last child. Each man must be allowed to decide for himself whether he will want no more children and whether or not to have a vasectomy.

   An important counseling task is to help a man think through his decision clearly and fully. For example, family planning providers can help him think about possible life changes (such as a change of partner or loss of existing children) and how these changes would affect his decision. (See page 9/10–2.)

7. **How can providers help a man decide about vasectomy?**
   - Provide clear, complete information about vasectomy and other family planning methods.
   - Discuss thoroughly his feelings about having children and ending his fertility.
   - If possible, arrange for him to talk with men who have already had vasectomies.
   - Review the 6 key points of informed consent to be sure the man understands what it means to have a vasectomy. (See page 9/10–1.)

8. **Is it possible to check to see if a vasectomy is working?**

   Yes. A provider looks in a microscope for sperm in a semen specimen collected either through masturbation or in a condom. If the provider sees no sperm, the vasectomy is working.

9. **How can health care providers who do not perform vasectomies help men get vasectomies?**
   - Learn where vasectomies are performed in the area and set up a referral system.
   - Find training to perform vasectomies. For more information about training, contact:
     - In-country training institutions.
     - **AVSC International**, 440 Ninth Avenue, New York, New York 10001, USA.
     - **The Johns Hopkins Program for International Education in Reproductive Health (JHPIEGO)**, Brown's Wharf, 1615 Thames Street, Suite 200, Baltimore, Maryland 21231, USA.

Chapter 11
Condoms

Key Points

▶ **Condoms prevent pregnancy *and* sexually transmitted diseases (STDs), including HIV/AIDS.**

▶ **Condoms work if used correctly every time.** Many men do not use them consistently, however. Therefore condoms are only somewhat effective as commonly used.

▶ **Can be used along with other family planning methods for STD/HIV prevention and extra protection from pregnancy.**

▶ **Some men object to condoms** because their use interrupts sex, reduces sensation, or embarrasses them.

Chapter 11
Condoms

Contents

Introduction to Condoms 11–3

Deciding About Condoms 11–4
    How Do They Work? 11–4
    How Effective? 11–4
    Advantages and Disadvantages 11–5
    Medical Eligibility Checklist 11–6

Female Condoms 11–7

Starting Condoms 11–8
    Providing Condoms 11–8
    Explaining How to Use 11–9

Following Up 11–12
    Helping Clients at Any Routine Return Visit . . . 11–12
    Managing Any Problems 11–13

Important Points for the User to Remember 11–15

Questions and Answers 11–16

Introduction to Condoms

- A condom is a sheath, or covering, made to fit over a man's erect penis.

- Also called rubbers, sheaths, skins, and prophylactics, and known by many different brand names. Most condoms are made of thin latex rubber. Some condoms are coated with a dry lubricant or with spermicide. Different sizes, shapes, colors, and textures may be available.

- "Female condoms" that are inserted into a woman's vagina are available in some places. (See page 11–7.)

Deciding About Condoms

How Do They Work?

Condoms help prevent both pregnancy and sexually transmitted diseases (STDs). Used correctly, they keep sperm and any disease organisms in semen out of the vagina. Condoms also stop any disease organisms in the vagina from entering the penis.

How Effective?

IMPORTANT: Must be used correctly every time to be highly effective. Many men do not use condoms correctly or do not use them every time they have sex. Thus they may risk causing pregnancy, getting STDs, or giving STDs to their partners.

Somewhat effective for preventing pregnancy as commonly used— 14 pregnancies per 100 women in the first year of use (1 in every 8).

Effective for preventing pregnancy when used correctly every time— 3 pregnancies per 100 women in first year of use (1 in every 33).

Help prevent sexually transmitted diseases. During sex, condoms are the best protection against catching STDs or giving STDs to a partner. Condoms can stop sexual transmission of many diseases including HIV/AIDS, gonorrhea, syphilis, chlamydia, and trichomoniasis. Condoms probably protect somewhat, but not as well, against herpes, genital wart virus (HPV), and other diseases that can cause sores on skin not covered by condoms.

In general, studies show that condom users have about two-thirds as much risk of getting gonorrhea, trichomoniasis, or chlamydial infection as people who never use condoms. Condom users have less than half the risk of HIV infection, which leads to AIDS. These studies included some people who used condoms incorrectly or inconsistently, however.

People who use condoms correctly every time face even less risk of disease. They can reduce their risk of STDs to a very low level.

Advantages and Disadvantages

ADVANTAGES

- Prevent STDs, including HIV/AIDS, as well as pregnancy, when used correctly with every act of sexual intercourse.
- Help protect against conditions caused by STDs—pelvic inflammatory disease, chronic pain, and possibly cervical cancer in women, infertility in both men and women.
- Can be used to prevent STD infection during pregnancy.
- Can be used soon after childbirth.
- Safe. No hormonal side effects.
- Help prevent ectopic pregnancies.
- Can be stopped at any time.
- Offer occasional contraception with no daily upkeep.
- Easy to keep on hand in case sex occurs unexpectedly.
- Can be used by men of any age.
- Can be used without seeing a health care provider first.
- Usually easy to obtain and sold in many places.
- Enable a man to take responsibility for preventing pregnancy and disease.
- Increased sexual enjoyment because no need to worry about pregnancy or STDs.
- Often help prevent premature ejaculation (help the man last longer during sex).

Disadvantages

- Latex condoms may cause itching for a few people who are allergic to latex. Also, some people may be allergic to the lubricant on some brands of condoms.
- May decrease sensation, making sex less enjoyable for either partner.
- Couple must take the time to put the condom on the erect penis before sex.
- Supply must be ready even if the woman or man is not expecting to have sex.
- Small possibility that condom will slip off or break during sex.
- Condoms can weaken if stored too long or in too much heat, sunlight, or humidity, or if used with oil-based lubricants—and then may break during use.
- A man's cooperation is needed for a woman to protect herself from pregnancy and disease.
- Poor reputation. Many people connect condoms with immoral sex, sex outside marriage, or sex with prostitutes.
- May embarrass some people to buy, ask partner to use, put on, take off, or throw away condoms.

MEDICAL ELIGIBILITY CHECKLIST FOR

Condoms

Only one medical condition prevents use of condoms—*severe allergy to latex rubber* (severe redness, itching, swelling after condom use). You can learn of this condition by asking the client. You do not have to perform tests or examinations.

If the client is at risk of STDs, including HIV/AIDS, he or she may want to keep using condoms despite the allergy. (See page 11–13.)

In general, anyone CAN use condoms safely and effectively if not allergic to latex.

Female Condom—New Method for Women

- A woman-controlled method to protect against STDs including HIV/AIDS *and* against pregnancy.
- A sheath made of thin, transparent, soft plastic. Before sex a woman places the sheath in her vagina. During sex the man's penis goes inside the female condom.

Effectiveness similar to male condoms and to other vaginal methods. Pregnancies per 100 women in first year of use: *As commonly used—21. Used correctly and consistently—5.*

Some advantages:	Some disadvantages:
• Controlled by the woman.	• Expensive at this time.
• Designed to prevent both STDs and pregnancy.	• Only somewhat effective as commonly used.
• No medical conditions appear to limit use.	• Usually needs partner's okay.
	• Supply must be on hand.
• No apparent side effects; no allergic reactions.	• Woman must touch her genitals.

How used: Some time before sex, the woman places the closed end of the sheath high in her vagina. The closed end contains a flexible, removable ring to help with insertion. A larger flexible ring around the open end of the sheath stays outside the vagina.

- Meant for one-time use.
- Can be used with other family planning methods to add STD protection.

Where available: As of 1997, public and private sources provide female condoms in the US and many European countries. Research is going on in many places, and the method is being introduced in a number of developing countries.

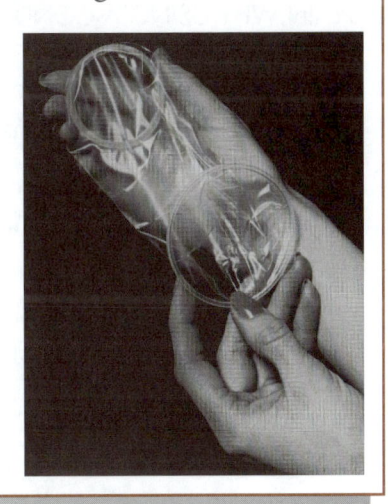

DECIDING About Condoms 11–7

Starting Condoms

Providing Condoms

IMPORTANT: A person who chooses condoms benefits from good counseling. At the same time, condoms should be made widely available, even where counseling is not possible.

A provider who listens to a client's concerns, answers questions, and gives clear, practical information, including how to discuss condom use with one's sex partner, will help the client use condoms with success and satisfaction.

FOLLOW THIS PROCEDURE

1. **Give each client a 3-month supply of condoms if possible—or more.** How often people have sex varies, but 40 condoms probably will last most clients for at least 3 months. Ask clients how many they will need.

2. **Give clients spermicides, too, if they want extra protection** and spermicides are available. Counsel about spermicide use. (See page 13–10.)

EXPLAIN WHY USING A CONDOM **EVERY TIME** IS IMPORTANT

1. Just one unprotected act of sexual intercourse can lead to pregnancy or sexually transmitted disease (STD).

2. Looking at a person cannot tell you if he or she has an STD. A person with an STD, including HIV/AIDS, can look perfectly healthy.

3. A person cannot always tell if he or she has an STD, including HIV infection.

Explaining How to Use

IMPORTANT: Whenever possible, show clients how to put on and take off a condom. Use a model, a stick, a banana, or 2 fingers to demonstrate putting on the condom. Suggest to a new user that he practice putting on a condom by himself before he next has sex.

GIVE SPECIFIC INSTRUCTIONS

1. **Put the condom on the erect penis before the penis touches the vagina.**

   - Hold the pack at its edge and open by tearing from a ribbed edge.
   - Hold the condom so that the rolled rim is facing up, away from the penis.
   - Pull the foreskin back if the penis is uncircumcised.
   - Place the condom on the tip of the penis.
   - Unroll the condom all the way to the base of the penis. The condom should unroll easily. If it does not, it is probably backwards. If more condoms are available, throw this one away and use a new condom. If this is the only condom available, turn it over and try again.

Putting On a Condom

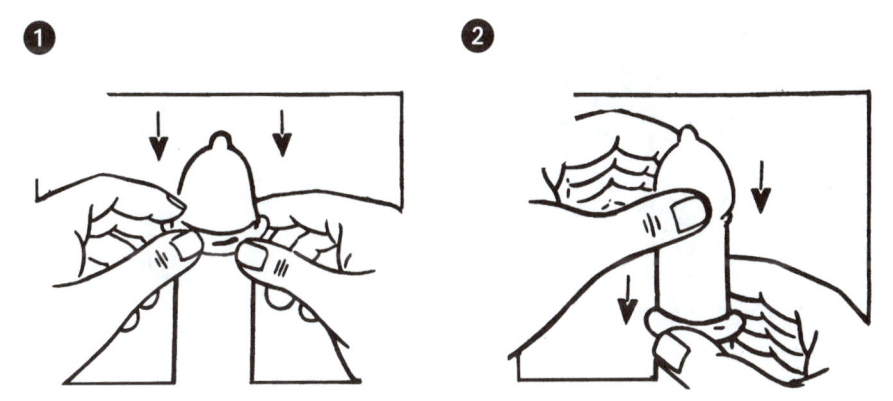

Hold the condom with the rim away from the body and unroll all the way to base of penis.

STARTING Condoms 11–9

2. **Any lubricant used should be water-based.** Good lubricants include spermicides, glycerine, and specially made products. Water can be used, also. They help keep condoms from tearing during sex. Natural vaginal secretions also act as a lubricant.

   Do not use lubricants made with oil. Most of them damage condoms. **Do NOT use** cooking oil, baby oil, coconut oil, mineral oil, petroleum jelly (such as *Vaseline®*), skin lotions, suntan lotions, cold creams, butter, cocoa butter, or margarine.

3. **After ejaculation** hold the rim of the condom to the base of the penis so it will not slip off. The man should pull his penis out of the vagina before completely losing his erection.

4. **Take off the condom** without spilling semen on the vaginal opening.

5. **Throw the condom away** in a pit latrine (toilet), burn it, or bury it. Do not leave it where children will find it and play with it. Do not use a condom more than once.

Taking Off a Condom

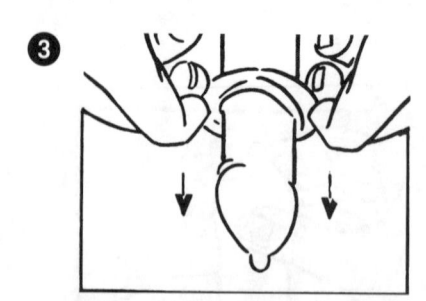

Slip off the condom without spilling semen.

Burn the used condom, throw it in the latrine, or bury it.

Disposing of a Used Condom

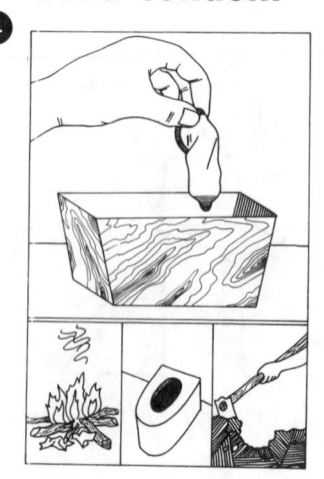

If a condom breaks:

- Immediately insert a spermicide into the vagina, if spermicide is available. Also, washing both penis and vagina with soap and water should reduce the risk of STDs and pregnancy.
- Some clients may want to use emergency oral contraception to prevent pregnancy. (See pages 5–20 through 5–25.)

GIVE TIPS ON CARING FOR CONDOMS

1. Store condoms in a cool, dark place, if possible. Heat, light, and humidity damage condoms.
2. If possible, use lubricated condoms that come in square wrappers and are packaged so that light does not reach them. Lubrication may help prevent tears.
3. Handle condoms carefully. Fingernails and rings can tear them.
4. Do not unroll condoms before use. This may weaken them. Also, an unrolled condom is difficult to put on.
5. Always use a different condom if the one you have:
   - Has torn or damaged packaging,
   - Has a manufacturing date on the package that is more than 5 years past,
   - Is uneven or changed in color,
   - Feels brittle, dried out, or very sticky.

EXPLAIN SPECIFIC REASONS TO SEE A NURSE OR DOCTOR

Urge clients to return or see a doctor or nurse if they or their sex partners:

- Have symptoms of STDs such as sores on the genitals, pain when urinating, or a discharge (drip). (See Chapter 16.)
- Have an allergic reaction to condoms (itching, rash, irritation). (See page 11–13.)

Other specific reasons to return: need more condoms, dissatisfied with condoms for any reason, have any questions or problems.

Following Up

Helping Clients at Any Routine Return Visit

ASK QUESTIONS

At any return visit:

1. Ask if the client has any questions or anything to discuss.

2. Ask the client about his or her experience with condoms, whether the client is satisfied, and whether the client has any problems. Is the client able to use a condom correctly every time? Also, you can check if the client knows how to use a condom; ask the client to put a condom on a model or a stick. Give any information and advice that the client needs. If the client has problems that cannot be resolved, help the client choose another method.

   IMPORTANT: Urge clients at risk for STDs including HIV/AIDS to keep using condoms despite any dissatisfaction. Explain that only condoms protect against STDs during sex.

3. If clients are satisfied:
   - Give them plenty of condoms.
   - Remind them to return if they or their sex partners have symptoms of STDs, such as sores on the genitals, pain when urinating, or a discharge (drip), or are dissatisfied with condoms.
   - Give clients spermicide if they want extra protection. Counsel about spermicide use. (See page 13–10.)
   - Invite them to return again at any time that they have questions or concerns.

Managing Any Problems

If the client reports any problems with condoms:

1. Do not dismiss the client's concerns or take them lightly.

2. If the client is not satisfied after counseling, help the client think about STD risk (see page 16–5). If the client has or might get an STD, encourage continued condom use. If not, help the client choose another method if he or she wishes.

For this problem:	Try this suggestion:
Condom or lubricant causes itching or rash on genitals	1. Suggest using water as a lubricant (if additional lubricant is desired). 2. If itching continues, clients (and possibly their partners) should be assessed for infection. 3. If there is no infection and allergy to latex seems likely, help the client choose another method *unless the client is at risk for STDs.* If the client is using lubricated condoms or condoms with spermicide: 1. Recommend a dry condom or one without spermicide. (Can use water to lubricate.) 2. If the problem continues, help the client choose another method *unless the client is at risk for STDs.*

FOLLOWING UP on Condoms

For this problem:	Try this suggestion:
Condom or lubricant causes itching or rash on genitals *(continued)*	**IMPORTANT:** For clients at risk of STDs including HIV/AIDS: Urge continued use of condoms despite discomfort. Explain that the only ways to be reasonably sure of not getting STDs are: • Using condoms every time you have sex, or • Having sex with only one partner who does not have an STD and does not have any other partners, or • Not having sex (abstinence). **Note:** Plastic condoms and condoms made of purified rubber are becoming available in some places. They may be a good choice for people allergic to latex.
Man cannot maintain an erection while putting on or using a condom	• Often due to embarrassment. Discuss how to make condom use more enjoyable and less embarrassing. If the woman puts the condom on for the man, this may make use more enjoyable. Explain that, with experience, most couples are less embarrassed. • Suggest a small amount of water or water-based lubricant on the penis and extra lubricant on the outside. This may increase sensation and help maintain an erection.

IMPORTANT POINTS FOR THE USER TO REMEMBER ABOUT

Condoms

▶ **Condoms protect against pregnancy *and* sexually transmitted diseases (STDs), including HIV/AIDS.**

▶ **Condoms work well when used correctly with *every* act of sexual intercourse.** But a condom cannot work when it is not used. Have a condom on hand before you need it, and be sure to use it.

▶ **Easy to use with a little practice.**

1. Put the condom on before your penis touches your partner. (This is especially important for STD prevention.) Putting a condom on can become a regular part of love play.

2. Hold the condom with the rolled rim away from the body. Unroll the condom over the erect penis. The condom should unroll easily. No need to stretch it.

3. Be careful not to spill semen when withdrawing your penis or taking off the condom.

4. Do not use a condom more than once. Throw the used condom away in a latrine or bury it.

If condoms cause itching, see a health care provider.

▶ **Condoms seldom break if used properly.**
New condoms seldom break if used as described. Water or a water-based lubricant on the outside of the condom can help prevent breaks. Never use oil-based lubricants such as *Vaseline*® or butter. Store condoms in a cool, dry place if possible. Do not use a condom that is sticky, dried-out, or comes from a torn or open package.

▶ You are **welcome back any time** you want more condoms, help or advice, or another method.

IMPORTANT INFORMATION About Condoms   11–15

Questions and Answers

1. **Is the condom an effective family planning method?**

   Yes, but only if condoms are used correctly every time the user has sex. As they are commonly used, condoms are only somewhat effective. This is because many users do not use them every time.

2. **How effective are condoms at preventing sexually transmitted diseases (STDs)?**

   Condoms can provide excellent protection against STDs, including HIV/AIDS, when used correctly every time a person has sexual intercourse of any kind (vaginal, anal, or oral). Unfortunately, many people use condoms incorrectly or do not use them every time with all partners. The best protections against STDs are either abstinence or else sex only with a faithful and uninfected partner.

3. **Can the AIDS virus (HIV) get through a condom?**

   No. Condoms can prevent AIDS and other sexually transmitted diseases. HIV is very small, but it cannot pass through an unbroken latex condom. Condoms made from animal intestines may not be as safe, however. Some disease-causing organisms probably can pass through them.

4. **Will condoms make a man weak and impotent (unable to have an erection)?**

   Not for most men. Impotence has many causes. Some causes are physical, and some are emotional. A few men may have trouble keeping an erection when using condoms. They may be embarrassed about using condoms. Condoms themselves do not cause impotence, however. In fact, some men find that condoms help them keep an erection longer.

5. **Do condoms make sex less enjoyable?**

   Some people find that they enjoy sex less when using condoms, but many enjoy sex as much or even more because they are free from worry about pregnancy or STDs. Also, sexual intercourse and the intense pleasure before ejaculation may last longer.

6. **How can a woman get her sex partner to use condoms?**

   Men have different reasons for not using condoms. Often their reasons are based on rumors or misunderstanding.

   A woman can talk to her sex partner. She might tell him:

   - Condoms prevent pregnancy and serious illness and even can save a person's life.
   - Using condoms correctly is easy with a little practice, and sex can be just as enjoyable.
   - Many couples use condoms. They are not just for prostitutes.
   - She knows he would not intentionally infect her with a disease, but many people have STDs, including HIV/AIDS, without knowing it.
   - Some men last longer during sex when they use condoms, and this makes sex more enjoyable for both the man and the woman.

   It is not easy to get some men to use condoms, and no one way always works. Still, every approach must be tried. The risks are too high not to try.

7. **Aren't condoms used mostly by prostitutes?**

   No. Married couples all over the world use condoms. In Japan more married couples use condoms than any other family planning method. Because of the high risk of STDs, however, it is especially important to use a condom whenever having sex with a prostitute.

QUESTIONS & ANSWERS About Condoms 11–17

8. **Do condoms often break during sex?**

   A small percentage of condoms break. When used properly, they seldom break. Condoms are more likely to break if a woman's vagina is dry. More love play before sex often makes a woman's vagina wetter. Water-based lubricant on the outside of the condom helps, too.

   IMPORTANT: Never use any oil or lubricants made with oil, such as petroleum jelly or skin cream. They weaken latex rubber very quickly and make condoms more likely to break.

9. **Does a person need to use condoms to protect against STDs when having oral or anal sex?**

   Yes. STDs can be passed from one person to another during any sex act that involves penetration (inserting the penis into any part of another person's body). All clients should be urged to use a condom when having oral, genital, or especially anal sex with someone who may have an STD—or if the client has an STD.

Chapter 12
Intrauterine Devices (IUDs)

Key Points

▶ Very effective, reversible, long-term method.

▶ TCu-380A IUD, the most widely available IUD, lasts at least 10 years.

▶ Menstrual periods may be heavier and longer, especially at first.

▶ Inserted and removed from the uterus by a specially trained provider using infection-prevention techniques.

▶ Can be inserted after childbirth by provider with special training. No effect on breastfeeding.

▶ Not a good method for a woman at high risk of getting sexually transmitted diseases (STDs). Could lead to pelvic inflammatory disease.

Chapter 12

Intrauterine Devices (IUDs)

Contents

	Introduction to IUDs	12–3
	Deciding About the IUD	12–4
	How Does It Work?	12–4
	How Effective?	12–4
	Advantages and Disadvantages	12–5
	Medical Eligibility Checklist	12–7
	Starting the IUD	12–10
	When to Start	12–10
	Providing the IUD	12–11
	Explaining How to Use	12–14
	Following Up	12–17
	Helping Clients at the Routine Return Visit	12–17
	Managing Any Problems	12–18
	Important Points for the User to Remember	12–25
	Questions and Answers	12–26

12–2 Essentials of Contraceptive Technology

Introduction to IUDs

- An intrauterine device (IUD) usually is a small, flexible plastic frame. It often has copper wire or copper sleeves on it. It is inserted into a woman's uterus through her vagina.

- Almost all brands of IUDs have one or two strings, or threads, tied to them. The strings hang through the opening of the cervix into the vagina. The user can check that the IUD is still in place by touching the strings. A provider can remove the IUD by pulling gently on the strings with forceps.

- IUDs are also called IUCDs (intrauterine contraceptive devices). Specific IUDs are called "the loop," *Lippes Loop* (no longer available in most countries), copper T, TCu-380A, MLCu-375 (*Multiload*), *Nova T*, *Progestasert*, and LNG-20.

The type now most widely used is:

- **Copper-bearing** IUDs (made of plastic with copper sleeves and/or copper wire on the plastic). TCu-380A and MLCu-375 are this type. This chapter focuses on copper-bearing IUDs.

Less widely available are:

- **Hormone-releasing** IUDs (made of plastic; steadily release small amounts of the hormone progesterone or another progestin such as levonorgestrel). LNG-20 and *Progestasert* are this type.

- **Inert**, or unmedicated IUDs (made of plastic or stainless steel only). *Lippes Loop* was this type—all plastic.

Deciding About the IUD

How Does It Work?

IUDs work chiefly by preventing sperm and egg from meeting. Perhaps the IUD makes it hard for sperm to move through the woman's reproductive tract, and it reduces the ability of sperm to fertilize an egg. Possibly could prevent egg from implanting in wall of uterus.

How Effective?

TCu-380A IUD (widely available and lasts at least 10 years):

Very effective—0.6 to 0.8 pregnancies per 100 women in first year of use (1 in every 125 to 170).

Rates for the **MLCu-375** (which lasts 5 years) are nearly as low.

Various other copper-bearing and inert IUDs:

Effective as commonly used—3 pregnancies per 100 women in first year of use (about 1 in every 30).

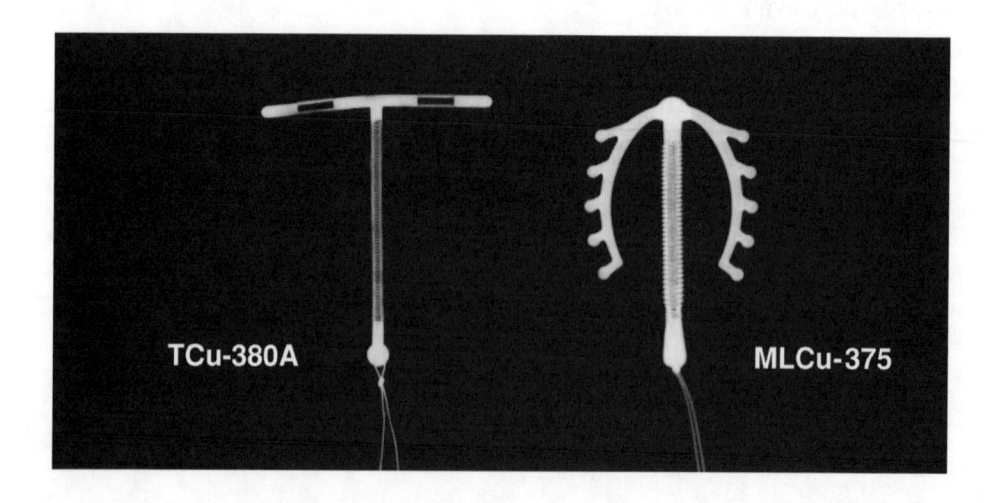

TCu-380A   MLCu-375

12–4 Essentials of Contraceptive Technology

Advantages and Disadvantages

ADVANTAGES

- A single decision leads to effective long-term prevention of pregnancy.

- Long-lasting. The most widely used IUD (outside China), the TCu-380A, lasts at least 10 years. Inert IUDs never need replacement.

- Very effective. Little to remember.

- No interference with sex.

- Increased sexual enjoyment because no need to worry about pregnancy.

- No hormonal side effects with copper-bearing or inert IUDs.

- Immediately reversible. When women have their IUDs removed, they can become pregnant as quickly as women who have not used IUDs.

- Copper-bearing and inert IUDs have no effect on amount or quality of breast milk.

- Can be inserted immediately after childbirth (except hormone-releasing IUDs) or after induced abortion (if no evidence of infection).

- Can be used through menopause (one year or so after last menstrual period).

- No interactions with any medicines.

- Helps prevent ectopic pregnancies. (Less risk of ectopic pregnancy than in women not using any family planning method.)

Disadvantages

- **Common side effects** (*not* signs of sickness):
  - Menstrual changes (common in the **first 3 months** but likely to lessen after 3 months):
    - Longer and heavier menstrual periods,
    - Bleeding or spotting between periods,
    - More cramps or pain during periods.
- Other, uncommon side effects and complications:
  - Severe cramps and pain beyond the first 3 to 5 days after insertion.
  - Heavy menstrual bleeding or bleeding between periods, possibly contributing to anemia. More likely with inert IUDs than with copper or hormone-releasing IUDs.
  - Perforation (piercing) of the wall of the uterus (very rare if IUD properly inserted).
- Does not protect against sexually transmitted diseases (STDs) including HIV/AIDS. Not a good method for women with recent STDs or with multiple sex partners (or partners with multiple sex partners).
- Pelvic inflammatory disease (PID) is more likely to follow STD infection if a woman uses an IUD. PID can lead to infertility.
- Medical procedure, including pelvic exam, needed to insert IUD. Occasionally, a woman faints during the insertion procedure.
- Some pain and bleeding or spotting may occur immediately after IUD insertion. Usually goes away in a day or two.
- Client cannot stop IUD use on her own. A trained health care provider must remove the IUD for her.
- May come out of the uterus, possibly without the woman's knowing (more common when IUD is inserted soon after childbirth).
- Does not protect against ectopic pregnancy as well as it does against normal pregnancy.
- The woman should check the position of the IUD strings from time to time. To do this, she must put her fingers into her vagina. Some women may not want to do this.

MEDICAL ELIGIBILITY CHECKLIST FOR

Copper-Bearing IUDs

Ask the client the questions below. If she answers NO to ALL of the questions, then she CAN use an IUD if she wants. If she answers YES to a question below, follow the instructions:

1. Do you think you are pregnant?

☐ No ☐ **Yes** ▶ Assess whether pregnant (see page 4–6). Do not insert IUD. Give her condoms or spermicide to use until reasonably sure that she is not pregnant.

2. In the last 3 months have you had vaginal bleeding that is unusual for you, particularly between periods or after sex?

☐ No ☐ **Yes** ▶ If she has unexplained vaginal bleeding that suggests an underlying medical condition, do not insert IUD until the problem is diagnosed. Evaluate by history and during pelvic exam. Diagnose and treat as appropriate, or refer.

3. Did you give birth more than 48 hours but less than 4 weeks ago?

☐ No ☐ **Yes** ▶ Delay inserting an IUD until 4 or more weeks after childbirth. If needed, give her condoms or spermicide to use until then.

4. Do you have an infection following childbirth?

☐ No ☐ **Yes** ▶ If she has puerperal sepsis (genital tract infection during the first 42 days after childbirth), do not insert IUD. Refer for care. Help her choose another effective method.

(Continued on next page)

Using the Medical Eligibility Checklist

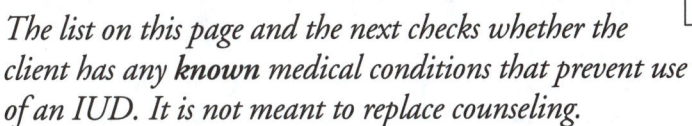

*The list on this page and the next checks whether the client has any **known** medical conditions that prevent use of an IUD. It is not meant to replace counseling.*

*The questions in the checklist refer to **known conditions**. Generally, you can learn of these conditions by asking the client. You do not usually have to perform laboratory tests.*

MEDICAL ELIGIBILITY CHECKLIST FOR COPPER-BEARING IUDs *(continued)*

Note: Assure confidentiality before asking remaining questions.

5. Have you had a sexually transmitted disease (STD) or pelvic inflammatory disease (PID) in the last 3 months? Have an STD, PID, or any other infection in the female organs now? (Signs and symptoms of PID: severe pelvic infection with pain in lower abdomen and possibly also abnormal vaginal discharge, fever, or frequent urination with burning.) If she has no tenderness in the abdomen or when the cervix is moved, however, she probably does not have pelvic infection.

☐ No   ☐ **Yes** ▶ Do not insert IUD now. Urge her to use condoms for STD protection. Refer or treat client and partner(s). IUD can be inserted 3 months after cure unless reinfection is likely.

6. Are you infected with HIV? Do you have AIDS?

☐ No   ☐ **Yes** ▶ If she has AIDS, is infected with HIV, or is being treated with any medicines that make her body less able to fight infections, careful clinical judgement should be made. In general, do not insert IUD unless other methods are not available or acceptable. Whatever method she chooses, urge her to use condoms. Give her condoms.

7. Do you think you might get an STD in the future? Do you or your partner have more than one sex partner?

☐ No   ☐ **Yes** ▶ If she is at risk of STDs, explain that STDs can lead to infertility. Urge her to use condoms for STD protection. Do not insert IUD. Help her choose another method.

8. Do you have any cancer in the female organs or pelvic tuberculosis?

☐ No   ☐ **Yes** ▶ Known *cervical, endometrial, or ovarian cancer; benign or malignant trophoblast disease; pelvic tuberculosis:* Do not insert IUD. Treat or refer for care as appropriate. Help her choose another effective method.

Be sure to explain the health benefits and risks and the side effects of the method that the client will use. Also, point out any conditions that would make the method inadvisable when relevant to the client.

Many Women Can Use Copper-Bearing IUDs

**In general, women CAN use IUDs safely and effectively.*
IUDs can be used in any circumstances by women who:**

- Smoke cigarettes,
- Have just had an abortion or miscarriage (if no evidence of infection or risk of infection),
- Take antibiotics or anticonvulsants,
- Are fat or thin,
- Are breastfeeding.

Also, women with these conditions CAN use IUDs in any circumstances:

- Benign breast disease,
- Breast cancer,
- Headaches,
- High blood pressure,
- Irregular vaginal bleeding (after evaluation),
- Blood clotting problems,
- Varicose veins,
- Heart disease (disease involving heart valves may require treatment with antibiotics before IUD insertion),
- History of stroke,
- Diabetes,
- Liver or gallbladder disease,
- Malaria,
- Schistosomiasis (without anemia),
- Thyroid disease,
- Epilepsy,
- Nonpelvic tuberculosis,
- Past ectopic pregnancy,
- Past pelvic surgery.

*Characteristics and conditions listed in this box are in WHO Eligibility Criteria category 1. Women with characteristics and conditions in WHO category 2 also can use this method. With proper counseling, women of any age or number of children can use IUDs. (Age less than 20 and having no children are characteristics in WHO Eligibility Criteria category 2.) See Appendix, page A–1.

DECIDING About IUDs 12–9

Starting the IUD

When to Start

Woman's situation	When to start

Having menstrual cycles	• Any time during the menstrual cycle (not just during menstruation) if it is reasonably sure that the woman is not pregnant (see page 4–6) and has a healthy uterus. If a woman has been using a reliable contraceptive or has not been having sex, the best time to insert her IUD is *when she asks for it.*
	
	• During menstruation. Possible advantages:
	  – If true menstrual bleeding, pregnancy is ruled out.
	  – Insertion may be easier.
	  – Any minor bleeding caused by insertion is less likely to upset the client.
	  – Insertion may cause less pain.
	
	Possible disadvantages of insertion during menstruation:
	  – Pain from pelvic infection may be confused with pain of menstrual period. IUD should not be inserted if a woman has a pelvic infection.
	  – May also be harder to identify other signs of infection.

After childbirth	• During hospital stay after childbirth, if she has decided voluntarily in advance. The IUD is best inserted within 10 minutes after delivery of the placenta. Can be inserted any time within 48 hours after childbirth. (Special training required.)

Woman's situation	When to start
After childbirth *(continued)*	• If not immediately after childbirth, as early as 4 weeks after childbirth for copper T IUD such as TCu-380A. At least 6 weeks after childbirth for other IUDs.
After miscarriage or abortion	• Immediately if no infection present. • If infection present, treat and help the client choose another effective method. After 3 months, if no infection remains, reinfection is not likely, and she is not pregnant, the IUD can be inserted.
When stopping another method	• Immediately.

Providing the IUD

IMPORTANT: A woman who chooses the IUD benefits from good counseling.

A provider who listens to a woman's concerns, answers her questions, and gives clear, practical information about side effects, especially probable bleeding changes and possible pain after insertion, will help the woman use the IUD with success and satisfaction.

IMPORTANT: All women who choose IUDs must have access to IUD removal. **All family planning programs that offer IUDs must have qualified staff to remove them, or they must set up convenient referral arrangements for removals.**

Inserting the IUD

Learning IUD insertion takes training and practice under direct supervision. The following description of procedures is a summary and not detailed instructions. All family planning providers should know about IUD insertion so that they can tell their clients about it.

1. The provider follows proper infection-prevention procedures. Generally, the health care provider will insert a **new, presterilized IUD that was individually packaged.**

2. "No-touch" insertion technique is preferred. "No-touch" technique includes: (1) Loading the IUD in the inserter while both parts are still in the sterile package; (2) Cleaning the cervix with antiseptic before IUD insertion; (3) Being careful not to touch the vaginal wall or speculum blades with the uterine sound or loaded IUD inserter; (4) Passing both the uterine sound and the loaded IUD inserter only *once* through the cervical canal.

3. The woman is **asked to tell the provider if she feels discomfort or pain** at any time during the procedure. Ibuprofen may be given 30 minutes before insertion to reduce cramping and pain.

4. The health care provider **conducts a careful pelvic examination** (speculum and bimanual) and checks the position of the uterus to make sure that the woman can use an IUD safely and effectively.

5. The provider carefully **cleans the cervix and vagina** several times with an antiseptic solution such as iodine.

6. *Working slowly and gently,* the provider **inserts the IUD,** *following the manufacturer's instructions.*

7. After the insertion, the provider asks the client how she feels and, if she feels dizzy when sitting, suggests that she lie quietly for 5 or 10 minutes. Any cramping probably will not last long.

IMPORTANT: **Postpartum insertion:** Only providers who have special training should insert IUDs after childbirth. Proper insertion technique is important to reduce the risk of expulsion. An IUD can be inserted just after delivery of the placenta or up to 48 hours after childbirth. An IUD can be inserted after vaginal delivery or after cesarean (surgical) delivery.

Removing the IUD

Possible reasons for removal:

- The client requests removal.

    IMPORTANT: Providers must not refuse or delay when the client asks to have her IUD removed, whatever her reason, whether it is personal or medical.

- Any side effects that make the client want her IUD removed, including pain.
- A medical reason for removal:
    - Pregnancy,
    - Acute pelvic inflammatory disease (endometritis or salpingitis),
    - Perforation of the uterus,
    - IUD has come out of place (partial expulsion),
    - Abnormal, very heavy bleeding that puts the woman's health at risk.
- When the effective lifespan of a copper-bearing or hormone-releasing IUD has passed.
- When the woman reaches menopause (at least one year after her last period).

To remove the IUD:

- Removing an IUD is usually simple. It can be done any time throughout the menstrual cycle. Removal may be somewhat easier during menstruation, when the cervix is dilated.
- Proper infection-prevention procedures are followed.
- The health care provider pulls the IUD strings slowly and gently with forceps.
- If removal is not easy, the provider may dilate the cervix using a uterine sound or alligator forceps or refer the client to a specially trained provider.

Explaining How to Use

Follow this procedure

1. Plan with the woman for a return visit in 3 to 6 weeks—for example, after a menstrual period—for checkup and pelvic examination. This checkup and exam make sure that her IUD is still in place and no infection has developed. The visit can be at any time convenient for her when she is not menstruating. After this one return visit, no further routine visits are required.

2. Make sure she knows:
   - Exactly what kind of IUD she has and what it looks like.
   - When to have her IUD removed or replaced. (For the TCu-380A IUD, 10 years after insertion.) Discuss how to remember the year to return. If she wants a new IUD, it can be inserted as soon as her old IUD is removed.
   - When she visits health care providers, she should tell them that she has an IUD.

IMPORTANT: Provide the client with a written record of month and year of IUD insertion and month and year when it should be removed.

Give specific instructions

A woman who chooses an IUD should know what will happen during the insertion procedure (see page 12–12). She also should understand the following:

1. She can expect:
   - Some cramping pain for the first day or two after insertion. She can take aspirin, paracetamol, or ibuprofen.
   - Some vaginal discharge for a few weeks after insertion. This is normal.
   - **Heavier menstrual periods**. Possible **bleeding between menstrual periods**, especially during the first few months after IUD insertion.

2. **Checking the IUD.** Sometimes IUDs come out. This can happen especially in the first month or so after insertion or during a menstrual period. An IUD can come out without the woman feeling it.

   A woman should check that her IUD is in place:
   - **Once a week** during the first month after insertion.
   - **After noticing any possible symptoms of serious problems.** (See page 12–16.)
   - **After a menstrual period**, from time to time. IUDs are more likely to come out along with menstrual blood.

   To check her IUD, a woman should:
   1. Wash her hands.
   2. Sit in a squatting position.
   3. Insert 1 or 2 fingers into her vagina as far as she can until she feels the strings. She should return to the health care provider if she thinks the IUD might be out of place.

      IMPORTANT: She should not pull on the strings. She might pull the IUD out of place.
   4. Wash her hands again.

   Note: After postpartum insertion, strings do not always come down through the cervix.

EXPLAIN SPECIFIC REASONS TO SEE A NURSE OR DOCTOR

Describe the possible symptoms of serious problems that require medical attention. Serious complications of IUD use are rare. Still, a woman should see a doctor or nurse if she has any of these symptoms of more serious problems. The IUD may or may not cause these problems.

- **Missed menstrual period**, or thinks she might be **pregnant**, especially if she also has symptoms of ectopic pregnancy: abnormal vaginal bleeding, abdominal pain or abdominal tenderness, fainting. A woman who develops these symptoms must seek care at once. (See "Note on ectopic pregnancy," page 12–23.)

- Thinks she may have been exposed to a **sexually transmitted disease, or she has HIV/AIDS**.

- When checking her IUD strings, she thinks the IUD might be out of place. For example, she finds:
  - **Strings missing or strings seem shorter or longer.**
  - **Something hard in her vagina or at the cervix.** It may be part of the IUD.

- **Increasing or severe pain in the lower abdomen**, especially if also fever and/or bleeding between menstrual periods (signs and symptoms of pelvic inflammatory disease).

OTHER SPECIFIC REASONS TO RETURN TO THE CLINIC

- Her sex partner feels the IUD strings during sex and this bothers him. At the clinic she can have the strings cut shorter.
- Heavy or prolonged bleeding that bothers the client.
- She or her partner is not pleased with the IUD.
- Copper-bearing or hormonal IUD has reached the end of its effectiveness: She needs it removed or replaced.
- She wants the IUD removed for any reason at any time.
- She has questions.
- She wants another family planning method.

Following Up

Helping Clients at the Routine Return Visit (3 to 6 Weeks after IUD Insertion)

FOLLOW THIS PROCEDURE

Conduct a pelvic exam as appropriate.

Definitely conduct a pelvic exam if you suspect:
- Sexually transmitted disease or pelvic inflammatory disease.
- The IUD is out of place.

ASK QUESTIONS

1. Ask if the client has any questions or anything to discuss.
2. Ask the client about her experience with the IUD, whether she is satisfied, and whether she has any problems. Give her any information or help that she needs and invite her to return again any time she has questions or concerns. If she has problems that cannot be resolved, help her choose another method.
3. Remind her of the reasons for returning. (See page 12–16.)
4. Remind her how long her IUD will keep working and when it should be removed.
5. Ask if she has had any health problems since her last visit.
   - If she has developed any condition that means she should not use an IUD (see pages 12–7 and 12–8), take out the IUD. Help her choose another method.
   - She may be able to keep using the IUD, however, even if she has developed (1) *unexplained abnormal vaginal bleeding* that may suggest pregnancy or an underlying medical condition or (2) *cervical, endometrial, or ovarian cancer*. See "Managing Any Problems" (pages 12–20 and 12–22).

Managing Any Problems

If the client reports any of the common side effects of IUDs, such as menstrual changes:

1. Do not dismiss the woman's concerns or take them lightly.
2. If the woman is worried but wants to continue the method, reassure her that such side effects are not usually dangerous or signs of danger.
3. If the woman is not satisfied after treatment and counseling, ask her if she wants the IUD removed. If so, remove the IUD or refer for removal even if her problems with the IUD would not harm her health. If she wants a new method, help her choose one.

For this problem:	**Try this suggestion:**
Irregular bleeding, prolonged or heavy bleeding (Prolonged bleeding = more than 8 days. Heavy bleeding = twice as long or twice as much as usual for her.)	*Evidence of infection or other abnormality?* • Conduct a pelvic exam to look for cervical disease, ectopic pregnancy, or pelvic inflammatory disease (PID). Refer for care if appropriate. • She can continue using her IUD while her condition is being evaluated. (For more about PID, see page 12–20. For more about ectopic pregnancy, see page 12–23.) *No evidence of infection or other abnormality, LESS THAN 3 MONTHS since IUD insertion, and bleeding is within normal and expected range?* • Reassure her that her changes in menstrual bleeding are normal and will probably lessen over time. • Name foods containing iron and suggest that she eat more of them if possible. If possible, give her iron tablets (ferrous sulfate up to 200 mg 3 times a day for 3 months).

For this problem:	Try this suggestion:

Irregular bleeding, prolonged or heavy bleeding *(continued)*	• Ask if she wants to keep her IUD.
	  – If she does, ask her to return in about 3 months for another checkup. If the bleeding bothers her, you may give her ibuprofen or other nonsteroidal anti-inflammatory drugs (but NOT aspirin) to help reduce it.
	  – If not, remove the IUD and help her choose another method.
	
	No evidence of infection or other abnormality and MORE THAN 3 MONTHS since IUD insertion?
	
	• If the **client wishes** or if **bleeding or pain is severe**, remove the IUD. Help her choose another method.
	
	• If an abnormal condition is causing irregular or heavy bleeding, treat or refer for care.
	
	• If **very heavy bleeding**, check for signs of severe anemia—pale under fingernails and inside eyelids. If found:
	  – Recommend IUD removal and help her choose another method.
	  – Give her enough iron tablets for 3 months.
	  – If she wants to keep using an IUD but has an inert IUD, replace it with a new copper-bearing IUD. Ask her to come for a checkup in 3 to 6 weeks.

For this problem:	Try this suggestion:
Unexplained abnormal vaginal bleeding that suggests pregnancy or an underlying medical condition	• She can continue using her IUD while her condition is being evaluated. • Evaluate and treat any underlying medical problem, or refer for care.
Lower abdominal pain that suggests pelvic inflammatory disease (PID)	1. **Diagnose.** Take history and do abdominal and pelvic exams. If pelvic exam is not possible, do an external genital exam. If one or more of the following is found, **refer to a capable provider at once:** • Missed a menstrual period, her period is late, or she is pregnant, • Recently given birth or had an abortion, • Pain or tenderness when pressure is put on the abdomen during exam, • Vaginal bleeding, • A pelvic mass. If she has none of the above conditions, diagnose as PID if she has one or more of the following (the more conditions she has, the stronger the diagnosis): • Oral temperature of 38.3°C (101°F) or higher, • Abnormal cervical or vaginal discharge, • Pain when moving the cervix during pelvic exam, • Tenderness in the area of fallopian tube or ovary, • Recent sex partner with urethral discharge or treated for gonorrhea.

For this problem:	Try this suggestion:
Lower abdominal pain that suggests pelvic inflammatory disease (PID) *(continued)*	**Note:** Diagnosis can be difficult. PID signs and symptoms may be mild or absent. Also, the common signs and symptoms of PID often also occur with other abdominal conditions, such as ectopic pregnancy or appendicitis. 2. **Treat or immediately refer for treatment. Treat for gonorrhea, chlamydia, *and* anaerobic infections such as trichomoniasis—all 3** (see Chapter 16). 3. **Generally, remove the IUD if physical examination or laboratory tests point to PID.** (Where PID management and follow-up are possible, some experienced clinicians may leave the IUD in place.) If diagnosis is uncertain and follow-up is possible, treat with antibiotics without taking out the IUD, and watch carefully for results of treatment. If diagnosis is uncertain and follow-up is *not* possible, take out the IUD and start antibiotics. 4. **Follow up.** If the woman does not improve in 2 or 3 days after starting treatment, or if she develops a tubal abscess, she should be sent to hospital. Otherwise, schedule another follow-up for just after she has finished taking all of her medicine. 5. **Treat sex partner(s).** Urge the client to have her sex partner or partners come for STD treatment.

FOLLOWING UP on IUDs

For this problem:	Try this suggestion:
Active sexually transmitted disease (STD) now or in the last 3 months, or acute purulent cervicitis (a pus-like discharge from the opening of the cervix).	• Remove the IUD. • Diagnose and treat the STDs, or refer. (See Chapter 16.)

Pregnancy	• If the IUD strings are visible and pregnancy is in the first trimester (less than 13 weeks):
	   – Explain that it is best to remove the IUD to avoid severe infection. Explain that she will have a slightly increased risk of spontaneous abortion.
	   – If she consents, remove the IUD or refer for removal. Explain that she should see a nurse or doctor if she has excessive bleeding, cramping, pain, abnormal vaginal discharge, or fever.
	• If the strings cannot be found and/or the pregnancy is beyond the first trimester:
	   – Explain that she is at risk of serious infection, which could threaten her life. Given this risk, if she does not want to continue the pregnancy, and if therapeutic termination of pregnancy is legally available, refer according to clinic guidelines.

For this problem:	Try this suggestion:
Pregnancy *(continued)*	– If client wants to or must continue her pregnancy, make clear that she faces increased risk of spontaneous abortion and infection. Her pregnancy should be followed closely by a nurse or doctor. She should see a nurse or doctor if she has excessive bleeding, cramping, pain, abnormal vaginal discharge, or fever.

IMPORTANT: Note on ectopic pregnancy: Pregnancies among users of IUDs are few. When pregnancy occurs, however, 1 in every 30 is ectopic. IUDs, especially the TCu-380A, offer significant protection against ectopic pregnancy, but they still sometimes occur. Ectopic pregnancy is life-threatening and requires immediate treatment.

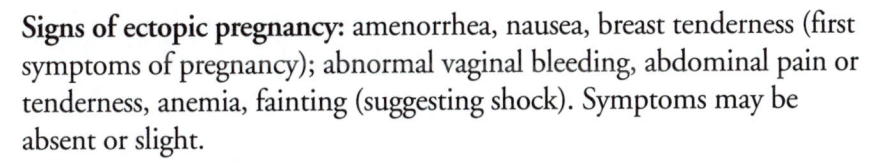

Signs of ectopic pregnancy: amenorrhea, nausea, breast tenderness (first symptoms of pregnancy); abnormal vaginal bleeding, abdominal pain or tenderness, anemia, fainting (suggesting shock). Symptoms may be absent or slight.

Care: Anemia and/or fainting indicate a possible ruptured ectopic pregnancy, an emergency condition requiring immediate surgery. If nonruptured ectopic pregnancy is suspected, perform a pelvic exam only if facilities for immediate surgery are available. If they are not available, refer at once for definitive diagnosis and care.

For this problem:	Try this suggestion:

Partner complains about IUD strings	• Explain to woman (and partner, if possible) that what her partner feels is normal. Recommend that they try again.
	• Describe other options to the client:
	  – Strings can be cut shorter.
	  – The IUD can be removed.

IMPORTANT: When a woman seeks help, **make sure you understand what she wants. After counseling and discussion, ask her directly whether she wants to continue using her IUD or to have it removed.** Help her make her own decision without pressure.

If you do not find out and heed her true wishes, people may say that you forced her to continue using the IUD or that you refused to remove it. To avoid such rumors, **find out what your client wants, and do it.**

IMPORTANT POINTS FOR THE USER TO REMEMBER ABOUT

TCu-380A IUD

▶ **Little to do once the IUD is in place.**

- You may have cramps for the first few days, vaginal discharge or spotting for a few weeks, and somewhat heavier menstrual periods.

- Check the IUD strings to be sure the IUD remains in place. Always wash hands first. With your fingers, feel the IUD strings in the vagina. Check once a week for the first month and then after a menstrual period from time to time. If you think the IUD might be out of place, come to the clinic.

▶ **IUDs do not prevent sexually transmitted diseases (STDs) including HIV/AIDS.** If you think you might get an STD, use condoms regularly.

▶ **Please come back:**

- In 3 to 6 weeks after insertion for a routine checkup.

- If you have very heavy bleeding or bad pain in the belly (especially pain with fever), if you might get or have sexually transmitted disease (STD), if you might be pregnant, or if the IUD might be out of place.

- Any time you want help, advice, or another method.

- Any time you want the IUD removed, for any reason.

▶ **You can keep your TCu-380A IUD for 10 years.** The TCu-380A IUD may become less effective after 10 years. It needs to be taken out in _____ [month, year]. A trained family planning provider can take out your IUD. You can get a new IUD put in at the same time if you want.

IMPORTANT POINTS About IUDs 12–25

Questions and Answers

1. **Can the IUD travel from the woman's uterus to other parts of her body, such as her heart or her brain?**

   The IUD normally stays within the uterus like a seed within a shell. Very rarely, the IUD may come through the wall of the uterus and rest in the abdomen. This is probably due to a mistake during insertion and not to slow movement through the wall of the uterus. The IUD never travels to any other part of the body.

2. **Will the IUD prevent a woman from having babies after it is removed?**

   In general, no. A woman can become pregnant after her IUD is removed. But the IUD does not protect her from sexually transmitted diseases (STDs). A woman should understand that the IUD may somewhat increase her chances of getting pelvic inflammatory disease if she gets STDs. These infections could make her infertile. Therefore, it is important for a woman who uses an IUD to have sex with only one, uninfected man and for him to have sex only with her.

3. **Can a woman who has never had a baby use an IUD?**

   Yes, as long as she does not have sexually transmitted diseases and there is little chance that she will get any. The IUD is not the best method for a woman who has not had a baby and wants a baby in the future. Also, a woman who has not had children is more likely to expel the IUD because her uterus is small. When properly counseled, however, these women may choose IUDs.

4. **Can a woman get an IUD just after she has a baby?**

   Yes, if the person who inserts her IUD has been properly trained. The IUD can be inserted after a vaginal delivery or through the abdominal incision after a cesarean section (surgical delivery).

5. **Can a woman get an IUD just after abortion or miscarriage?**

   Yes. An IUD can be inserted after an abortion or miscarriage unless she has a pelvic infection. Insertion following miscarriage after 16 weeks gestation requires special training.

6. **Must an IUD be inserted only during a woman's menstrual period?**

   No. An IUD can be inserted at any time during her menstrual cycle if it is reasonably sure that the woman is not pregnant. During her period may be a good time because she is not likely to be pregnant, and insertion may be easier for some women. It is not as easy to see signs of infection during menstruation, however. Some providers like to insert the IUD midway through the menstrual cycle because the mouth of the cervix is a little wider then.

7. **Should antibiotics be given before IUD insertion to prevent infection?**

   Not necessarily. When IUD insertion is done correctly with well-screened clients, there is little risk of infection for healthy women, and antibiotics are not necessary for IUD insertion. In any case, most recent research suggests that antibiotics do not significantly reduce the risk of pelvic inflammatory disease (PID).

8. **Can a woman be too young or too old to use an IUD?**

   No. There is no minimum or maximum age, so long as the woman is not at risk for a sexually transmitted disease and is properly counseled about the advantages and disadvantages of the IUD. An IUD should be removed from the woman after menopause—at least one year after her last menstrual period.

9. **Can a woman get her IUD on the same day that she has her initial counseling?**

   Yes. If it is reasonably certain that she is not pregnant and has no infections, there is no medical reason for a separate visit. It may be inconvenient for a woman to come back again. Also, she may become pregnant before she returns to have her IUD inserted.

QUESTIONS & ANSWERS About IUDs 12–27

10. **Can a woman with diabetes use an IUD?**

    Yes. IUDs are safe for women with diabetes. Women with diabetes are at greater risk of many infections, however. They should see a nurse or doctor if they notice possible signs of sexually transmitted disease or other infection, particularly just after IUD insertion.

11. **Should a woman have a "rest period" after using her IUD for several years or after the IUD reaches its recommended time for removal?**

    No. This is not necessary, and it may be harmful. There is less risk of pelvic infection in replacing an IUD at one time than in 2 separate procedures. Also, a woman could become pregnant before her new IUD is inserted.

12. **When does a copper IUD need to be replaced?**

    The latest models of copper-bearing IUDs are effective for many years. The TCu-380A has been approved by the US Food and Drug Administration for 10 years of use. (It probably can prevent pregnancy even longer.)

13. **Will the IUD cause discomfort to a woman's partner during sex?**

    Generally, no. Sometimes a man can feel the strings. If this bothers him, cutting the strings shorter should solve the problem. The woman should be told beforehand, however, that this will mean she will not be able to feel the strings to check her IUD, and removing her IUD may be more difficult. A man may feel discomfort during sex if the IUD has started to come out through the cervix. If a women suspects this, she should see a doctor or nurse immediately.

Chapter 13
Vaginal Methods

Key Points

▶ **Spermicides, diaphragm, and cap—methods controlled by a woman, for use when needed.**

▶ **Safe.** Minor side effects or none for most women.

▶ **Only somewhat effective as commonly used,** but more effective with consistent and correct use. Clients need clear instructions on correct use. Practice inserting a diaphragm or cap will help.

▶ A woman may find it **difficult to interrupt sex to insert** a vaginal method. She **can place spermicide, diaphragm, or cap in her vagina ahead of time**, however.

▶ **May help prevent some sexually transmitted diseases (STDs) somewhat**, but this has not been proved.

Chapter 13
Vaginal Methods

Contents

Introduction to Vaginal Methods 13–3

Deciding About Vaginal Methods 13–4
    How Do They Work? 13–4
    How Effective? 13–4
    Advantages and Disadvantages 13–5
    Medical Eligibility Checklist 13–8

Starting Vaginal Methods 13–9
    When to Start 13–9
    Providing Vaginal Methods 13–9
    Explaining How to Use 13–10

Following Up 13–14
    Helping Clients at Any Routine Return Visit . . . 13–14
    Managing Any Problems 13–15

Important Points for the User to Remember 13–17

Questions and Answers 13–18

Introduction to Vaginal Methods

Vaginal methods are contraceptives that a woman places in her vagina shortly before sex. There are several vaginal methods:

- **Spermicides**, including foaming tablets or suppositories, melting suppositories, foam, melting film, jelly, and cream.
- **Diaphragm**, a soft rubber cup that covers the cervix. Should be used with spermicidal jelly or cream.
- **Cervical cap**—like the diaphragm but smaller. Not widely available outside North America, Europe, Australia, and New Zealand.

Diaphragm

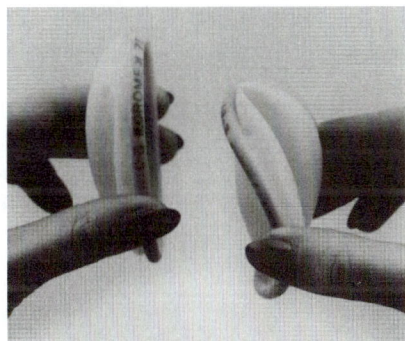

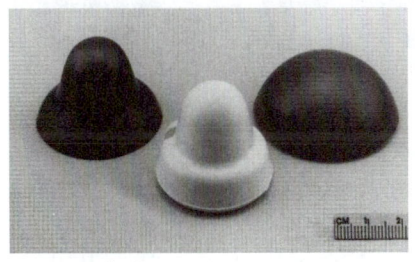

Cervical Caps   *Spermicides*

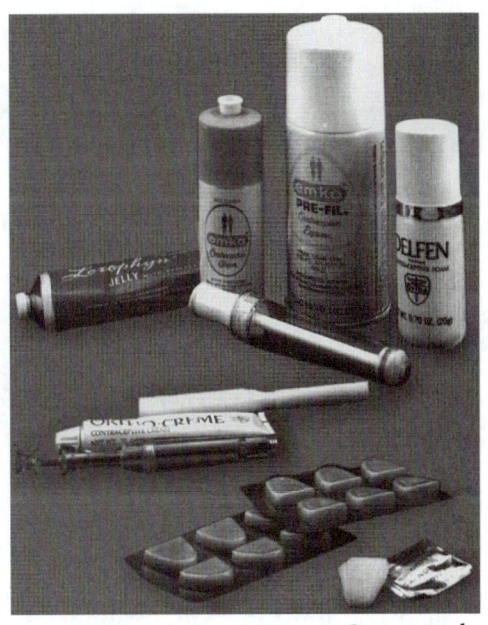

INTRODUCTION to Vaginal Methods   13-3

Deciding About Vaginal Methods

How Do They Work?

- **Spermicides** kill sperm or make sperm unable to move toward the egg.
- **Diaphragms and cervical caps** block sperm from entering the uterus and tubes, where sperm could meet an egg.

How Effective?

IMPORTANT: Effectiveness depends on whether a woman uses a vaginal method correctly every time she has sex and on which vaginal method she uses.

Pregnancies per 100 Women in First Year of Use

	Spermicides	Diaphragm	Cervical cap for women who have **not** had children	Cervical cap for women who **have** had children
As commonly used	26 *somewhat effective* (1 in every 4)	20 *somewhat effective* (1 in every 5)	20 *somewhat effective* (1 in every 5)	40 *poorly effective* (1 in every 2 or 3)
Used consistently and correctly	6 *effective* (1 in every 17)	6 *effective* (1 in every 17)	9 *effective* (1 in every 11)	26 *somewhat effective* (1 in every 4)

Vaginal methods may help to prevent some sexually transmitted diseases (STDs) (and possibly HIV/AIDS, although studies have not shown this so far). It is not clear whether vaginal methods prevent STDs as well as condoms do. Still, using vaginal methods alone is better than not using either a vaginal method or a condom. Also, a woman-controlled method may be used more consistently than a condom.

Advantages and Disadvantages

ADVANTAGES OF ALL VAGINAL METHODS

- Safe, woman-controlled methods that almost every woman can use.
- Help prevent some STDs and conditions caused by STDs—pelvic inflammatory disease (PID), infertility, ectopic pregnancy, and possibly cervical cancer. May offer some protection against HIV/AIDS, but not demonstrated yet.
- Offer contraception just when needed.
- Prevent pregnancy effectively if used correctly with every act of sexual intercourse (except cervical cap for women who have had children).
- No side effects from hormones.
- No effect on breast milk.
- Can be stopped at any time.
- Easy to use with a little practice.

Additional Advantages of Spermicide

- Can be inserted as much as one hour before sex to avoid interrupting sex.
- May increase vaginal lubrication.
- Can be used immediately after childbirth.
- No need to see a health care provider before using.

Additional Advantages of Diaphragm or Cervical Cap Used with Spermicide

- Diaphragm can be inserted up to 6 hours before sex to avoid interrupting sex. Cap may be inserted even earlier since it protects for up to 48 hours after insertion.

DISADVANTAGES OF ALL VAGINAL METHODS

- Side effects:
  - Spermicide may cause irritation to woman or her partner, especially if used several times a day.
  - Spermicide may cause local allergic reaction (rarely) in the woman or her partner.
  - Can make urinary tract infections more common. (A woman can avoid this by always urinating after sex.)
- Effectiveness requires having method at hand and taking correct action before each act of sexual intercourse.
- Require woman or her partner to put fingers or inserter into her vagina. (Should wash hands first.)
- Interrupt sex if not inserted beforehand.
- Spermicide may be messy.
- May be hard to conceal from partner.

Additional Disadvantages of Spermicide

- Melting types must be placed in vagina at least 10 minutes before the man ejaculates but not more than 1 hour before.
- Some types may melt in hot weather.
- Foaming tablets may cause warm sensation.
- In theory, irritation caused by use several times a day may increase STD/HIV risk.

Additional Disadvantages of Diaphragm and Cervical Cap Used With Spermicide

- Requires fitting by a family planning provider, involving pelvic examination.
- May be difficult to remove. Diaphragm can tear as the woman removes it (rare).

- Woman may need a different size diaphragm after childbirth.
- Cervical cap appears to be less effective for women who have given birth.
- Diaphragm or cap should be washed with mild soap and clean water after each use.
- Diaphragm needs careful storage to avoid developing holes.

Using the Medical Eligibility Checklist

*The list on the next page checks whether the client has any **known** medical conditions that prevent use of vaginal methods. It is not meant to replace counseling.*

*The questions in the checklist refer to **known conditions**. Generally, you can learn of these conditions by asking the client. You do not usually have to perform laboratory tests or physical examinations. (A pelvic examination is needed for a diaphragm or cap.)*

IMPORTANT: Nonmedical providers can safely offer spermicides to all women. Nonmedical providers include retailers and community-based distributors.

MEDICAL ELIGIBILITY CHECKLIST FOR

Vaginal Methods

Ask the client the questions below. If she answers NO to ALL of the questions, then she CAN use vaginal methods if she wants. If she answers YES to a question below, follow the instructions.

1. Have you recently had a full-term delivery or second-trimester spontaneous or induced abortion? If so, when?

   ☐ No   ☐ Yes ▶ Diaphragm and cervical cap generally should not be fitted until 6 to 12 weeks after childbirth or second-trimester abortion, depending on when the uterus and cervix return to normal. Can use spermicide alone.

2. Are you allergic to latex?

   ☐ No   ☐ Yes ▶ She should not use a latex diaphragm or cap.

3. Have you ever been told that your vagina, cervix, or uterus has an unusual shape or position?

   ☐ No   ☐ Yes ▶ May be impossible or ineffective for her to use a diaphragm or cap. A pelvic exam may be necessary to determine whether diaphragm or cap can be correctly placed and will stay in place.

4. Do you have a medical condition that makes pregnancy dangerous? (See pages 4–13 through 4–18.)

   ☐ No   ☐ Yes ▶ She may want a more effective method. She may use vaginal methods, however, if she makes an informed choice and receives proper instruction on effective use.

5. Have you ever had toxic shock syndrome?

   ☐ No   ☐ Yes ▶ Generally should not use diaphragm or cervical cap. Can use spermicides alone or another method.

Be sure to explain the health benefits and risks and the side effects of the method that the client will use. Also, point out any conditions that would make the method inadvisable when relevant to the client.

Starting Vaginal Methods

When to Start

A woman can begin using a vaginal method any time during her monthly cycle and soon after childbirth, abortion, or miscarriage.

The diaphragm and cervical cap generally should **not** be fitted, however, in the first 6 to 12 weeks after full-term delivery or second-trimester spontaneous or induced abortion, depending on when the uterus and cervix return to their normal sizes. If needed, a woman can use spermicide alone or with condoms until then.

Providing Vaginal Methods

IMPORTANT: A woman who chooses a vaginal method benefits from good counseling.

A friendly provider who listens to a woman's concerns, answers her questions, and gives clear, practical information, especially about the importance of consistent use, will help clients use vaginal methods with success and satisfaction.

You can follow these steps to provide vaginal methods:

1. **Give her plenty of spermicide**—up to a year's supply, if possible.

2. **Explain how to use** vaginal methods, including insertion and, for diaphragm and cervical cap, removal (see pages 13–10 to 13–13).

3. If she chooses a diaphragm or cap, **arrange for proper fitting and placement** with a specifically trained provider. Refer if necessary.

4. **Plan a return visit** when she will need to get more spermicide if she does not prefer to get it elsewhere.

5. **Invite the client to come back any time** she has questions, problems, or wants another method.

Explaining How to Use

IMPORTANT: For all vaginal methods, the woman must use the method **each time** she has sexual intercourse.

Spermicide

Inserting spermicide

1. The woman inserts the spermicide in her vagina before each time she has sexual intercourse.
2. She inserts more spermicide before each act of sexual intercourse and ejaculation of semen into her vagina.
3. She does not douche for at least 6 hours after sex.

Type of spermicide	How to insert
Foam or cream	Any time less than 1 hour before sex, the woman squeezes foam or cream from the can or tube into a plastic applicator. She inserts the applicator deep into her vagina and pushes its plunger. With foam, she must shake the can strongly just before filling the applicator.
Tablets, suppositories, film	Less than 1 hour but more than 10 minutes before sex, the woman inserts a tablet, suppository, or film deep into her vagina with an applicator or with her fingers. Film must be folded in half and inserted with dry fingers near the cervix, or else the film will stick to the fingers and not the cervix.

Storing spermicide

Most spermicides—especially some suppositories—should be stored in a cool, dry place, if possible, or they may melt. If kept dry, foaming tablets are not so likely to melt in hot weather.

13–10 Essentials of Contraceptive Technology

Diaphragm

Inserting the diaphragm

The woman inserts the diaphragm with spermicide in the proper position in the vagina before having sexual intercourse.

1. The woman holds the diaphragm with the dome down (like a cup).
2. She squeezes about a tablespoon of spermicidal cream or jelly into the cup of the diaphragm and around the rim.
3. She presses opposite sides of the rim together and, with dome side toward palm of hand, pushes the diaphragm into the vagina as far as it goes. (See drawing, page 13–12.)
4. With a finger, she touches the diaphragm to make sure that it covers the cervix. Through the dome of the diaphragm, the cervix feels like the tip of the nose.
5. For each additional act of intercourse, she uses an applicator to insert additional spermicide. She does NOT remove the diaphragm.

Removing the diaphragm

1. The woman leaves the diaphragm in place for **at least 6 hours** after the man's last ejaculation. She does NOT leave the diaphragm in for more than 24 hours. Doing so might increase the risk of toxic shock syndrome.*
2. She inserts a finger into the vagina until she feels the rim of the diaphragm.
3. She gently slides a finger under the rim and pulls the diaphragm down and out. She is careful not to tear the diaphragm with a fingernail.
4. She washes the diaphragm with mild soap and clean water after each use. She checks for holes by filling it with water or by holding it up to the light.
5. She dries the diaphragm and stores it in a clean, dark, cool place, if possible.

---

* Toxic shock syndrome is a rare but serious illness caused by bacteria. A few cases have been reported in diaphragm users. The longer a diaphragm or cap is left in place, the more the bacteria can grow. Symptoms are sudden high fever, body rash like sunburn, vomiting, diarrhea, dizziness, sore throat, and muscle aches. A woman who develops these symptoms should go at once to the nearest health center. Treatment with antibiotics and intravenous fluids is very effective.

Checking Proper Placement of a New Diaphragm or Cervical Cap

An experienced user of diaphragm or cap or else a specifically trained provider must show a new user how to place the device within the vagina. She should allow the woman to practice privately, and then she should check placement.

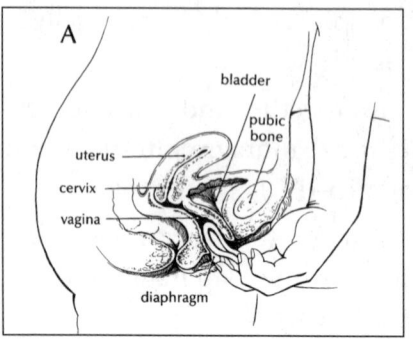

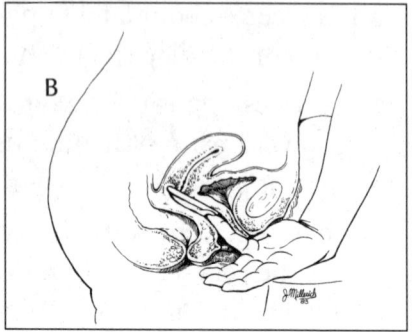

To insert a diaphragm, a woman squeezes its sides together and pushes it into her vagina as far as it will go (A). Then with her finger she checks that the diaphragm fits snugly behind the pubic bone and covers the cervix (B).

CERVICAL CAP

Inserting the cervical cap

The woman inserts the cervical cap with spermicide in the proper position in the vagina before having sexual intercourse.

1. She fills the dome of the cap 1/3 full with spermicidal cream or jelly.

2. She squeezes the rim of the cap between thumb and index finger, and, with the dome side toward the palm of the hand, slides the cap into the vagina as far as it goes.

3. She uses a finger to locate the cervix, which feels like the tip of the nose. She presses the rim of the cap around the cervix until it is completely covered. She sweeps a finger around the cap rim to be sure the cervix is covered.

4. She does not need additional spermicide for additional acts of intercourse that occur within 48 hours after insertion, as long as she keeps the cap in place.

Removing the cervical cap

1. The woman leaves the cap in for at least 6 hours after the man's last ejaculation. She does NOT leave the cap in for more than 48 hours. Doing so could cause a bad odor and may increase the risk of toxic shock syndrome.*
2. She inserts a finger into the vagina until she feels the rim of the cap.
3. She presses on the cap rim until the seal against the cervix is broken; then she tilts the cap off the cervix.
4. She hooks a finger around the rim and pulls it sideways out of the vagina.
5. She washes the cap with mild soap and clean water after each use. She checks for holes by filling it with water or by holding it up to the light.
6. She dries the cap and stores it in a clean, dark, cool place, if possible.

EXPLAIN SPECIFIC REASONS TO RETURN TO THE PROVIDER

Urge the client to return for any of these reasons:

- For more spermicide.
- When a diaphragm or cap wears out, gets thin, develops holes, or becomes stiff. It needs to be replaced.
- After delivery or abortion to check the fit of her diaphragm or cervical cap.
- She or her partner has an allergic reaction (itching, rash, irritation). (See page 13–15.)
- She stops using the method.
- She has any questions or problems or wants another method.

* See footnote on page 13–11.

Following Up

Helping Clients at Any Routine Return Visit

IMPORTANT: A scheduled return visit is not necessary. At any time convenient for the client, she can return for more spermicide or for advice on diaphragm or cap use and fit.

Ask questions

At any return visit:

1. Ask if the client has any questions or anything to discuss.

2. Ask the client about her experience with the method, whether she is satisfied, and whether she has any problems. Give her any information or help that she needs and invite her to return again any time she has questions or concerns. If she has problems that cannot be resolved, help her choose another method.

3. Ask if she has had any health problems since her last visit.

    - If she has developed *allergy to latex, a medical condition that makes pregnancy dangerous,* or *toxic shock syndrome* or recently had a *full-term delivery or second-trimester spontaneous or induced abortion*, see page 13–8 for instructions. If appropriate, help her choose another method.

    - If she has developed *urinary tract infection*, see "Managing Any Problems," page 13–15.

13–14 Essentials of Contraceptive Technology

Managing Any Problems

If the client reports any problems with vaginal methods:

1. Do not dismiss the woman's concerns or take them lightly.
2. Help her with any problems. If she wants to keep using the method, encourage her to keep using it with every act of intercourse.
3. If she is not satisfied after counseling and advice, help her choose another method if she wishes.

For this problem:	**Try this suggestion:**
Allergic reaction or sensitivity to spermicide, such as burning or itching	• Check for infection (signs: abnormal vaginal discharge, redness and/or swelling of the vagina, and itching of the vulva), and treat or refer as appropriate. • If no infection, suggest a different type or brand of spermicide.
Urinary tract infection	• Treat with antibiotics such as ampicillin or trimethoprim plus sulfamethoxazole for 10 to 14 days. • Suggest that the woman urinate soon after sex to help prevent future infections. Also suggest that she drink plenty of fluids, urinate often, and eat food containing vitamin C, such as oranges, grapefruit, and limes, if possible. • If infection is frequent or recurrent, check that the diaphragm is not too tight. (You should be able to fit a gloved finger in front of the rim.) Also consider possibility of STD. • Continued use of the diaphragm is usually not recommended for a woman who has chronic or recurrent urinary tract infection that does not respond to treatment.

FOLLOWING UP on Vaginal Methods

For this problem:	Try this suggestion:
Pain from pressure on bladder or rectum with diaphragm use	• Check diaphragm fit and look for vaginal lacerations. If diaphragm is too large, fit with smaller model.
Difficulty inserting diaphragm or cap	• Give additional advice on insertion. Have her try insertion in the clinic and then check placement. • Her sex partner sometimes can help with insertion.
Sudden high fever, body rash, vomiting, diarrhea, dizziness, and muscle aches (very rare)	• The woman should be taken immediately to the nearest health center. She may have toxic shock syndrome. • If she has toxic shock syndrome, treatment with antibiotics and intravenous fluids is very effective and should be given right away.
Vaginitis with diaphragm use	• Suggest that she clean her diaphragm thoroughly after each use and make sure it is dry before using it again.
Unusual vaginal discharge with diaphragm use	• Suggest that she remove the diaphragm promptly *(but no sooner than 6 hours after having sex)* and clean it after each use.
Vaginal lesion with diaphragm use	• Suggest that she use another method temporarily and give her supplies. • Check diaphragm fit and how the client removes her diaphragm.

IMPORTANT POINTS FOR THE USER TO REMEMBER ABOUT

Vaginal Methods—Spermicide, Diaphragm, Cervical Cap

▶ These are **methods that women control and can use when needed.**

▶ **Must be used correctly every time for best protection.** Vaginal methods are only somewhat effective as most women use them. They are more effective when used correctly every time.

▶ **May help protect against some sexually transmitted diseases (STDs) somewhat,** but this has not been proved. Condoms give the best protection against passing disease during sex.

▶ You can **insert any spermicide up to 1 hour before sex. Place it high in the vagina.** Insert foaming tablets, films, and suppositories **at least 10 minutes before sex. Do not douche for at least 6 hours after sex.**

▶ You can **insert a diaphragm or cervical cap ahead of time** when you might have sex. After sex **leave the diaphragm or cap in place and do not douche for at least 6 hours.**

▶ With diaphragm or cervical cap, **use plenty of spermicidal jelly or cream** for best protection.

▶ Please **come back for more spermicide before your supply runs out.**

▶ You are **welcome back any time** you want help, advice, or another method.

IMPORTANT POINTS About Vaginal Methods   13–17

Questions and Answers

1. **Do spermicides cause birth defects?**

   No. The best evidence is that spermicides do not cause birth defects. Spermicides do not harm the baby even if a woman uses them while pregnant.

2. **Do spermicides cause cancer?**

   No. In fact, spermicides, diaphragms, and cervical caps may help prevent cancer of the cervix.

3. **Is the diaphragm uncomfortable for the woman?**

   No, not if it is fitted and inserted correctly. The woman and her partner generally cannot feel the diaphragm during sex. The provider selects the right size diaphragm for each woman so that it fits and does not hurt.

4. **If a woman uses the diaphragm without spermicide, will it work at all?**

   Yes, but without the spermicide, the diaphragm will be less effective. Therefore using a diaphragm without spermicide is not recommended.

5. **Could a woman leave a diaphragm in all day?**

   Although not usually recommended, a woman who wants to use the diaphragm but may not always be able to put it in before sex could leave it in all day. She should remove it and wash it every day to avoid urinary tract infections and toxic shock syndrome.

6. **Can a woman use lubricants with a diaphragm or cap?**

   Oil-based lubricants can damage the latex rubber in a diaphragm or cap. Therefore a woman should not use oil-based vaginal lubricants or medications along with diaphragm or cap. These include petroleum jelly (*Vaseline*), mineral oil, hand lotion, vegetable oil, butter, margarine, and cocoa butter as well as common vaginal yeast creams.

   She can use contraceptive jelly or a water-soluble lubricant specifically made for use with latex condoms.

7. **Do vaginal methods protect against sexually transmitted diseases (STDs) including HIV/AIDS?**

   Spermicides can kill organisms that cause some STDs. The diaphragm and cervical cap can help block these organisms. They may also offer some protection against HIV, which causes AIDS, but this has not been shown. The best protection during sex may be using both a condom and spermicide together, every time. If only one method is used, the condom is best. But a woman-controlled vaginal method might be used more regularly than condoms when a woman cannot convince her partner to use condoms.

Chapter 14
Fertility Awareness-Based Methods Including Periodic Abstinence

Key Points

▸ **A woman learns how to tell when the fertile time of her menstrual cycle starts and when it ends.**

▸ **With this knowledge, a couple can avoid pregnancy.** They can abstain from sex, or they can use a barrier method or withdrawal during the fertile time.

▸ **Only moderately effective as commonly used.** Can be effective if used correctly.

▸ **Usually need close cooperation between sex partners and full commitment from the man.**

▸ **No physical side effects.** Methods that involve long abstinence can be difficult for some couples.

▸ **May be hard to use during fever or vaginal infection, after childbirth, or while breastfeeding.**

Chapter 14
Fertility Awareness-Based Methods Including Periodic Abstinence

Contents

- Introduction to Fertility Awareness-Based Methods 14–3
- Deciding About Fertility Awareness-Based Methods . . . 14–4
    - How Do They Work? 14–4
    - How Effective? 14–4
    - Advantages and Disadvantages 14–6
    - Medical Eligibility Checklist 14–8
- Using Fertility Awareness-Based Methods 14–10
    - When to Start 14–10
    - Teaching Fertility Awareness-Based Methods . . . 14–10
    - Explaining How to Use 14–11
- Following Up 14–15
    - Helping Clients at Any Routine Return Visit . . . 14–15
    - Managing Any Problems 14–16
- Important Points for the User to Remember 14–17
- Questions and Answers 14–18

Introduction to Fertility Awareness-Based Methods

"Fertility awareness" means that a woman learns how to tell when the fertile time of her menstrual cycle starts and ends. (The fertile time is the time when she can become pregnant.)

A woman can use several ways to tell when her fertile time begins and ends:

- **Calendar calculation:** A woman can count calendar days to identify the start and end of the fertile time. The number of days depends on the length of previous menstrual cycles.

- **Cervical secretions:** When a woman sees or feels cervical secretions, she may be fertile. Can be just a sense of vaginal wetness.

- **Basal body temperature (BBT):** A woman's resting body temperature goes up slightly around the time of ovulation (release of an egg), when she could become pregnant.

- **Feel of the cervix:** As the fertile time begins, the opening of the cervix feels softer, opens slightly, and is moist. When she is not fertile, the opening is firmer and closed. (Seldom used as the only sign.)

A woman may use one of these or a combination. To tell when the fertile time **starts**, she can use *calendar calculations* and *cervical secretions*. To tell when the fertile time **ends**, she can use *BBT*, *cervical secretions*, and *calendar calculation*. (For details, see pages 14–10 through 14–14.)

Deciding About Fertility Awareness-Based Methods

How Do They Work?

Fertility awareness helps a woman know when she could become pregnant. The couple avoids pregnancy by changing their sexual behavior during fertile days. They can:

- **Abstain from vaginal intercourse**—avoiding vaginal sex completely during the fertile time. Also called **periodic abstinence** and **Natural Family Planning (NFP)**.

- **Use barrier methods**—condoms, diaphragm and spermicide, or spermicide alone.

- **Use withdrawal**—taking the penis out of the vagina before ejaculation. Also called coitus interruptus and "pulling out." Or they can have other sexual contact without vaginal intercourse.

How Effective?

Note: The pregnancy rates in this section are for periodic abstinence only.

IMPORTANT: Effectiveness of periodic abstinence varies more than for any other family planning method. For highest effectiveness, couples should never guess about the fertile time. They should abstain completely from sexual intercourse during fertile times.

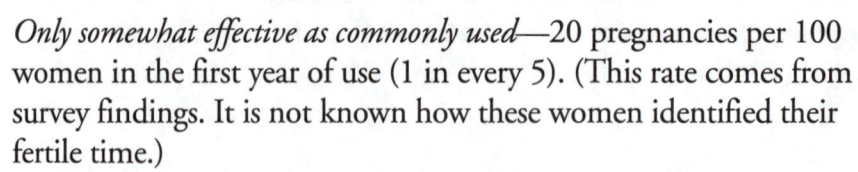

Only somewhat effective as commonly used—20 pregnancies per 100 women in the first year of use (1 in every 5). (This rate comes from survey findings. It is not known how these women identified their fertile time.)

Effective or very effective when used consistently and correctly—

Consistent Use of Single-Indicator Methods

Cervical secretions: 3 pregnancies per 100 women in first year of use (1 in every 33).

Basal body temperature: 1 pregnancy per 100 women in first year of use (when intercourse takes place only after ovulation and before next menstrual period; see page 14–11).

Calendar: 9 pregnancies per 100 women in first year of use (1 in every 11).

Consistent Use of Multiple-Indicator Method

Sympto-thermal or multi-index (usually cervical secretions + BBT, and perhaps also calendar calculations and feeling the cervix): 2 pregnancies per 100 women in the first year of use (1 in every 50).

Note: There is little information on effectiveness of fertility awareness used with barrier methods or withdrawal. Some couples find using barrier methods during the fertile time easier—and thus possibly more effective—than avoiding sex.

Couples who regularly use barrier methods also can use fertility awareness and avoid sex while the woman is fertile. This may be more effective than using barrier methods alone.

DECIDING About Fertility Awareness

Advantages and Disadvantages

Advantages

- Once learned, can be used to avoid pregnancy or to become pregnant, according to the couple's wishes.
- No physical side effects.
- Very little or no cost.
- Can be used by most couples if they are committed to it.
- Effective if used correctly and consistently.
- Once learned, may require no further help from health care providers.
- Can be learned from trained volunteers. Contact with medical personnel is not necessary.
- Immediately reversible.
- Periodic abstinence is acceptable to some religious groups that reject or discourage use of other methods.
- No effect on breastfeeding or breast milk. No hormonal side effects.
- Involves men in family planning.
- Educates people about women's fertility cycles.

Disadvantages

- Usually only somewhat effective.
- Takes up to 2 or 3 cycles to learn how to identify fertile time accurately using cervical secretions and BBT. Less time to learn the calendar method, although it is best if a woman has records of the last 6 to 12 cycles to identify the fertile time.
- If using periodic abstinence, requires long periods without vaginal intercourse—8 to 16 days each menstrual cycle. Abstinence may be difficult for some couples.
- Will not work without continuing cooperation and commitment of both the woman and the man.

- Can become unreliable or hard to use if the woman has a fever, has a vaginal infection, is breastfeeding, or has any other condition that changes body temperature, cervical mucus, or menstrual cycle length.
- After childbirth, may be hard to identify the fertile time until menstrual cycle becomes regular again.
- Calendar method may not be effective for women with irregular menstrual cycles.
- May be very difficult to practice if a woman has more than one sex partner.
- Most methods require women or couples to keep careful daily records and pay close attention to body changes.
- Does not protect against sexually transmitted diseases (STDs) including HIV/AIDS.

   IMPORTANT: Ask the client if she might have or get a sexually transmitted disease (STD). (Has more than one sex partner? Partner has more than one partner? Could this happen in future?)

   If she has or might get an STD, urge her to use condoms regularly. Give her condoms.

Using the Medical Eligibility Checklist

*The list on the next page checks whether the client has any **known** medical conditions that might interfere with use of fertility awareness-based methods. It is not meant to replace counseling.*

*The questions in the checklist refer to **known conditions**. Generally, you can learn of these conditions by asking the client. You do not usually have to perform laboratory tests or physical examinations.*

DECIDING About Fertility Awareness   14–7

MEDICAL ELIGIBILITY CHECKLIST FOR

Fertility Awareness-Based Methods

Ask the client the questions below. If she answers NO to ALL questions, she CAN use any fertility awareness-based method if she wants. If she answers YES to any question, follow the instructions. No conditions restrict use of these methods, but some conditions can make them harder to use effectively.

---

1. Do you have a medical condition that would make pregnancy especially dangerous? (See page 4–13.)

   ☐ No   ☐ Yes ▶ She may want to choose a more effective method. If not, stress careful use of fertility awareness-based methods to avoid pregnancy.

---

2. Do you have irregular menstrual cycles? Vaginal bleeding between periods? Heavy or long monthly bleeding?
   For younger women: Are your periods just starting?
   For older women: Have your periods become irregular, or have they stopped?

   ☐ No   ☐ Yes ▶ Predicting her fertile time with only the calendar method may be hard or impossible. She can use basal body temperature (BBT) and/or cervical mucus, or she may prefer another method.

---

3. Did you recently give birth or have an abortion? Are you breastfeeding? Do you have any other condition that affects the ovaries or menstrual bleeding, such as stroke, serious liver disease, hyperthyroid, hypothyroid, or cervical cancer?

   ☐ No   ☐ Yes ▶ These conditions do not restrict use of fertility awareness-based methods. But these conditions may affect fertility signs, making fertility awareness-based methods hard to use. For this reason, a woman or couple may prefer a different method. If not, they may need more counseling and follow-up to use the method effectively.

---

4. Do you have any infections or diseases that may change cervical mucus, basal body temperature, or menstrual bleeding—such as sexually transmitted disease (STD) or pelvic inflammatory disease (PID) in the last 3 months, or vaginal infection?

   ☐ No   ☐ Yes ▶ These conditions may affect fertility signs, making fertility awareness-based methods hard to use. Once an infection is treated and reinfection is avoided, however, a woman can use fertility awareness-based methods more easily.

MEDICAL ELIGIBILITY CHECKLIST FOR FERTILITY AWARENESS *(continued)*

5. Do you take any drugs that affect cervical mucus, such as mood-altering drugs, lithium, tricyclic anti-depressants, or anti-anxiety therapies?

☐ No   ☐ **Yes** ▶ Predicting her fertile time correctly may be difficult or impossible if she uses only the cervical mucus method. She can use BBT and/or the calendar method, or she may prefer another method.

Be sure to explain the health benefits and risks and the side effects of the method that the client will use. Also, point out any conditions that would make the method inadvisable when relevant to the client.

Most Women Can Use Fertility Awareness-Based Methods

In general, most women CAN use fertility awareness-based methods safely and effectively. Fertility awareness-based methods can be used in any circumstances by women who:

- Are fat or thin,
- Have no children,
- Have children,
- Smoke cigarettes.

Also, women with these conditions CAN use fertility awareness-based methods in any circumstances:

- Mild high blood pressure,
- Deep vein thrombosis or pulmonary embolism,
- Varicose veins,
- Mild or severe headaches,
- Painful menstruation,
- Uterine fibroids,
- Endometriosis,
- Ovarian cysts,
- Iron deficiency anemia,
- Viral hepatitis,
- Malaria.

DECIDING About Fertility Awareness

Using Fertility Awareness-Based Methods

When to Start

Once trained, a woman or couple can begin using fertility awareness-based techniques at any time. Before starting to use the calendar method, a woman must record the length of her menstrual cycles for at least 6 months.

Immediately after childbirth or abortion: Once bleeding stops after delivery, cervical secretions can be used, but with difficulty. The calendar method and BBT are unreliable.

Some providers encourage women to begin monitoring their fertility before marriage or before they become sexually active. In this way women can learn to detect their fertile times before they face any risk of pregnancy. For couples already sexually active, a trainer may recommend a cycle of abstinence so that a woman can learn to observe her fertility signs.

Teaching Fertility Awareness-Based Methods

IMPORTANT: A woman or couple who chooses to use fertility awareness-based methods needs good counseling to use these methods most effectively and confidently.

A friendly provider who listens to a woman or couple's concerns, answers their questions, and gives clear, practical information and advice will help clients use fertility awareness-based methods with success and satisfaction.

Health care providers, volunteers, counselors, and couples experienced with fertility awareness methods can counsel and train others.

Trainers should be able to:

- Help a woman and her partner learn to recognize fertility signs.
- Encourage couples repeatedly to avoid sex or to use withdrawal or barrier methods during the fertile time. Also, be able to counsel couples about any problems with abstinence.
- Provide materials to chart body changes, such as special, expanded-scale BBT thermometers, calendars, and paper or notebooks, if possible.
- Tell couples about other methods or refer them to a source of information, supplies, and services for other methods if the couple asks.

Explaining How to Use

IMPORTANT: Couples who choose to use fertility awareness-based methods usually need personal guidance from a trained counselor, usually over several months. During this time the couple must use another method or avoid intercourse.

*Some trainers emphasize specific sets of rules, called by such names as the cervical mucus, Billings, or ovulation method, the basal body temperature (BBT) method, and the sympto-thermal method. Here, specific rules of behavior are highlighted in **dark type**.*

For all fertility awareness-based methods: The couple avoids unprotected vaginal intercourse during the fertile time.

Cervical Secretions To Identify Start and End of the Fertile Time:

1. A woman checks every day for any cervical secretions. She may feel wetness at the opening of her vagina or see secretions on her finger, underpants, or tissue paper. **As soon as she notices any secretions, the couple avoids sex, uses a barrier method, or uses withdrawal.**

2. The secretions have a peak day, when they are most slippery, stretchy, and wet. **The couple continues to avoid sex, use withdrawal, or use a barrier method until 4 days after the peak day.**

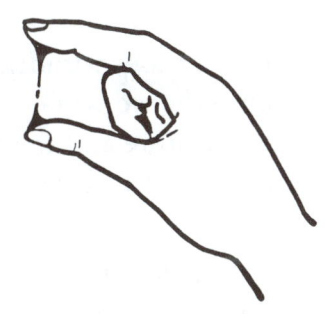

Avoid Sex
Secretions—especially when slippery, wet, and can be stretched—mean the couple should avoid sex or use withdrawal or a barrier method until the 4th day after the peak day.

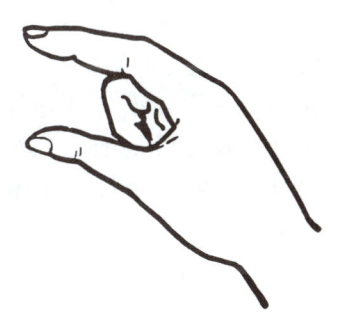

Can Have Sex
No secretions mean the woman probably cannot become pregnant. She can have unprotected vaginal sex.

3. In a few days the secretions become sticky, pasty, or crumbly, or the woman has no secretions at all. The couple can have unprotected sex until menstrual bleeding begins again.
4. Some trainers recommend that couples avoid unprotected sex during menstrual bleeding because cervical secretions could be hard to notice. The chances of pregnancy in the first 5 or 6 days of the cycle are slight, however.
5. After menstrual bleeding stops, the woman may have several days with no secretions. Sex is usually considered safe during this time. It should be limited to every second day, however, because vaginal fluids and semen could be confused with secretions. Spermicides, vaginal infections, and some drugs also affect the normal pattern of a woman's secretions. **The couple does not have unprotected vaginal sex if they are unsure whether there are secretions.**

Basal Body Temperature (BBT) to Identify End of the Fertile Time:
1. The woman must take her body temperature in the same way, either orally, rectally, or vaginally, at the same time *each morning* before she gets out of bed. She must know how to read a thermometer and must record her temperature on a special graph.
2. The woman's temperature rises 0.2° to 0.5°C (0.4° to 1.0°F) around the time of ovulation (about midway through the menstrual cycle for many women).
3. **The couple avoids sex, uses a barrier method, or uses withdrawal from the first day of menstrual bleeding until the woman's temperature has risen above her regular temperature and stayed up for 3 full days.** This means that ovulation has occurred and passed.
4. After this, the couple can have unprotected sex (over the next 10 to 12 days) until her next menstrual bleeding period begins.

Cervical Secretions + Basal Body Temperature To Identify the Start and End of the Fertile Time:

Users identify fertile and infertile days by combining BBT and cervical secretion observations and instructions and, often, other signs and symptoms of ovulation.

1. **The couple starts avoiding unprotected sex when the woman senses cervical secretions.** For more protection the couple can start avoiding sex with the first day of menstrual bleeding.

2. **The couple keeps avoiding unprotected intercourse until *both* the fourth day after peak cervical secretions *and* the third full day after the rise in temperature (BBT).** If one of these events happens without the other, the couple waits for the other event before having unprotected sex.

3. Other signs and symptoms of ovulation include: abdominal pain, cervical changes, and breast tenderness. Also, the calendar method may help identify the start of the fertile time.

Calendar (Rhythm) Method To Identify Start and End of the Fertile Time:

1. Before relying on this method, the woman records the number of days in each menstrual cycle for at least 6 months. The first day of menstrual bleeding is always counted as day 1.

2. The woman subtracts 18 from the length of her *shortest* recorded cycle. This tells her the estimated first day of her fertile time. Then she subtracts 11 days from the length of her *longest* recorded cycle. This tells her the last day of her fertile time. **The couple avoids sex, uses a barrier method, or uses withdrawal during the fertile time.**

    Example:
    - If her recorded cycles vary from 26 to 32 days,
        26 – 18 = 8. Start avoiding unprotected sex on day 8.
        32 – 11 = 21. Okay to have unprotected sex again after day 21.

USING Fertility Awareness 14–13

- She must avoid unprotected sex from day 8 through day 21 of her cycle (14 days of avoiding unprotected sex).

The calendar method may require 16 days or more in a row of avoiding sex or using withdrawal or a barrier method in each cycle, especially for women with irregular menstrual cycles. This much abstinence may be too restrictive for some couples. For this reason the BBT method or barrier methods during fertile days are often recommended along with the calendar method.

EXPLAIN REASONS TO RETURN

Trainers should encourage the woman or couple to meet with them several times during the first few cycles to discuss their experience with the method and to receive encouragement or guidance.

Also:

- When they have any questions or problems with the method,
- If the woman's situation changes in ways that can affect fertility signs—for example, when the woman has just had a baby, is breastfeeding, or is close to menopause,
- If they stop using the method,
- If they want another method.

Following Up

Helping Clients at Any Routine Return Visit

ASK QUESTIONS

At any return visit:

1. Ask if the client or couple has any questions or anything to discuss.

2. Ask the client or couple about their experience with the method, whether they are satisfied, and whether they have any problems. Review the couple's observations and any records of fertility signs that they have kept. Check whether they are using the method correctly. Give them any information or help they need. If they have any problems that cannot be resolved, help them choose another method.

3. Ask if the woman has had any health problems since her last visit. If she has developed any conditions that will make fertility awareness-based methods difficult to use or too unreliable (see checklist on pages 14–8 and 14–9), help the woman or couple to decide if they should choose another method. If she has developed any conditions that would make pregnancy especially dangerous (see page 4–13), help her choose a more effective method if she is willing.

PLAN FOR THE NEXT VISIT

If the woman or couple are satisfied with the method, encourage them to continue using fertility awareness-based methods and to continue abstaining from sex or using barrier methods during the fertile time.

If they need more training, counsel them now and plan as needed for their next visit to check that they are satisfied with the method and using it correctly.

Managing Any Problems

For inability to abstain from sex during the fertile time:

Difficulty with abstinence is the most common problem with fertility awareness-based methods. Discuss the problem openly with the couple and help them feel at ease, not embarrassed.

- Discuss possible use of condoms or vaginal methods or sexual contact without vaginal intercourse that the couple can enjoy during the fertile time.
- If the problem cannot be resolved and leads to marital disputes or may lead to unintended pregnancy, suggest that the couple also use condoms or spermicide or else choose another method.

IMPORTANT POINTS FOR THE USER TO REMEMBER ABOUT

Fertility Awareness-Based Methods

▸ Only somewhat effective as commonly used.

▸ Be aware of body changes. Remember the rules:
  - *Cervical secretions*: Avoid unprotected sex from the first day of any cervical secretions or feeling of vaginal wetness until the 4th day after the peak day of slippery secretions.
  - *Basal body temperature (BBT):* Avoid unprotected sex from the first day of menstrual bleeding until body temperature has risen and stayed up for 3 full days.
  - *Calendar, or rhythm:* Determine the fertile time through calendar calculations. Avoid unprotected sex between the first and last days of the estimated fertile time.
  - *Cervical secretions + BBT*: Avoid unprotected sex from the first day of cervical secretions until *both* the 4th day after the peak day of slippery secretions *and* the 3rd full day after the rise in body temperature.

▸ **If sensing body changes is difficult…**
Infections in the vagina and other illnesses can upset the usual changes in cervical mucus and body temperature. You may need to avoid sex or use another method until the illness is cured.

▸ **If avoiding sex is difficult…**
If acceptable, you can use condoms, diaphragm, spermicide, or withdrawal during the fertile time or have sexual contact without putting the penis in the vagina. Also, you are welcome to more counseling, and you can choose another method.

▸ **Come back any time for help.**
Fertility awareness-based methods take training, practice, and commitment. Please come back to your family planning provider any time you have questions or problems.

▸ **These methods do not prevent sexually transmitted diseases (STDs) including HIV/AIDS.** If you think you might get an STD, use condoms regularly.

❓ Questions and Answers

1. **Can only highly educated couples use fertility awareness-based methods for family planning?**

    No. Couples with little or no formal schooling can use fertility awareness-based methods effectively. All couples must be highly motivated, well-trained, and committed to avoiding sex or using withdrawal or barrier methods during the fertile time.

2. **Are fertility awareness-based methods unreliable for contraception?**

    For many women, these methods can provide reliable information about the fertile days. If the couple consistently uses periodic abstinence, withdrawal, or a barrier method during the woman's fertile time, fertility awareness-based methods can be effective. In general, however, pregnancy rates are higher among users of these methods than among women using most other methods (see page 4–20).

Chapter 15
Lactational Amenorrhea Method (LAM)

Key Points

▶ LAM—a contraceptive method based on breastfeeding.

▶ A woman uses LAM when:
- Her baby gets **little or no other food or drink except breast milk,** and she **breastfeeds often,** both day and night, AND
- Her **menstrual periods have not returned,** AND
- Her **baby is less than 6 months old.**

▶ Effective for up to 6 months after childbirth.

▶ Protects the milk supply by avoiding pregnancy.

▶ The woman should be planning to start another family planning method.

Chapter 15
Lactational Amenorrhea Method (LAM)

Contents

Introduction to LAM 15–3
Deciding About LAM 15–4
    How Does It Work? 15–4
    How Effective? 15–4
    Advantages and Disadvantages 15–4
    Medical Eligibility Checklist 15–6
Starting LAM 15–7
    When to Start 15–7
    Providing LAM 15–8
    Explaining How to Use 15–9
Following Up 15–11
    Helping Clients at Any Routine Return Visit . . . 15–11
    Managing Any Problems 15–12
Important Points for the User to Remember 15–14
Questions and Answers 15–15

Introduction to LAM

- The Lactational Amenorrhea Method (LAM) is the use of breastfeeding as a temporary family planning method. ("Lactational" means related to breastfeeding. "Amenorrhea" means not having menstrual bleeding.)

- LAM provides natural protection against pregnancy and encourages starting another method at the proper time. A woman is naturally protected against pregnancy when:
  - Her baby gets at least 85% of his or her feedings as breast milk, and she breastfeeds her baby often, both day and night, AND
  - Her menstrual periods have not returned, AND
  - Her baby is less than 6 months old.

- If she keeps breastfeeding very often, her protection from pregnancy may last longer than 6 months and perhaps as long as 9 or 12 months.

- LAM makes sure that the baby gets needed nutrients and protection from disease provided by breast milk. Breastfeeding is the healthiest way to feed most babies during the first 6 months of life. Along with other foods, breast milk can be a major part of the child's diet for 2 years or more.

Deciding About LAM

How Does It Work?

Stops ovulation (release of eggs from ovaries) because breastfeeding changes the rate of release of natural hormones.

How Effective?

Effective as commonly used—2 pregnancies per 100 women in the first 6 months after childbirth (1 in every 50).

Very effective when used correctly and consistently—0.5 pregnancies per 100 women in the first 6 months after childbirth (1 in every 200).

IMPORTANT: Correct and consistent use means:

(1) The baby gets at least 85% of his or her feedings as breast milk, and the mother breastfeeds often, both day and night, AND

(2) The mother's menstrual periods have not returned, AND

(3) The baby is less than 6 months old.

If any of these is *not* true, the woman should:

- Use another method for effective family planning—one that does not interfere with breastfeeding. (See page 4–8.)
- Keep breastfeeding her baby if possible, even while starting to give the baby other food.

Advantages and Disadvantages

ADVANTAGES

- Effectively prevents pregnancy for at least 6 months and maybe longer if a woman keeps breastfeeding often, day and night.
- Encourages the best breastfeeding patterns.
- Can be used immediately after childbirth.
- No need to do anything at time of sexual intercourse.
- No direct cost for family planning or for feeding the baby.
- No supplies or procedures needed to prevent pregnancy.

- No hormonal side effects.
- Counseling for LAM encourages starting a follow-on method at the proper time.
- Breastfeeding practices required by LAM have other health benefits for baby and mother including:
  - Provides the healthiest food for the baby.
  - Protects the baby from life-threatening diarrhea.
  - Helps protect the baby from life-threatening diseases such as measles and pneumonia by passing the mother's immunities to the baby.
  - Helps develop close relationship between mother and baby.

DISADVANTAGES

- Effectiveness after 6 months is not certain.
- Frequent breastfeeding may be inconvenient or difficult for some women, especially working mothers.
- No protection against sexually transmitted diseases (STDs) including HIV/AIDS.
- If the mother has HIV (the virus that causes AIDS), there is a small chance that breast milk will pass HIV to the baby.

IMPORTANT: Ask her if she might have or get a sexually transmitted disease (STD). (Has more than one sex partner? Partner has more than one partner? Could this happen in future?)

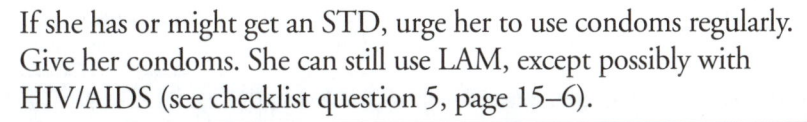

If she has or might get an STD, urge her to use condoms regularly. Give her condoms. She can still use LAM, except possibly with HIV/AIDS (see checklist question 5, page 15–6).

Using the Medical Eligibility Checklist

The list on the next page checks whether the client can use LAM. It is not meant to replace counseling.

*The questions in the checklist refer to **known conditions**. No medical conditions rule out LAM, and LAM has no known ill effects on a woman's health. Medical conditions that prevent or limit breastfeeding, however, can limit use of LAM. Generally, you can learn of these conditions by asking the client. You do not usually have to perform laboratory tests or physical examinations.*

MEDICAL ELIGIBILITY CHECKLIST FOR

Lactational Amenorrhea Method (LAM)

Ask the client the questions below. If she answers NO to ALL of the questions, then she CAN use LAM. If she answers YES to a question below, follow the instructions.

1. Is your baby 6 months old or older?

   ☐ No ☐ **Yes** ▶ She cannot use LAM. Help her choose another method. If she is breastfeeding, a nonhormonal method is best.

2. Has your menstrual period returned? (Bleeding in the first 8 weeks after childbirth does not count.)

   ☐ No ☐ **Yes** ▶ After 8 weeks since childbirth, if a woman has 2 straight days of menstrual bleeding, or her menstrual period has returned, she cannot use LAM. Help her choose another method. If she is breastfeeding, a nonhoronal method is best.

3. Have you begun to breastfeed less often? Do you regularly give the baby other food or liquid?

   ☐ No ☐ **Yes** ▶ If the baby's feeding pattern has just changed, explain that she must fully or nearly fully breastfeed — day and night — to protect against pregnancy. At least 85% of her baby's feedings should be breastfeeds.

   If she is not fully or nearly fully breastfeeding, she cannot use LAM as effectively. Help her choose another nonhormonal method.

4. Has a health care provider told you not to breastfeed your baby?

   ☐ No ☐ **Yes** ▶ If she is not breastfeeding, she cannot use LAM. Help her choose another method. A woman should not breastfeed if she is taking mood-altering drugs, reserpine, ergotamine, antimetabolites, cyclosporine, cortisone, bromocriptine, radioactive drugs, lithium, or certain anticoagulants, if her baby has a specific infant metabolic disorder, or possibly if she has active viral hepatitis. All others can and should breastfeed for the health benefits.

5. Do you have AIDS? Are you infected with HIV, the virus that causes AIDS?

   ☐ No ☐ **Yes** ▶ Where infectious diseases kill many babies, she should be encouraged to breastfeed. HIV may be passed to the baby in breast milk, however. When infectious diseases are a low risk and safe, affordable other food for the baby is available, advise her to feed her baby that other food. Help her choose a family planning method other than LAM. (Some other infectious conditions, such as active viral hepatitis, also can be transmitted during breastfeeding.)

Be sure to explain the health benefits and risks and the side effects of the method that the client will use. Also, point out any conditions that would make the method inadvisable when relevant to the client.

Most Women Can Use LAM After Childbirth

In general, most women CAN use LAM safely and effectively.* LAM can be used in any circumstances by women who:

- Smoke cigarettes,
- Are young or old,
- Are fat or thin.

Also, women with these conditions CAN use LAM in any circumstances:

- Benign breast disease,
- Breast cancer,
- Headaches,
- High blood pressure,
- Varicose veins,
- Valvular heart disease,
- Diabetes,
- Iron deficiency anemia,
- Malaria,
- Sickle cell disease,
- Gallbladder disease,
- Thyroid disease, or
- Uterine fibroids.

The only conditions that limit use of LAM are conditions that make breastfeeding difficult or that rule out breastfeeding (see checklist questions 4 and 5, page 15–6).

*Characteristics and conditions listed in this box are in WHO Eligibility Criteria category 1. Women with characteristics and conditions in WHO category 2 also can use this method. See Appendix, page A–1.

Starting LAM

When to Start

Start breastfeeding as soon as possible after the baby is born.

- In the first few days after childbirth, breast milk contains substances very important to the baby's health.
- Early and frequent breastfeeding helps the mother produce enough milk to keep her baby well-fed and healthy. It also ensures effective protection from pregnancy.

IMPORTANT: A woman can start LAM at any time if she meets the conditions required for using the method. See chart below.

Can a Woman Use LAM?

Ask the mother, or advise her to ask herself, these 3 questions:

1. Have your menstrual periods returned?

2. Are you regularly giving the baby much other food besides breast milk or allowing long periods without breastfeeding, either day or night?

3. Is your baby more than 6 months old?

If YES → The mother's chance of pregnancy is increased. For continued protection, advise her to begin using a complementary family planning method and to continue breastfeeding for the child's health.

If the answer to ALL of these questions is NO

But, when the answer to any ONE of these questions becomes YES

She can use LAM. There is only a 1% to 2% chance of pregnancy at this time.*

*The mother may choose to use a complementary family planning method *at any time*, however.

Providing LAM

IMPORTANT: A woman who chooses LAM benefits from good counseling.

A provider who listens to a woman's concerns, answers her questions, and gives clear, practical information about LAM, especially how to breastfeed properly and when to start a follow-on contraceptive method, will help the woman use LAM with success and satisfaction.

Explaining How to Use

Give specific instructions

A woman who uses LAM should be encouraged to:

1. **Breastfeed often.** An ideal pattern is at least 8 to 10 times a day including at least once at night. No daytime feedings regularly more than 4 hours apart, and no night feedings regularly more than 6 hours apart.

   IMPORTANT: Some babies may not want to breastfeed 8 to 10 times a day and may want to sleep through the night. These babies may need more encouragement to breastfeed enough.

2. **Breastfeed properly.** Counsel her on breastfeeding technique and diet.

3. **Start other foods** when the baby is **6 months old**. Breastfeed before giving other food, if possible. If the baby's hunger is satisfied first by breast milk, this will help ensure good nutrition and will encourage breast milk production.

   IMPORTANT: The baby may breastfeed less after starting to eat other foods. Therefore LAM may no longer be as effective. An additional family planning method is recommended.

4. **Start another family planning method when:**

   - Her menstrual periods return (bleeding in the first 56 days, or 8 weeks, after childbirth is not considered menstrual bleeding), OR
   - She stops fully or nearly fully breastfeeding, OR
   - Her baby is 6 months old (about the time the baby starts sitting up), OR
   - She no longer wants to rely on LAM for family planning.

If possible, give her another method now that she can start later, when needed. For example, if she has no condition that would prevent using progestin-only oral contraceptives, she can be given these pills along with instructions for taking them (see pages 6–9 and 6–10).

Encourage her to return when she needs more supplies or she needs or wants another method.

For more about other methods during breastfeeding, see pages 4–8 and 4–9.

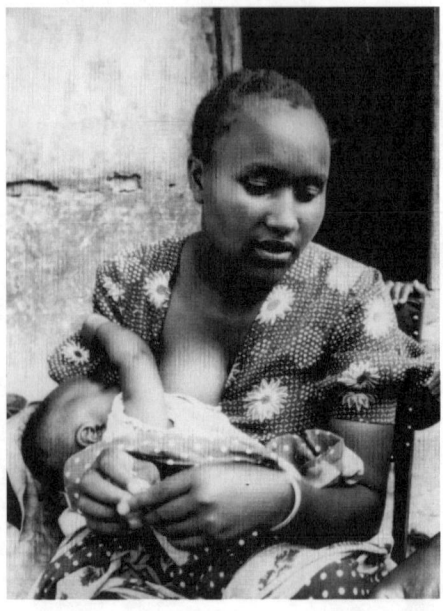

Following Up

Helping Clients at Any Routine Return Visit

ASK QUESTIONS

At any return visit:

1. Ask if the client has any questions or anything to discuss.

2. Ask the client about her experience with breastfeeding, whether she is satisfied, and whether she has any problems. Give her any information or help that she needs and invite her to return any time she has questions or concerns. If she has problems that cannot be resolved, help her choose another family planning method but encourage her to continue breastfeeding as much as possible.

3. Ask if:

   - Her menstrual period has returned, OR
   - Her baby is no longer breastfeeding fully or nearly fully, OR
   - Her baby is 6 months old or older.

   If ANY of these changes has occurred, LAM no longer applies. Help her choose another method. If the new method cannot be started that day, provide enough condoms or spermicide to last until she can start her new method.

4. Ask if she has had any health problems since her last visit.

   - If she has started any *medicines* listed in question 4 on page 15–6, has *active viral hepatitis*, or has been infected with *HIV*, see answers to questions 4 and 5, page 15–6.

PLAN FOR HER NEXT VISIT

If she has not developed any conditions that mean she should not use LAM:

- Plan for her next visit when she will need to choose another method. If possible, give condoms and spermicide or progestin-only oral contraceptives now in case she needs them.

Managing Any Problems

If the client reports any problems with using LAM:

1. Do not dismiss the woman's concerns or take them lightly.

2. Give help and advice about breastfeeding technique, as appropriate, and encourage her to continue breastfeeding for the health of the baby as well as for protection against pregnancy.

3. If the woman is not satisfied with LAM after counseling and discussion, help her choose another method if she wishes. Encourage her to continue breastfeeding, even if she chooses another family planning method. Encourage her to choose a barrier method, an IUD, or a progestin-only method such as progestin-only oral contraceptives, *Norplant* implants, or DMPA injectable contraceptive. These methods do not appear to interfere with breastfeeding.

For this problem:	Try this suggestion:
Not enough milk supply	*Is she breastfeeding often enough?* Feeding the baby more often increases milk supply. Just after childbirth she should breastfed her baby at least every 1 to 3 hours.
	Is she getting little sleep and rest? Is she under great stress? If so, her milk supply may decrease. Suggest that she ask relatives or friends to help with her work at home.

For this problem:	Try this suggestion:
Not enough milk supply *(continued)*	*Has she been eating and drinking enough?* She should drink plenty of fluid every day and eat plenty of healthy food.
Sore nipples	*Are her nipples cracked?* If so, assure her that they will heal. She can continue breastfeeding. To aid in healing, she should: • Feed more often, starting on the less sore nipple. • Let her nipples dry in the air after breastfeeding. She may not be holding the baby in the right position. Advise her on proper breastfeeding techniques. Examine for signs of thrush (fungus infection).
Sore breasts	*Does she have a fever and feel tired? Are her breasts red and tender?* Her breasts may be infected. Treat with antibiotics according to clinic guidelines. Advise her to: • Continue breastfeeding often. • Get more rest. *If no signs of infection, are her breasts tender only in certain places? Do they have lumps? Are they full, hard, and tender?* These signs may point to plugged milk ducts or engorgement (congestion). Advise her to: • Vary her position when breastfeeding. • Get more rest. She may not be holding the baby in the right position. Advise her on proper breastfeeding techniques. Explain signs of infection and tell her to return right away if she sees those signs—fever, fatigue, red and tender breasts.

FOLLOWING UP on Lactational Amenorrhea Method (LAM)

IMPORTANT POINTS FOR THE USER TO REMEMBER ABOUT

Lactational Amenorrhea Method (LAM)

▶ For best protection against pregnancy:
- Breastfeed often, day and night.
- Almost all the baby's feedings should be breast milk.

▶ **Effective protection from pregnancy.**

▶ You will need another family planning method when any 1 of these 3 things happens:
- Your period starts again.
- Your baby is getting much food besides breast milk regularly.
- Your baby is 6 months old (about the time that the baby first sits up).

▶ **Plan for a follow-on method.** You can get supplies ahead of time.

▶ You are **welcome back any time** you want help, advice, or another method.

▶ **LAM does not prevent sexually transmitted diseases (STDs) including HIV/AIDS.** If you think you might get an STD, use condoms regularly along with LAM.

Questions and Answers

1. **Is LAM an effective method of family planning?**

   Yes. Breastfeeding is effective if the woman's monthly menstrual period has not returned, she is fully or nearly fully breastfeeding, and her baby is less than 6 months old.

2. **When should a mother start giving her baby other foods besides breast milk?**

   Usually when the baby is 6 months old. When women start giving other foods, they should always breastfeed before offering the other foods. Then the baby's hunger is first satisfied by breast milk. Also, frequent breastfeeding encourages milk production. Along with other foods, breast milk can be a major part of the child's diet for 2 years or more.

3. **If the mother has AIDS or is infected with HIV, the AIDS virus, can the baby get it from the mother's milk?**

   Yes. There is a small chance that a mother can pass the virus to her baby through her breast milk. Still, in most of the world babies are more likely to die because of infectious diseases than from HIV in breast milk. Unless she can always get suitable food for her baby, a woman with HIV should fully breastfeed her baby if she can. The World Health Organization (WHO) advises that, where infectious diseases kill many infants, women infected with HIV should breastfeed to pass immunities to their babies. Where risk of infectious disease is slight and other safe, affordable food is available, WHO advises infected women to use the safe alternative.

Chapter 16
Sexually Transmitted Diseases Including HIV/AIDS

Key Points

▶ Prevention is better than cure.

▶ The ABCs prevent STDs: Abstain, Be Faithful, Consistently Use Condoms.

▶ All health care providers can do something to help prevent and treat STDs. AT LEAST, they can:

- Quickly assess clients' STD risk.

- Make clients aware of STD risk and teach them the ABCs.

- Encourage people to seek care if they suspect STDs. Many STDs can be treated and cured.

- Distribute condoms and, if possible, spermicides.

- Recognize STD symptoms.

- Refer cases for diagnosis and treatment. Tell clients that their sex partners also need treatment.

Some family planning providers also can diagnose and treat STDs themselves.

Chapter 16
Sexually Transmitted Diseases Including HIV/AIDS

Contents

Introduction to Sexually Transmitted Diseases	16–3
Family Planning Providers and STDs	16–4
Why Should Family Planning Providers Know About STDs?	16–4
How Can Health Care Providers Help Fight STDs?	16–4
Dealing with STDs	16–6
Checklist for Recognizing STD Risk	16–6
Preventing STDs	16–8
Recognizing STDs	16–8
Getting Treated	16–9
Dealing with HIV and AIDS	16–10
What Are HIV and AIDS?	16–10
How Is HIV Carried and Spread?	16–10
How Can HIV/AIDS Be Prevented?	16–11
Symptoms and Likely Diagnosis of Common STDs and Other Genital Infections	16–12
Treatments for Common STDs and Other Genital Infections	16–17
Important Points for the Client to Remember	16–22

Introduction to Sexually Transmitted Diseases

Sexually transmitted diseases (STDs) are diseases that can spread from one person to another by sexual contact. STDs can cause pain, and some can cause infertility and death if not treated. Some common curable STDs are gonorrhea, trichomoniasis, chlamydial infection, and syphilis.

AIDS refers to Acquired Immune Deficiency Syndrome. AIDS is caused by the human immunodeficiency virus (HIV). HIV can be transmitted by sexual contact, by blood, and from a pregnant woman to her child during pregnancy, childbirth, or, occasionally, by breastfeeding. As of 1997 AIDS has no definite cure. Treatments have improved the quality and length of life for people with HIV/AIDS, however.

Each year there are more than 333 million new cases of curable STDs, 1 million new cases of HIV infection, and millions of other viral STDs such as herpes and hepatitis B. STDs are more common than malaria.

Family Planning Providers and STDs

Why Should Family Planning Providers Know About STDs?

- STDs are common. They cause much suffering and disability. All health care providers have a responsibility to do what they can about STDs.

- Family planning clients may ask about changes or conditions of their sex organs. These could be signs of STDs or other reproductive tract infections. To help clients, providers should recognize signs of STDs and either promptly treat or refer for treatment.

- Providers can recognize STD risk (see pages 16–6 and 16–7), and they can recommend and teach STD prevention.

- Women who currently have an STD or are likely to get an STD should not use IUDs. Providers should diagnose and treat known STDs before inserting an IUD. (See Chapter 12.)

- Men and women who have several sex partners have more chances of getting STDs. Sex workers and the clients of sex workers are most likely to get STDs. Female sex workers also usually want to avoid pregnancy, and so they may come to family planning providers. Reaching the people at greatest STD risk is an important way to limit the spread of these diseases.

How Can Health Care Providers Help Fight STDs?

All health care providers, including family planning providers, can do something to fight STDs. Some ways to fight STDs are listed here. Programs and providers can choose ways that fit their resources, their clients' needs, and available services for referral.

- Routinely tell clients how to prevent STDs and how to know if they have an STD (see pages 16–6 and 16–7). Find or make posters or signs, too.

- Encourage people to seek care if they suspect infection or if they develop symptoms, and tell them where to find care.
- Ask standard questions to find out if clients are likely to get an STD. See checklist, page 16–6.
- Encourage people who might get STDs to use condoms or, if condoms are not possible, spermicide—even if they also use another family planning method.
- Make condoms available—free, if necessary. In some countries, social marketing programs may be able to provide condoms for sale at low prices.
- If you cannot provide them, find out where condoms are available in the community, and tell clients. If condoms are not available, try to talk with shop owners about selling them, or find another supplier.
- Learn which STDs are common in your area, know their symptoms, and recognize them among your clients.
- Offer diagnosis and treatment, if possible. If not, arrange for referral.
- Know and use good infection-prevention techniques in the clinic because many STDs can be spread in body fluids, especially blood. (See page 4–10.)
- Help educate the community. Mass-media and person-to-person programs help clients recognize their risk and change their sexual behavior. They also can encourage people to seek treatment.

Dealing with STDs

Because family planning clients usually are sexually active people, they need to know about STDs. They need to know:

- If they risk getting STDs,
- How to prevent STDs.

And, if they risk getting STDs, they also need to know:

- How to recognize STD symptoms, and
- How to get treated for STDs.

Checklist for Recognizing STD Risk

Answering these questions can help a person recognize if he or she is likely to get STDs. The answers also can guide the family planning provider: If the client is likely to get STDs, the client needs a supply of condoms and possibly spermicide and also counseling about avoiding STDs, recognizing possible symptoms, and getting treatment if symptoms appear. If the client has any symptoms, the client also needs diagnosis and treatment, or referral.

Sex workers and their clients face the highest risk of getting STDs. Among people with lower risk, in many countries STD rates are highest among people under age 20.

▶ Ask the client the questions below.*

1. **Do you have more than one sex partner? Does your partner? Have you or your partner had any other sex partners in the last several months? If so, do you sometimes have sex without a condom? Could this happen in the future?**

    ☐ No   ☐ Yes

*NOTE: Question 1 alone does not particularly help to tell if a person without symptoms already HAS an STD. In women, many STDs do not always cause obvious symptoms. Also, conditions in women that are not STDs may have the same symptoms as STDs. By comparison, in men STDs are usually easier to detect. Men are more likely to have symptoms, and there are fewer other possible causes.

▶ **If YES to question 1, the client may be likely to get an STD.** Urge the client to use condoms, try to have a mutually faithful relationship, or abstain (see "Preventing STDs," next page). If YES to question 1, go on to ask questions 2 and 3.

FOR A WOMAN

2. Do you have any of the following?

   - **Unusual discharge** from your vagina?
     ☐ No   ☐ Yes

   - **Itching or sores** in or around your vagina?
     ☐ No   ☐ Yes

   - **Pain or burning** when you urinate?
     ☐ No   ☐ Yes

FOR A MAN

2. Do you have any of the following?

   - **Pain or burning** when you urinate?
     ☐ No   ☐ Yes

   - **Open sores** anywhere in your genital area?
     ☐ No   ☐ Yes

   - **Pus** coming from your penis?
     ☐ No   ☐ Yes

   - **Swollen testicles or penis?**
     ☐ No   ☐ Yes

3. **Do you think your sex partner might have an STD?** Does he/she have open sores anywhere in the genital area? Does he have pus coming from his penis? OR Does she have an unusual discharge from her vagina?

▶ **If YES to any parts of question 1 and either 2 or 3, these symptoms may be caused by an STD.** Diagnose and treat, or refer. Urge that the client avoid sex until 3 days after treatment is done and symptoms are gone. Urge these clients to bring or send their sex partners for care.

DEALING WITH STDs 16–7

Preventing STDs

People can avoid STDs by changing their sexual behavior. They can follow any of the ABCs—**A**bstain, **B**e mutually faithful, and **C**onsistently **U**se **C**ondoms:

A **Abstain from sex.** This is the only guaranteed protection.

or

B **Be mutually faithful.** Always have sex with the same person. This person also must not have sex with anyone else and must not have an STD.

> **IMPORTANT:** You usually cannot tell if a person has an STD just by looking at him or her. People with STDs, including HIV, usually do not look sick.

or

C **Consistently Use Condoms.** Use them every time and use them correctly.

To prevent STDs, people at risk should use condoms even when they use another family planning method. If a woman's sex partner will not use condoms, she should try to use spermicide. Spermicides may not stop HIV/AIDS, however. The diaphragm and cervical cap also may help prevent some STDs somewhat. (See Chapter 11—Condoms, and Chapter 13—Vaginal Methods.)

Recognizing STDs

People who might get an STD need to know:
- The common signs and symptoms of STDs,
- Where to seek care if symptoms appear,
- To protect their sex partners by avoiding sex if symptoms appear.

Common symptoms of STDs are listed in question 2 of the checklist on page 16–7. For more information about symptoms, see pages 16–12 through 16–16.

Any of these symptoms could mean STD infection. These symptoms might have other causes, however, especially in women. Some people, especially women, may have no symptoms at all, especially early in the infection. They can still give the infection to their sex partners, however.

Getting Treated

Many STDs can be treated and cured, especially in their early stages. Some, such as HIV and herpes, cannot be cured, but sometimes their effects can be stopped for a time.

Prevention is better than treatment, however. Even when the STD itself is cured, sometimes scarring or infertility can follow.

A person who thinks that she or he may have an STD should:

1. Get diagnosed and treated immediately.

2. Take all of the medicine according to instructions, even if symptoms go away. The medicine can cause some side effects such as vomiting, diarrhea, or a rash. If any of these side effects occurs and is severe, the person must return to the clinic that provided the medicine. *All of the medicine must be taken for a lasting cure.*

3. Avoid sex with anyone until 3 days after treatment is finished *and* all symptoms are gone.

4. Tell his or her sex partner or partners so that they can get treated, too. Unless all sex partners are treated at the same time, they will infect each other again and again. It is especially important that a man tell a woman. This is because many women do not have symptoms until the STD has reached a more serious stage.

5. If friends have symptoms, urge them to seek care. Urge them not to have sex until they are treated. If friends have multiple sex partners, urge them to use condoms and/or spermicide and to see a health care provider for a check-up.

For more information about treatment, see pages 16–17 to 16–21.

Dealing with HIV and AIDS

What Are HIV and AIDS?

HIV is the virus that causes AIDS. AIDS reduces the body's ability to fight other diseases. People with HIV/AIDS get sick very easily with certain diseases, such as pneumonia, tuberculosis, and diarrhea. Most people with AIDS die from diseases that their bodies no longer can fight.

A person who does not look sick can still pass HIV to others. A person may have HIV for years before any symptoms appear.

Other STDs increase a person's chances of getting HIV or spreading it to others. Clients with STDs need to seek treatment and, if possible, to be tested for HIV and counseled.

How Is HIV Carried and Spread?

HIV is carried in body fluids. The most important are:

- Semen,
- Blood,
- Vaginal fluid.

HIV can be spread through:

- Vaginal sexual intercourse,
- Anal intercourse,
- Sharing intravenous needles with an infected person,
- Transfusions of infected blood,
- Other activities that allow semen, blood, or vaginal fluid to enter the mouth, anus, or vagina or to touch an open cut or sore.
- A pregnant woman with HIV is able to pass HIV to her fetus during pregnancy or childbirth. Sometimes, a woman passes HIV to her baby through her breast milk. Still, where many babies die from infectious diseases, women with HIV should breastfeed their babies.

HIV is **not** spread by kissing, shaking hands, or sharing food, clothing, or toilets.

How Can HIV/AIDS Be Prevented?

HIV/AIDS can be prevented in the same way that other STDs are prevented. Follow the **ABCD**s:

A Abstain from sex.

or

B Be mutually faithful. Have sex with only one partner, who also is not infected. This person also must not have sex with anyone else and must not share hypodermic needles with others.

or

C Consistently use Condoms.

ALSO

D Do not use a hypodermic needle that has not been sterilized or soaked in bleach.

Symptoms and Likely Diagnosis of Common STDs and Other Genital Infections

Infections That Cause Painful Urination or Unusual Genital Discharge

Likely Diagnosis	Typical Symptoms
Gonorrhea and/or chlamydia Difficult to diagnose. For treatments, see pages 16–17 and 16–18.	**For a woman:** • Unusual vaginal discharge. • Unusual vaginal bleeding. • Lower abdominal pain. A woman can have gonorrhea or chlamydial infection for several months without symptoms. **For a man:** • Painful urination. • Drops of pus from his penis. In men symptoms usually appear soon after infection. Without treatment, gonorrhea and chlamydial infection can cause sterility. If an infected woman gives birth, her baby could get infected and go blind unless treated.

Likely Diagnosis	Typical Symptoms
Trichomoniasis For treatments, see page 16–18.	**For a woman:** • Vaginal burning and itching. • Foamy, green-yellow fluid with a bad smell from the vagina. • Pain or burning when urinating. **For a man:** • Watery, white fluid from the penis. • Pain or burning when urinating.
Bacterial vaginosis A common infection, not sexually transmitted. Can come from douching, pregnancy, or antibiotics. Treatments same as for trichomoniasis. See page 16–18.	**For a woman:** • Gray, sticky fluid from the vagina (with a fishy smell especially after sex).
Candidiasis Rarely sexually transmitted. A very common genital infection. For treatments, see page 16–18.	**For a woman:** • Intense vaginal burning and itching. • Clumpy white fluid in and around the vagina. **For a man:** • Itchiness of the genitals. • White fluid under the foreskin (if uncircumcised).

SYMPTOMS and LIKELY DIAGNOSIS of Common STDs and Other Genital Infections

STDs That Cause Sores on the Genitals

Likely Diagnosis	Typical Symptoms
Syphilis An inexpensive screening test for syphilis is widely available. For treatments, see page 16–19.	• Painless sore on the penis, vagina, or anus. Sore may last only a few days, usually goes away without treatment, and women may not notice it. But the disease keeps spreading throughout the body. • Weeks or months later, the person may have: — Sore throat, — Skin rashes, and/or — Mild fever. All these symptoms may disappear. Without treatment, however, syphilis causes heart disease, paralysis, insanity, and even death. A pregnant woman can pass syphilis to her fetus before birth.
Chancroid For treatments, see page 16–20.	• Soft, painful sore on penis, vagina, or anus. • Swollen lymph nodes in the groin that contain pus, may open and drain pus, and scar up. In women, symptoms may not appear or may be difficult to notice.

Likely Diagnosis	Typical Symptoms
Lymphogranuloma venereum For treatments, see page 16–20.	**Early:** • Swollen lymph nodes in the groin that may open and drain pus. Very common in men. Less common in women. • Painful, oozing sores around the anus. More common in women than in men. **Late:** • Enlarged genitals, abscesses around the anus, narrowed rectum, anal fistula.
Genital herpes For treatments, see pages 16–20 and 16–21.	• One or more very painful small blisters around the vagina, on the penis, or around the anus. • Blisters burst open and dry up to become scabs. Sores can last for 3 weeks or more with first infection and then disappear. • New blisters usually appear from time to time because the virus stays in the body. Blisters last a shorter time than on first infection.
Granuloma inguinale (donovanosis) For treatments, see page 16–21.	• Lumps under the skin in the genital area, most often between the scrotum and thighs on men or between the labia and vagina on women. • Lumps grow, then break down into beefy, red ulcers. • Ulcers are painless but bleed when touched. If not treated, can lead to destruction of the genital organs.

SYMPTOMS and LIKELY DIAGNOSIS of Common STDs and Other Genital Infections

STD That Causes Warts

Likely Diagnosis	Typical Symptoms
Genital human papillomavirus (HPV) An STD caused by a virus. Certain subtypes are responsible for most cases of cervical cancer. For treatment, see page 16–21.	• Warts on or near penis, vagina, or anus. Warts may not appear or may be difficult to notice.

Treatments for Common STDs and Other Genital Infections

These treatments are based largely on 1998 recommendations of the US Centers for Disease Control and Prevention.

> **IMPORTANT:** Various treatments are listed below. For the appropriate likely diagnosis, choose ONE treatment from the list. Choose a treatment known to be effective in your area. Consult supervisors if you are not sure. You can place an **X** or ✔ in a box (☐) to mark the appropriate treatment for your area.

Gonorrhea and/or chlamydial infection

If possible, test, or refer patient to a convenient place for test and treatment. (Gonorrhea test alone is useful because it may rule out that disease.) If not possible to test, both gonorrhea and chlamydial infection can be treated at the same time. Give ONE treatment from EACH group, below and at the top of the next page.

Gonorrhea treatments (choose ONE)

☐ Ciprofloxacin, 500 mg tablet by mouth as a single dose. (Do NOT give to pregnant or breastfeeding women.)

☐ Ceftriaxone, 125 mg intramuscular injection as a single dose.

☐ Cefixime, 400 mg by mouth as a single dose.

☐ Ofloxacin, 400 mg by mouth as a single dose AND azithromycin, 1 g by mouth as a single dose. (Do NOT give ofloxacin to pregnant or breastfeeding women.)

☐ Spectinomycin, 2 g intramuscular injection as a single dose.

Treatments that may be useful in countries where the disease is not commonly resistant to these medications:

☐ Kanamycin, 2 g intramuscular injection as a single dose.

☐ Trimethoprim, 80 mg/sulphamethoxazole, 400 mg; 10 tablets by mouth daily for 3 days. (Do NOT give to pregnant or breastfeeding women.)

In most areas of the world, penicillin and tetracycline are no longer effective against gonorrhea.

▶ Tell patient to avoid sex until treatment is completed and symptoms are gone. Urge that sex partner(s) get treated.

Treatments for chlamydial infection (choose ONE)

☐ Azithromycin, 1 g by mouth as a single dose.

☐ Doxycycline, 100 mg by mouth 2 times daily for 7 days.
(Do NOT give to pregnant or breastfeeding women.)

☐ Tetracycline, 500 mg by mouth 4 times daily for 7 days.
(Do NOT give to pregnant or breastfeeding women.)

Treatment for pregnant or breastfeeding women:

☐ Amoxicillin, 500 mg by mouth 3 times daily for 7 days.

☐ Erythromycin, 500 mg by mouth 4 times daily for 7 days.

▶ Tell patient to avoid sex for 7 days after treatment starts. Urge that sex partner(s) get treated.

Trichomoniasis/Bacterial vaginosis treatments (choose ONE)

☐ Metronidazole, 2 g by mouth as a single dose.

☐ Metronidazole, 500 mg by mouth 2 times daily for 7 days.

(Do NOT give metronidazole to pregnant women before the fourth month of pregnancy.)

▶ Tell patient not to drink alcohol while taking metronidazole. It may cause nausea and vomiting. Urge that sex partner(s) get treated. Tell patient to avoid sex until treatment is completed and symptoms are gone in both partners.

Pelvic inflammatory disease treatment

Treat for gonorrhea, chlamydia, and trichomonias—all 3. (See pages 12–20 and 12–21.)

Candidiasis treatments (choose ONE)

For women:

☐ Nystatin, 100,000 unit tablet inserted in vagina once daily for 14 days.

☐ Miconazole, 200 mg suppository inserted in vagina once daily for 3 days; or 100 mg suppository inserted in vagina once daily for 7 days.

☐ Clotrimazole, 500 mg tablet inserted in vagina as a single dose; or 100 mg tablet once daily for 7 days; or two 100 mg tablets once daily for 3 days.

For men:

☐ Nystatin, miconazole, or clotrimazole cream or ointment, applied to infected area 2 times a day for 7 days.

Syphilis treatments
For early disease—primary, secondary, or latent syphilis of 2 years or less (choose ONE)

For anyone without penicillin allergy:

☐ Benzathine penicillin G, 2.4 million units total, in 2 intramuscular injections during 1 clinic visit; give 1 injection in each buttock.

☐ Aqueous procaine penicillin G, 1.2 million units in 1 intramuscular injection once daily for 10 days.

Allergic to penicillin* (men and nonpregnant women only):

☐ Doxycycline, 100 mg by mouth 2 times daily for 14 days.

☐ Tetracycline, 500 mg by mouth 4 times daily for 14 days.

Allergic to penicillin (pregnant women only):

☐ Erythromycin, 500 mg by mouth 4 times daily for 14 days. Not highly effective. Urge these women to bring their babies within 7 days after birth for treatment for congenital syphilis.

▶ Urge that sex partner(s) get treated.

Late latent syphilis or latent syphilis of unknown duration

For anyone without penicillin allergy:

☐ Benzathine penicillin G, 7.2 million units total, administered as intramuscular injections in 3 doses of 2.4 million units each at 1-week intervals.

Allergic to penicillin (men and nonpregnant women only):

☐ Same as for early disease but treat for 4 weeks rather than 14 days.

Allergic to penicillin (pregnant women only):

☐ Same as for early disease but treat for 4 weeks rather than 14 days.

Congenital syphilis (choose ONE)

☐ Procaine penicillin G, 50,000 unit per kg of body weight, as one intramuscular injection daily for 10 days.

☐ Aqueous crystalline penicillin G, 100,000 to 150,000 U per kg of body weight per day, given as 50,000 units/kg intravenously every 12 hours for the first 7 days of life and every 8 hours thereafter for the next 3 days.

If more than 1 day of treatment is missed, the entire course should be restarted.

---

*Typical symptoms of true allergy to penicillin are the symptoms of anaphylaxis, including severe facial swelling, widespread itching and hives, difficulty breathing and swallowing, sudden drop in blood pressure, weak and rapid pulse, nausea, vomiting, abdominal cramps, diarrhea, confusion, dizziness, and possible loss of consciousness. Symptoms occur within 20 minutes after penicillin injection. In general, treatment involves maintaining an airway and giving oxygen and epinephrine.

Chancroid treatment (choose ONE)

- ☐ Azithromycin, 1 g by mouth as a single dose.
- ☐ Ceftriaxone, 250 mg intramuscular injection as a single dose.
- ☐ Erythromycin, 500 mg by mouth 4 times daily for 7 days.
- ☐ Ciprofloxacin, 500 mg by mouth 2 times daily for 3 days. (Do NOT give to pregnant or breastfeeding women or people under age 18.)
- ☐ Trimethoprim, 80 mg/sulphamethoxazole, 400 mg; 2 tablets by mouth 2 times daily for 7 days. (Use only in area where it has been proved effective against chancroid and its effectiveness can be regularly monitored. Do NOT give to pregnant or breastfeeding women.)

▶ Re-examine in 3 to 7 days. Sex partner(s)—even those with no symptoms—should be treated if they had sex with patient within 10 days before patient's symptoms started or since symptoms started.

Lymphogranuloma venereum treatment (choose ONE)

- ☐ Doxycycline, 100 mg by mouth 2 times a day for 21 days. (Do NOT give to pregnant or breastfeeding women.)
- ☐ Erythromycin, 500 mg by mouth 4 times a day for 21 days.
- ☐ Tetracycline, 500 mg by mouth 4 times a day for 14 days. (Do NOT give to pregnant or breastfeeding women.)

▶ Urge that sex partner(s) be tested and treated.

Genital herpes treatment

▶ Clients should not have sex when blisters are present—not even with a condom. Herpes can be spread even when no blisters are present, but a condom may provide some protection.

No cure available. The client should keep the infected area clean and try not to touch the sores. Antibiotic ointments may help.

Duration of symptoms can be shortened if treatment begins early in an outbreak. If not started early, treatment may be ineffective.

For first outbreak give acyclovir, 200 mg by mouth 5 times a day for 7 to 10 days or 400 mg 3 times a day for 7 to 10 days.

For recurrences of blisters, give acyclovir, 200 mg by mouth 5 times a day for 5 days. If the client has outbreaks more than 6 times a year, treat with acyclovir, 400 mg by mouth 2 times a day for 1 year and then reassess.

- ▶ Urge that sex partners be evaluated and counseled and, if they have symptoms, treated.
- ▶ A woman with herpes can infect her baby during childbirth. This is very dangerous for the baby and requires medical attention.

Granuloma inguinale (donovanosis) treatment (choose ONE)

- ☐ Trimethoprim, 80 mg/sulfamethoxazole, 400 mg, 2 tablets by mouth twice daily for at least 21 days or until sores heal. (Do NOT give to pregnant or breastfeeding women.)
- ☐ Tetracycline, 500 mg by mouth 4 times a day for at least 14 days or until sores heal. (Do NOT give to pregnant or breastfeeding women.)
- ☐ Doxycycline, 100 mg by mouth 2 times a day for at least 21 days or until sores heal. (Do NOT give to pregnant or breastfeeding women.)
- ☐ Erythromycin, 500 mg by mouth 4 times a day for 21 days, or until sores heal.
- ▶ Urge that sex partner(s) with symptoms get treated.

Human papilloma virus (HPV) treatment

No cure available. Can be treated chemically or surgically for cosmetic purposes. If warts grow rapidly, check for HIV infection.

IMPORTANT POINTS FOR THE CLIENT TO REMEMBER ABOUT

Preventing and Curing Sexually Transmitted Diseases (STDs)

▶ First, prevent STDs.

- **Some STDs cannot be cured.** This includes HIV/AIDS.
- **Remember—ABC prevents STDs:**
  - Abstain from sex.
  - Be faithful. Stay with just one sex partner.
  - Consistently use Condoms.
- **Protect yourself against AIDS.** Other STDs increase your risk of getting HIV/AIDS.

▶ If you have an STD:

- **Seek care quickly** if you think you might have an STD—even if you do not have symptoms.
- **Do not spread STDs:** If you think you might have an STD, avoid sex or at least use condoms with every sex partner. If you are told you have an STD and given medicine, avoid sex until 3 days after you have taken all of your medicine and you have no more symptoms.
- **Cure your infection:** Take all your medicine as directed even if symptoms go away or you feel better.
- **Help your sex partners get treatment:** Tell them to come for treatment or else bring them in.
- **Come back to make sure you are cured:** If you still have symptoms, you can get more medicine to cure your infection.
- **Protect your baby:** Go (or help your wife go) to an antenatal clinic within the first 3 months of pregnancy for a physical exam and syphilis test.

WHO Medical Eligibility Criteria for Starting Contraceptive Methods

The table on the following pages summarizes World Health Organization (WHO) medical eligibility criteria for starting contraceptive methods. These criteria are the basis for the Medical Eligibility Checklists in Chapters 5 through 15.

WHO Categories for Temporary Methods

WHO 1 **Can use** the method. **No restriction on use**.

WHO 2 **Can use** the method. **Advantages generally outweigh theoretical or proven risks.** Category 2 conditions could be considered in choosing a method. If the client chooses the method, more than usual follow-up may be needed.

WHO 3 **Should not use** the method unless a doctor or nurse makes a clinical judgement that the client can safely use it. **Theoretical or proven risks usually outweigh the advantages** of the method. Method of last choice, for which careful follow-up will be needed.

WHO 4 **Should not use** the method. Condition represents an **unacceptable health risk** if method is used.

Simplified 2-Category System

Where a doctor or nurse is not available to make clinical judgements, the WHO 4-category classification system can be simplified into a 2-category system as shown in this table:

WHO Category	With Clinical Judgement	With Limited Clinical Judgement
1	Use the method in any circumstances	Use the method
2	Generally use the method	Use the method
3	Use of the method not usually recommended unless other, more appropriate methods are not available or acceptable	Do not use the method
4	Method not to be used	Do not use the method

NOTE: In the table that follows, Category 3 and 4 conditions are shaded to indicate the mehtod should not be provided where clinical judgement is limited.

WHO Categories for Female Sterilization and Vasectomy

Accept No medical reason prevents performing the procedure in a routine setting.

Caution The procedure can be performed in a routine setting but with **extra preparation and precautions**.

Delay **Delay the procedure.** Condition must be treated and resolved before the procedure can be performed. Provide temporary methods.

Refer **Refer client** to a center where an experienced surgeon and staff can perform the procedure. Setting should be equipped for general anesthesia and other medical support. Provide temporary methods. (WHO calls this category "Special.")

NOTE: In the table that follows, "Delay" and "Refer" conditions are shaded.

WHO Medical Eligibility Criteria for Starting Contraceptive Methods

NA = not applicable to decision to use method.

a Sterilization is appropriate for women and men of any age, but only if they are sure they will not want children in the future.
b This condition may affect ovarian function and/or change fertility signs and symptoms and/or make methods difficult to learn and use.
c Shortly after menarche (age at first menstrual bleeding) and as menopause approaches, menstrual cycles may be irregular.
d Higher typical failure rates of this method may expose the user to an unacceptable risk of dangerous unintended pregnancy.
e With or without vascular disease.
f Breastfeeding may not be recommended with drugs used to treat this condition.
— Condition not listed by WHO for this method; does not affect eligibility for method use.

CONDITION	Combined OCs	Progestin-Only OCs	DMPA/NET EN	Norplant Implants	Female Sterilization	Vasectomy	Condoms	TCu-380A IUD	Spermicides	Diaphragm, Cervical Cap	Fertility Awareness-Based Methods	Lactational Amenorrhea Method (LAM)
Pregnant	NA	NA	NA	NA	Delay	—	1	4	1	1	—	—
Age												
Less than 18 (<20 for IUD)	1	1	2	1	Caution[a]	—[a]	1	2	1	1	1[b,c]	1
18 to 39	1	1	1	1	Accept.[a]	—[a]	1	1	1	1	1	1
40 to 45	2	1	2	1	Accept.[a]	—[a]	1	1	1	1	1[b,c]	1
Over 45	2	1	1	1	Accept.[a]	—[a]	1	1	1	1	1[b,c]	1
Smoking												
Less than age 35	2	1	1	1	Accept.[a]	—[a]	1	1	1	1	1	1
Age 35 and over												
& Light smoker (fewer than 15 cigarettes per day)	3	1	1	1	Accept.[a]	—[a]	1	1	1	1	1	1
& Heavy smoker (15 or more cigarettes per day)	4	1	1	1	Accept.[a]	—[a]	1	1	1	1	1	1
High blood pressure (hypertension)												
Systolic 140-159 or diastolic 90-99	3	1	2	1	Caution	—	1	1	1	1	1	1[f]
Systolic ≥ 160 or diastolic ≥ 100	4	2	3	2	Refer	—	1[d]	1	1[d]	1[d]	1[d]	1[f]
Adequately controlled hypertension where blood pressure can be monitored	3	1	2	1	Caution	—	1	1	1	1	1	1
Past hypertension where blood pressure cannot be evaluated	3	2	2	2	Caution	—	1	1	1	1	1	1
Diabetes												
Past elevated blood sugar levels during pregnancy	1	1	1	1	Accept	—	1	1	1	1	1	1
Diabetes without vascular disease												
Not treated with insulin	2	2	2	2	Caution	Caution	1	1	1	1	1	1
Treated with insulin	2	2	2	2	Caution	Caution	1[d]	1	1[d]	1[d]	1[d]	1
Diabetes with vascular disease or diabetes for more than 20 years	3/4[g]	2	3	2	Refer	Caution	1[d]	1	1[d]	1[d]	1[d]	1[f]

A–2 Essentials of Contraceptive Technology Appendix

	3/4	2	3	2	Refer	—	1	1	1	—	
Multiple cardiovascular risks[h]											
Thromboembolic disorder[i]											
Current thromboembolic disorder	4	3	3	3	Delay	—	1	1	1	1[f,j]	
Past thromboembolic disorder	4	3	3	3	Accept	—	1	1	1	1	
Ischemic heart disease[k]											
Current ischemic heart disease	4	2	3	2	Delay	—	1[d]	1	1[d]	1[f,j]	
Past ischemic heart disease	4	2	3	2	Caution	—	1[d]	1	1[d]	1	
Valvular heart desease											
Without complications	2	1	1	1	Caution	—	1	1	1	1	
With complications[l]	4	1	1	1	Refer	—	1[d]	2	1[d]	1[f,j]	
Varicose veins	1	1	1	1	Accept	—	1	1	1	1	
Superficial thrombophlebitis[m]	2	1	1	1	Accept	—	1	1	1	1	
Major surgery											
With prolonged immobilization or surgery on the legs	4	1	1	1	Delay	—	1	1	1	1[f,j]	
Without prolonged immobilization	2	1	1	1	Accept	—	1	1	1	1	
Stroke (past cerebrovascular accident)	4	2	3	2	Caution	1	1	1	1	1	
Headaches											
Non migraine headaches, mild or severe	1	1	1	1	Accept	—	1	1	1	1	
Migraine without focal neurological symptoms[n]	2	1	2	2	Accept	—	1	1	1	1	
Less than age 35	2	1	2	2	Accept	—	1	1	1	1[f]	
Age 35 and older	3	1	2	2	Accept	—	1	1	1	1[f]	
Migraine with focal neurological symptoms[n,o]	4	2	2	2	Accept	—	1	1	1	1[f]	
Vaginal bleeding patterns											
Irregular without heavy bleeding	1	2	2	2	Accept	—	1	1	1[p]	—	
Irregular with heavy or prolonged bleeding	1	2	2	2	Accept	—	2[q]	1	1[p]	—	
Unexplained abnormal vaginal bleeding	2	3	3	4	Accept	—	4	1	1[p]	—	

[h] Risk factors for arterial disease, such as age, smoking, diabetes, high blood pressure.
[i] Circulatory disease due to blood clots.
[j] LAM has no impact on this condition, but the condition may rule out breastfeeding.
[k] Heart disease due to blocked arteries.
[l] Pulmonary hypertension, risk of arterial fibrilation, history of subacute bacterial endocarditis, or taking anticoagulant drugs.
[m] Inflammation of a vein just beneath the skin.
[n] Focal neurological symptoms = blurred vision, temporary loss of vision, sees flashing lights or zigzag lines, or has brief trouble speaking or moving.
[o] Regardless of age.
[p] This condition may make the calendar method difficult of impossible to use effectively.
[q] Category 3 if client is anemic. Also, unusually heavy bleeding may indicate a serious underlying condition.
— Condition not listed by WHO for this method; does not affect eligibility for method use.

Appendix WHO MEDICAL ELIGIBILITY CRITERIA A–3

WHO Medical Eligibility Criteria for Starting Contraceptive Methods (continued)

CONDITION	Combined OCs	Progestin-Only OCs	DMPA/NET EN	Norplant Implants	Female Sterilization	Vasectomy	Condoms	TCu-380A IUD	Spermicides	Diaphragm, Cervical Cap	Fertility Awareness-Based Methods	Lactational Amenorrhea Method (LAM)
Breast cancer												
Current	4	4	4	4	Caution	—	1[d]	1	1[d]	1[d]	1[d]	1[f,j]
Past, with no evidence of disease in last 5 years	3	3	3	3	Accept	—	1	1	1	1	1	1
Breast lump (undiagnosed)	2	2	2	2	Accept	—	1	1	1	1	1	1
Benign breast disease	1	1	1	1	Accept	—	1	1	1	1	1	1
Family history of breast cancer	1	1	1	1	Accept	—	1	1	1	1	1	1
Cervical cancer (awaiting treatment)	2	1	2	2	Delay	—	1[d]	4	2[d]	1[d,r]	1[b,d]	1[f]
Noncancerous cervical lesions (cervical intraepithelial neoplasia)	2	1	2	2	Accept	—	1	1	1	1[r]	1[b]	1
Endometrial cancer	1	1	1	1	Delay	—	1[d]	4	1[d]	1[d]	1[d]	1[f]
Ovarian cancer	1	1	1	1	Delay	—	1	3	1	1	1	1
Benign ovarian tumors (including cysts)	1	1	1	1	Accept	—	1	1	1	1	1	1
Pelvic inflammatory disease (PID)												
Past PID (no known current risk of STDs)												
Became pregnant since PID	1	1	1	1	Accept	—	1	1	1	1	1	1
Has not become pregnant since PID	1	1	1	1	Caution	—	1	2	1	1	1	1
Current PID or in last 3 months[s]	1	1	1	1	Delay	—	1	4	1	1	1[b,t]	1
Sexually transmitted disease (STDs)[u]												
Current STD (including purulent cervicitis)[v]	1	1	1	1	Delay	Delay	1	4	1	1	1[b,t]	1
STD in last 3 months (no symptoms persisting after treatment)[v]	1	1	1	1	Accept	—	1	4	1	1	1[b]	1
Vaginitis without purulent cervicitis[v,w]	1	1	1	1	Accept	—	1	2[w]	1	1	1	1
Increased risk of STDs[x]	1	1	1	1	Accept	—	1	3	1	1	1	1

b This condition may affect ovarian function and/or change fertility signs and symptoms and/or make methods difficult to learn and use.

d Higher typical failure rates of this method may expose the user to an unacceptable risk of dangerous unintended pregnancy.

f Breastfeeding may not be recommended with drugs used to treat this condition.

j LAM has no impact on this condition, but the condition may rule out breastfeeding.

r Cervical cap not recommended.

s Including endometritis (inflammation of the lining of the uterus) following childbirth or abortion.

t Condition does not affect vaginal bleeding patterns; calendar method can be used.

u Barrier methods, especially condoms, are always recommended for prevention of STDs, including HIV/AIDS.

v Purulent cervicitis = a pus-like discharge from the opening of the cervix.

— Condition not listed by WHO for this method; does not affect eligibility for method use.

Urinary tract infection	—	—	—	—	—	—	—	—	—	—	—	—
HIV infection/AIDS[u]												
HIV infected	1	1	1	1	Accept	1[d]	1	1[y]	1[y]	1[d]	1	1[aa]
High risk of HIV infection[x]	1	1	1	1	Accept	1	2[a,b]	3	1	1	1	1[aa]
AIDS	1	1	1	1	Refer	1[d]	1	3[z]	1[d]	1[d]	1[d]	1[aa]
Gallbladder disease												
Current disease	3	2	2	2	Delay	—	1	1	1	1	1	1
Treated with medication	3	2	2	2	Accept	—	1	1	1	1	1	1
Without symptoms or surgically treated	2	2	2	2	Accept	—	1	1	1	1	1	1
Past cholestasis (jaundice)												
Related to pregnancy	2	1	1	1	Accept	—	1	1	1	1	1	1
Related to past combined oral contraceptive use	3	2	2	2	Accept	—	1	1	1	1	1	1
Viral hepatitis												
Active disease	4	3	3	3	Delay	—	1	1	1	1	1	1[f]
Carrier	1	1	1	1	Accept	—	1	1	1	1	1	1
Cirrhosis of the liver												
Mild (compensated)	3	2	2	2	Caution	—	1	1	1	1	1	1
Severe (decompensated)	4	3	3	3	Refer	—	1[d]	1	1[d]	1[b,d,t]	1[d]	1[f,j]
Liver tumors												
Benign	4	3	3	3	Caution	—	1	1	1	1[b,t]	1	1
Malignant	4	3	3	3	Caution	—	1[d]	1	1[d]	1[b,d,t]	1[d]	1[f,j]
Uterine fibroids	1	1	1	1	Caution	—	1	1	1	1	1	1
Past ectopic pregnancy	1	2	1	1	Accept	—	2[a,c]	1	1	1	1	1
Obesity (body mass index >30)	2	1	2	2	Caution	—	1	1	1[ad]	1	1	1

w In areas where STD incidence is high, vaginitis may indicate an STD.

x For example, currently has or will have more than one sex partner or a partner who has more than one partner.

y There is a potential increased risk of urinary tract infection with diaphragms and spermicides.

z For IUDs, HIV-infected or any other medical condition or medication that makes the body less able to fight infection.

aa In areas where infectious disease is the main cause of infant death, HIV-infected women should be advised to breastfeed. In other areas, if affordable alternatives to breastmilk are available, HIV-infected women should not breastfeed.

ab High dose of nonoxynol-9 spermicide may cause vaginal abrasions, which may increase risk of HIV infection.

ac Uterine fibroids distorting the uterine cavity; otherwise category 1.

ad Severe obesity may make diaphragm or cap placement difficult.

— Condition not listed by WHO for this method; does not affect eligibility for method use.

WHO Medical Eligibility Criteria for Starting Contraceptive Methods (continued)

CONDITION	Combined OCs	Progestin-Only OCs	DMPA/NET EN	Norplant Implants	Female Sterilization	Vasectomy	Condoms	TCu-380A IUD	Spermicides	Diaphragm, Cervical Cap	Fertility Awareness-Based Methods	Lactational Amenorrhea Method (LAM)
Thyroid												
Simple goiter	1	1	1	1	Accept	—	1	1	1	1	1	1
Hyperthyroid	1	1	1	1	Refer	—	1	1	1	1	1,b,t	1
Hypothyroid	1	1	1	1	Caution	—	1	1	1	1	1,b,t	1,f
Thalassemia (inherited anemia)	1	1	1	1	Caution	—	1	2	1	1	1	1
Trophoblast disease												
Benign	1	1	1	1	Accept	—	1	3	1	1	1	1
Malignant	1	1	1	1	Delay	—	1,d	4	1,d	1,d	1,d	1,f
Sickle cell disease	2	1	1	1	Caution	Accept	1,d	2	1,d	1,d	1,d	1
Coagulation (blood clotting) disorders	—	—	—	—	Refer	Refer	—	—	—	—	—	—
Iron deficiency anemia												
Hemoglobin 7 g/dl –10 g/dl	1	1	1	1	Caution	—	1	2	1	1	1	1
Hemoglobin less than 7 g/dl	1	1	1	1	Delay	—	1	2	1	1	1	1
Epilepsy	1	1	1	1	Caution	—	1	1	1	1	1	1,f
Schistosomiasis												
Without complications	1	1	1	1	Accept	—	1	1	1	1	1	1
With fibrosis of the liver	1	1	1	1	Caution	—	1,d	1	1,d	1,d	1,b,d,t	1,f
With severe fibrosis of the liver	4	3	3	3	Refer	—	1,d	1	1,d	1,d	1,b,d,t	1,f
Malaria	1	1	1	1	Accept	—	1	1	1	1	1	1

b This condition may affect ovarian function and/or change fertility signs and symptoms and/or make methods difficult to learn and use.

d Higher typical failure rates of this method may expose the user to an unacceptable risk of dangerous unintended pregnancy.

f Breastfeeding may not be recommended with drugs used to treat this condition.

t Condition does not affect vaginal bleeding patterns; calendar method can be used.

— Condition not listed by WHO for this method; does not affect eligibility for method use.

Drug interactions												
Taking the antibiotics rifampin (rifampicine) or griseofulvin	3	3	2	3	Caution	—	1	1	1	1	1	—
Taking other antibiotics[ae]	1	1	1	1	Accept	—	1	1	1	1	1	—
Taking anticonvulsants for epilepsy except valproic acid[af]	3	3	2	3	Caution	—	1	1	1	1	1	—
Allergy to latex	—	—	—	—	—	—	3[ag]	—	1	—	—	—
Other drug use												
Mood-altering drugs, lithium therapy, tricyclic antidepressants, ar anti-anxiety therapies	—	—	—	—	—	—	—	—	1	3	—	—
Parity												
Nulliparous (has no children)	1	1	1	1	Accept[ai]	Accept[ai]	1	2	1	1	1	—
Parous (has children)	1	1	1	1	Accept	Accept	1	1	1	2	1	1
Severe dysmenorrhea (pain during menstruation)	1	1	1	1	Accept	—	1	2	1	1	1	—[aj]
Tuberculosis												
Nonpelvic	1	1	1	1	Accept	—	1[d]	1	1[d]	1[d]	1[d]	1[ak]
Pelvic	1	1	1	1	Refer	—	1[d]	4	1[d]	1[d]	1[d]	1[ak]
Endometriosis	1	1	1	1	Refer	—	1	2	1	1	1	—
Anatomical abnormalities												
Distorted uterine cavity	—	—	—	—	—	—	4[ai]	—	—	—[am]	—	—
Other abnormalities not distorting the uterine cavity and not interfering with IUD insertion[an]	—	—	—	—	—	—	—	2	—	—	—	—
Past toxic shock syndrome	—	—	—	—	—	—	1	—	1	—	3	—
Breastfeeding												
Less than 6 weeks after childbirth	4	3	3	1	Accept	—	1	—[ao]	1	—[ao]	1	1
6 weeks to 6 months after childbirth (fully or almost fully breastfeeding)	3	1	1	1	Accept	—	1	—	1	1	1	1
6 months or more after childbirth	2	1	1	1	Accept	—	1	—	1	1	1[b]	—

ae Antibiotics other than rifampin and griseofulvin.

af Barbiturates, phenytoin, carbamezapine, primidone.

ag Allergy to latex is not a problem with plastic condoms, if available.

ah In order to protect infant health, breastfeeding is not recommended.

ai Counseling requires special care to ensure an informed choice is made.

aj Menstruation indicates need for another contraceptive method.

ak Decision to breastfeed should take into consideration the risks and benefits to the infant.

al Any abnormality distorting the uterine cavity so that proper IUD insertion is not possible.

am Diaphragm cannot be used in certain cases of prolapse; cap not acceptable for clients with severely distorted cervical anatomy.

an Including uterine fibroids, cervical stenosis, or cervical lacerations.

— Condition not listed by WHO for this method; does not affect eligibility for method use.

WHO Medical Eligibility Criteria for Starting Contraceptive Methods (continued)

CONDITION	Combined OCs	Progestin-Only OCs	DMPA/NET EN	Norplant Implants	Female Sterilization	Vasectomy	Condoms	TCu-380A IUD	Spermicides	Diaphragm, Cervical Cap	Fertility Awareness-Based Methods	Lactational Amenorrhea Method (LAM)
Postpartum (nonbreastfeeding women)												
Less than 21 days after childbirth	3	1	1	1	*	**	1	+	1	—	1[b]	—
21 or more days after childbirth	1	1	1	1	*	**	1	+	1	—[ao]	1[b]	—
Postabortion												
First trimester	1	1	1	1	—	—	1	1	1	1	1[b]	—
Second trimester	1	1	1	1	—	—	1	2	1	1[ap]	1[b]	—
After septic abortion[aq]	1	1	1	1	—	—	1	4	1	1	1[b]	—

*Additional conditions related to female sterilization:
Conditions that require delay: abdominal skin infection; acute bronchitis or pneumonia; emergency surgery; surgery for an infectious condition; systemic infection or severe gastroenteritis. Conditions that require referral to a special center: chronic asthma, bronchitis, emphysema, or lung infection; fixed uterus due to previous surgery or infection; abdominal wall or umbilical hernia. Conditions that require caution: Diaphragmatic hernia; kidney disease; elective surgery; severe nutritional deficiencies. Conditions that pose no special requirements: cesarian section.

Postpartum sterilization conditions that require delay: 7 days to 42 days after childbirth; severe preeclampsia/eclampsia; prolonged rupture of membranes (24 hours or more); severe hemorrhage; fever during or right after delivery; sepsis; severe trauma to the genital tract (cervical or vaginal tear at delivery). Postpartum sterilization conditions that require referral to a special center: uterine rupture or perforation. Postpartum sterilization conditions that pose no special requirements: less than 7 days after childbirth; more than 42 days after childbirth; mild preeclampsia. Postabortion sterilization conditions that require delay: severe sepsis or fever; severe hemorrhage; severe trauma to the genital tract; acute hematometra (excess blood in the uterus). Postabortion sterilization conditions that require referral to a special center: uterine perforation.

**Additional conditions related to vasectomy:
**Conditions that require delay: scrotal skin infection; active STD; balanitis; epididymitis or orchitis; systemic infection or severe gastroenteritis; filariasis or elephantiasis; intrascrotal mass. Condition that requires referral to a special center: inguinal hernia. Conditions that require caution: previous scrotal surgery or injury; large varicocele, large hydrocele; cryptorchidism. (In some circumstances, cryptorchidism may require referral.)*

†Additional conditions related to TCu-380A IUD, postpartum insertion (breastfeeding or nonbreastfeeding):
Condition that represent an unacceptable health risk (WHO 4): puerperal sepsis (genital tract infection during the first 42 days after childbirth). Condition that requires a doctor or nurse to make a clinical judgement that the client can safely use an IUD (WHO 3): 48 hours to 4 weeks postpartum. Condition for which advantages of IUD use generally outweigh theoretical or proven risks (WHO 2): less than 48 hours after childbirth. Condition that requires no restriction: More than 4 weeks after childbirth.

b *This condition may affect ovarian function and/or change fertility signs and symptoms and/or make methods difficult to learn and use.*

ao *Can start diaphragm use 6 weeks after childbirth.*

ap *Can start diaphragm use 6 weeks after second-trimester abortion.*

aq *That is, immediately after abortion involving genital tract infection.*

— *Condition not listed by WHO for this method; does not affect eligibility for method use.*

††Additional conditions related to LAM:
Conditions that represent an unacceptable health risk to the infant: use of reserpine, ergotamine, antimetabolites, cyclosporine, cortisone, bromocriptine, radioactive drugs, lithium, or anticoagulants. Conditions for which LAM has no effect on the condition, but the condition may prevent breastfeeding: sore nipples; mastitis (breast inflammation); congenital deformity of infant's mouth, jaw or palate; infant small for age, premature birth, or neonatal intensive care; past breast surgery; certain infant metabolic disorders. Condition that requires no restrictions (WHO 1): breast engorgement.

Suggested Reading

Angle, M. Guidelines for clinical procedures in family planning, a reference for trainers, 2nd ed. Chapel Hill, North Carolina, Program for International Training in Health (INTRAH), 1992.

Angle, M. Guidelines for clinical procedures in family planning, a reference for trainers. 2nd ed., revised (chapters 3–7). Chapel Hill, North Carolina, Program for International Training in Health (INTRAH), 1993.

AVSC International. Safe and voluntary surgical contraception: Guidelines for service programs. New York, AVSC International, 1995.

Blumenthal, P.D. and McIntosh, N. PocketGuide for family planning service providers, 1996–1998. 2nd edition. Baltimore, Johns Hopkins Program for International Education in Reproductive Health (JHPIEGO), 1996.

Cooperating Agencies Informed Choice Task Force. Informed choice: Report of the Cooperating Agencies Task Force. Baltimore, Johns Hopkins School of Public Health, Center for Communication Programs, 1989.

Hatcher, R.A., Trussell, J., Stewart, F., Stewart, G.K., Kowal, D., Guest, F., Cates, W., and Policar, M. Contraceptive technology. 16th ed. New York, Irvington, 1994.

Huezo, C.M. and Carignan, C.S. Medical and service delivery guidelines for family planning. London, International Planned Parenthood Federation (IPPF) in collaboration with AVSC International, 1997.

Labbok, M., Cooney, C., and Coly, S. Guidelines: Breastfeeding, family planning, and the Lactational Amenorrhea Method—LAM. Washington, D.C., Georgetown University, Institute for Reproductive Health, 1994.

McCann, M.F. and Potter, L.S. Progestin-only oral contraception: A comprehensive review. Contraception 50(6): S9-S195. December 1994.

McIntosh, N., Kinzie, B., and Blouse, A. IUD guidelines for family planning service programs, a problem-solving reference manual. 2nd ed. Baltimore, Johns Hopkins Program for International Education in Reproductive Health (JHPIEGO), 1993.

McIntosh, N., Blouse, A., and Shaefer, L. Norplant® guidelines for family planning service programs, a problem-solving reference manual. 2nd ed. Baltimore, Johns Hopkins Program for International Education in Reproductive Health (JHPIEGO), 1995.

Moreno, L. and Goldman, N. Contraceptive failure rates in developing countries: Evidence from the Demographic and Health Surveys. International Family Planning Perspectives 17(2): 44–49. 1991.

Murphy, E. M. and Steele, C. Client-provider interactions in family planning services: Guidance from research and program experience. In: Technical Guidance/Competence Working Group. Recommendations for updating selected practices in contraceptive use. Vol. 2. Chapel Hill, North Carolina, University of North Carolina, Program for International Training in Health, 1997. p. 187–194.

Population Council (PC). Norplant contraceptive subdermal implants: Guide to effective counseling. New York, PC, 1990.

Shelton, J.D., Angle, M.A., and Jacobstein, R.A. Medical barriers to access to family planning. Lancet 340(8831): 1334–1335. November 28, 1992.

Solter, C. Comprehensive reproductive health and family planning training curriculum, module 6: DMPA injectable contraceptive. Watertown, Massachusetts, Pathfinder International, August 1996.

Technical Guidance/Competence Working Group. Recommendations for updating selected practices in contraceptive use: Results of a technical meeting. Vols. 1 and 2. Chapel Hill, North Carolina, University of North Carolina, Program for International Training in Health, 1994 and 1997. (Condensed version published in **Population Reports**, *Family Planning Methods: New Guidance.* Baltimore, Johns Hopkins School of Public Health, Population Information Program, 1996.)

Tietjen, L., Cronin, W. and McIntosh, N. Infection prevention for family planning service programs, a problem-solving reference manual. Baltimore, Johns Hopkins Program for International Education in Reproductive Health (JHPIEGO), March 1992.

World Health Organization (WHO). Improving access to quality care in family planning: Medical eligibility criteria for contraceptive use. Geneva, WHO, Family and Reproductive Health, 1996.

World Health Organization (WHO). Injectable contraceptives, their role in family planning care. Geneva, WHO, 1990.

Population Reports, especially the following issues:

> Blackburn, R.D., Cunkelman, J.A., and Zlidar, V.M. Oral Contraceptives — An Update. **Population Reports**, Series A, No. 9. Baltimore, Johns Hopkins School of Public Health, Population Information Program, Spring 2000.
>
> Church, C.A. and Geller, J.S. Voluntary female sterilization: Number one and growing. Population Reports, Series C, No. 10. Baltimore, Johns Hopkins School of Public Health, Population Information Program, November 1990.
>
> Gardner, R., Blackburn, R.D., and Upadhyay, U.D. Closing the Condom Gap. **Population Reports**, Series H, No. 9. Baltimore, Johns Hopkins School of Public Health, Population Information Program, April, 1999.

Lande, R. New era for injectables. Population Reports, Series K, No. 5. Baltimore, Johns Hopkins School of Public Health, Population Information Program, August 1995.

Liskin, L., Benoit, E., and Blackburn, R. Vasectomy: New opportunities. Population Reports, Series D, No. 5. Baltimore, Johns Hopkins School of Public Health, Population Information Program, March 1992.

McCauley, A.P. and Geller, J.S. Decisions for Norplant programs. Population Reports, Series K, No. 4. Baltimore, Johns Hopkins School of Public Health, Population Information Program, September 1992.

Rinehart, W., Rudy, S., and Drennan, M. GATHER guide to counseling. Population Reports, Series J, No. 48. Baltimore, Johns Hopkins School of Public Health, Population Information Program, December 1998.

Treiman, K., Liskin, L., Kols, A., and Rinehart, W. IUDs—An update. Population Reports, Series B., No. 6. Baltimore, Johns Hopkins School of Public Health, Population Information Program, December 1995.

Glossary

abscess. Collection of **pus** surrounded by inflammation.

acquired immune deficiency syndrome (AIDS). A progressive, usually fatal condition (**syndrome**) that reduces the body's ability to fight certain infections. Caused by infection with HIV (human immunodeficiency virus).

acute purulent cervicitis. Inflammation of the **cervix** with a **pus**-like discharge.

AIDS. See **acquired immune deficiency syndrome**.

amenorrhea. Absence of **menstrual period**s (monthly vaginal bleeding).

anemia. Low levels of the oxygen-carrying material in the blood. Anemia results in decreased oxygen to the tissues of the body. Symptoms are often vague and may include chronic fatigue, irritability, dizziness, memory problems, shortness of breath, headaches, and bone pain. Mild anemia may have no noticeable symptoms. Anemia may result from excessive blood loss, blood cell destruction, or decreased blood cell formation. (See **hemoglobin, iron deficiency anemia**.)

anal fistula. An abnormal opening at or near the **anus**.

anus. The lower opening of the digestive tract (large intestine); the outlet of the **rectum**.

backup method. A family planning method such as condoms or spermicide that can be used temporarily for extra protection against pregnancy when needed—for example, when starting a new method, when supplies run out, and when a pill user misses several pills in a row.

bacterial vaginitis. Inflammation of the vagina caused by a bacterial infection.

bacterial vaginosis. A common vaginal condition caused by overgrowth of bacteria normally found in the vagina. Not generally sexually transmitted. Can come from douching, pregnancy, or antibiotics. Causes fishy-smelling discharge.

balanitis. Inflammation of the head (tip) of the **penis** and the **mucous membrane** beneath it.

Note: Words in **dark black type** also are defined in this glossary.

benign breast disease. A disease involving the presence of abnormal but not malignant (cancerous) breast tissue.

blood pressure. The force (pressure) of the blood against the walls of blood vessels, created chiefly by the heart as it pumps blood through the body. As the heart beats, pressure increases. As the heart relaxes between beats, pressure decreases. Normal blood pressure varies from moment to moment within each person. Generally, normal systolic (pumping) blood pressure is less than 140 mm HG, and normal diastolic (resting) blood pressure is less than 90 mm HG. (See **hypertension**.)

breakthrough bleeding. Vaginal bleeding between menstrual periods. (See also **spotting**.)

buboes. Bursting **lymph nodes**. (See **lymphogranuloma venereum**.)

candidiasis. A common infection of the skin or **mucous membranes** caused by a yeast-like fungus (usually *Candida albicans*); the most common cause of **vaginitis**. In women, symptoms include intense vaginal burning and itching and a clumpy, white fluid in and around the **vagina**. In men, symptoms include itching genitals and white fluid under the foreskin (if uncircumcised). Rarely sexually transmitted.

cardiovascular disease (or problems). Any disease or abnormal condition of the heart, blood vessels, or blood circulation. (See **cardiovascular system**, **circulatory system**.)

cardiovascular system. The system by which blood is circulated through the body. Consists of the heart and blood vessels.

cerebrovascular disease. Any disease of the blood vessels of the brain.

cervical mucus. A thick fluid plugging the opening of the **cervix**. Most of the time **cervical mucus** is thick enough to prevent **sperm** from entering the **uterus**. At midcycle, however, under the influence of **estrogen**, the mucus becomes thin and watery, and sperm can more easily pass into the uterus.

cervicitis. Inflammation of the **cervix**.

cervix. The lower portion of the **uterus** that extends into the upper **vagina**.

chancroid. A **sexually transmitted disease** caused by the bacillus (rod-shaped bacteria) *Hemophilus ducreyi*. Symptoms include soft and painful sores on the **penis**, **vagina**, or **anus**, and swollen **lymph nodes**. Symptoms may not appear or may be difficult to notice in women, but both women and men can transmit the disease.

chlamydia. A **sexually transmitted disease** caused by infection with the bacterium *chlamydia trachomatis*. Symptoms that women may notice include unusual vaginal discharge, irregular bleeding, bleeding after intercourse, or deep pain after and/or during sexual intercourse. Symptoms that men may notice include clear, mucus-like discharge from the **penis** and burning during urination. Chlamydia is dangerous because, if untreated, it can lead to **pelvic inflammatory disease**.

cholestasis. Reduced flow of bile secreted by the liver.

circulatory system. The system by which blood and **lymph** are circulated throughout the body. Includes the **cardiovascular system** and the **lymphatic system**.

cirrhosis (of the liver). A disease of the liver involving destruction of liver cells and diminished liver function. Can block blood flow to the liver, causing high **blood pressure** or **jaundice**.

conception. Union of an **ovum**, or egg cell, with a **sperm**. Also known as fertilization.

coronary artery disease. Narrowing of the arteries that supply blood to the myocardium (muscular middle layer of the heart wall). May eventually result in damage to the heart muscle.

cryptorchidism. Failure of one or both **testes** to descend into the **scrotum**.

depression. A mental condition typically marked by dejection, despair, lack of hope, and sometimes either extreme tiredness or agitation.

diabetes (diabetes mellitus). A chronic disorder caused by ineffective production or use of the hormone insulin secreted by the pancreas. People with diabetes (diabetics) are unable to use carbohydrates in food properly, causing glucose (sugar) to build up in the blood and urine. Symptoms include excessive urination and excessive thirst. Diabetics, especially if untreated, are at risk of developing serious long-term complications such as **nephropathy**, **neuropathy**, and **retinopathy**.

disinfect (medical instruments). To destroy all living microorganisms except some forms of bacteria. Also called high-level disinfection.

dysmenorrhea. Painful **menstrual period**s.

eclampsia. A major toxic condition of late pregnancy, labor, and the period immediately after delivery, characterized by convulsions (involuntary muscle contractions, or seizures). In serious cases, sometimes followed by coma and death. Eclampsia occurs as a complication of **preeclampsia**.

ectopic pregnancy. Pregnancy anywhere outside the **uterus**, such as in the **fallopian tubes** or **ovaries**. Ectopic pregnancy is an emergency since the **fetus** often grows to a size large enough to cause fatal internal bleeding in the mother's abdomen.

ejaculation. The release of **semen** from the **penis**.

elephantiasis. A chronic and often extreme swelling and hardening of skin tissue and tissue just beneath the skin, especially of the legs and **scrotum**, resulting from an obstruction in the **lymphatic system**. (See **filariasis**.)

embryo. The product of **conception** (fertilization of an egg by a **sperm**) during the first 8 weeks of its development. During the remainder of pregnancy it is know as the **fetus**.

emergency oral contraception. Combined or progestin-only oral contraceptives or specifically packaged pills used soon after unprotected sexual intercourse to prevent pregnancy.

endometrium. The membrane that lines the inner surface of the **uterus**.

endometriosis. A condition where endometrial tissue is located outside the **uterus**. The tissue may attach itself to the reproductive organs or to other organs in the abdominal cavity. May cause **pelvic adhesions** in the abdominal cavity and in the **fallopian tube**s. Endometriosis may also interfere with **ovulation** and with the **implantation** of the **embryo**. (See **endometrium**.)

engorgement (breast engorgement). A condition resulting when more milk accumulates in the breasts than the infant consumes. Engorgement may cause the breasts to feel hard, painful, and hot. Can usually be prevented (or relieved) by breastfeeding more often.

epididymis. A coiled, tubular organ attached to and lying on the testicle. Developing **sperm** reach maturity and develop their swimming capabilities within this organ. The matured sperm leave the epididymis through the **vas deferens**.

epididymitis. Inflammation of the **epididymis**.

epilepsy. A chronic disorder caused by disturbed brain function. Usually involves some disturbance of consciousness. May involve convulsions (involuntary muscle contractions, or seizures).

estrogen. Natural estrogens, especially the **hormone** estradiol, are secreted by a mature ovarian **follicle**, which surrounds the **ovum**, or egg. Responsible for female sexual development. The word estrogen is now used to describe synthetic drugs that have effects like those of an estrogen and are used in combined oral contraceptives and monthly injectable contraceptives.

fallopian tube. Either of a pair of slender ducts that connect the **uterus** to the region of each ovary. It carries the **ovum** from the ovary to the uterus and carries **sperm** from the uterus towards the ovary. **Fertilization** of the ovum by sperm usually takes place in the fallopian tube.

fertilization. See conception.

fetus. The product of **conception** from the end of the eighth week until birth. (See **embryo**.)

fibroid. A benign growth often found in or on the uterus. Fibroids are not harmful unless they cause pain or grow large enough to cause an obstruction.

fibrosis. The excess formation of fibrous tissue, as in reaction to organ damage; for example, fibrosis of the liver.

filariasis. A chronic parasitic disease caused by filarial worms. People usually become infected when they are bitten by mosquitoes that have been exposed to the worms. Living worms cause little tissue damage, but death of adult worms may lead to inflammation and permanent **fibrosis** clogging channels in the **lymphatic system**. Serious infections may lead to **elephantiasis**.

focal neurologic symptoms. Blurred vision, temporary loss of vision, seeing flashing lights or zigzag lines, or trouble speaking or moving. Occur with a type of **migraine**.

follicle. A small round structure in the **ovary**. Each follicle contains an egg. During **ovulation** the follicle on the surface of the ovary opens and releases a mature egg.

fully breastfeeding. Giving a baby no other food or liquid than breast milk. A woman described as nearly fully breastfeeding gives the baby some additional liquid or food, but at least 85% of the baby's feedings are breast milk.

gastroenteritis. Inflammation of the **mucous membrane** of both stomach and intestine.

genital herpes. A disease caused by the virus herpes simplex. Usually spread by sexual contact. Symptoms likely to be noticed include one or more very painful small blisters around the **vagina**, on the **penis**, or around the **anus**. These blisters may burst open and dry up to become scabs. Sores can last for 3 weeks or more and then disappear. New blisters usually appear from time to time because the virus stays in the body.

genital warts. Cluster-like growths on the **vulva**, the vaginal wall, and the **cervix** in women, and on the **penis** in men. Caused by **human papillomavirus**.

gestational diabetes. Diabetes that develops only during pregnancy. Occurs because the usual **hormone** production is changed and sugar is not utilized as efficiently.

gland. A cell or group of cells in the body that makes a substance (secretion) to be discharged and used in some other part of the body.

goiter. A chronic, noncancerous enlargement of the **thyroid gland**.

gonorrhea. A **sexually transmitted disease** caused by the bacterium *Neisseria gonorrhea*. It is transmitted by a person carrying the bacterium when one **mucous membrane comes into contact with another's**. Gonorrhea causes inflammation of the genital mucous membrane in both sexes. May also affect other parts of the body such as the anus and **cervix**. Symptoms include a **pus**-like discharge from the **penis** in men or the cervix in women and lower abdominal pain and fever in women. If not treated, gonorrhea can cause sterility.

granuloma inguinale. A **sexually transmitted disease** that causes lumps under the skin in the genital region, most often between the **scrotum** and thighs on men or between the **labia** and **vagina** on women.

groin. The depression between the thigh and the torso.

heart attack. A heart attack occurs when the flow of blood in a coronary artery is blocked long enough to cause some heart muscle to die. Also called myocardial infarction. (See also **ischemic heart disease**.)

heavy smoker. A person who smokes 15 or more cigarettes per day.

hemoglobin. The iron-containing material in red blood cells. Hemoglobin carries oxygen from the lungs to the tissues of the body.

hepatitis. Inflammation of the liver, usually caused by a virus but sometimes by a **toxin**.

hernia. The projection of an organ, part of an organ, or any bodily structure through the wall that normally contains it.

HIV. Human immunodeficiency virus, the cause of **acquired immune deficiency syndrome** (AIDS). HIV can be transmitted by sexual contact (heterosexual or homosexual), by contaminated blood products (especially blood transfusion), through contaminated needles or surgical instruments, and from mother to **fetus** or infant before or during birth. If the mother is infected with HIV, there is a small chance that the virus will be passed to the baby through breast milk.

hormone. A chemical substance formed in one organ or part of the body and carried in the blood to another organ or part. Affects the activity of other organs or parts of the body through chemical action.

human papillomavirus (HPV). A common, highly contagious **sexually transmitted disease** caused by a virus and spread by skin-to-skin contact. Symptoms include warts on or near the **penis**, **vagina**, or **anus**. Warts may not appear or may be difficult to notice. Certain subtypes of HPV are responsible for most cases of cervical cancer. (See **genital warts**.)

hydrocele. The collection of fluid in a body cavity, especially in the **testes** or along the **spermatic cord**.

hypertension. Higher **blood pressure** than normal. Normal blood pressure in adults varies from moment to moment within each person, but generally diastolic (resting) blood pressure from 90 to 99 mm HG is considered mild hypertension; 100 to 109, moderate hypertension; and 110 or greater, severe hypertension. Systolic (pumping) blood pressure from 140 to 159 mm HG is considered mild hypertension; 160 to 179, moderate hypertension; and 180 or greater, severe hypertension. (See **blood pressure**.)

hyperthyroid. Too much production of thyroid **hormones**. (See **thyroid gland**.)

hypothyroid. Not enough production of thyroid **hormones**. (See thyroid gland.)

implantation. The embedding of the **embryo** into tissue so it can establish contact with the mother's blood supply for nourishment. Implantation usually occurs in the **endometrium**; however, in an **ectopic pregnancy** it may occur elsewhere in the body.

inguinal hernia. A **hernia** in the **groin**.

iron deficiency anemia. Anemia resulting from a greater demand for iron than can be supplied. Commonly caused by chronic loss of blood, such as vaginal bleeding, or by poor diet. Usually successfully treated by iron supplements and a well-balanced diet.

ischemic heart disease, ischemia. ischemia is reduced blood flow (and thus reduced oxygen) to tissues of the body. When this reduced flow is in the coronary arteries (arteries of the heart), it is called ischemic heart disease or myocardial ischemia.

jaundice. A symptom of liver disease. A person with jaundice typically has abnormal yellowing of the skin and whites of the eyes.

labia. The inner and outer lips of the **vagina**.

laceration. A wound or irregular tear of the flesh.

LAM (Lactational Amenorrhea Method). A family planning method that relies on breastfeeding as natural protection against pregnancy for up to 6 months after childbirth. Women who use LAM must fully or nearly fully breastfeed to protect themselves from pregnancy. (See **fully breastfeeding**.)

laparoscope. A device consisting of a tube containing an optical system for viewing the inside of an organ or body cavity. Used in diagnosis and in some female sterilization procedures.

laparoscopy. A medical procedure performed using a **laparoscope** to see the inside of an organ or body cavity. Also, a type of female sterilization procedure (laparoscopic sterilization).

lesion. A diseased area of skin or other body tissue.

light smoker. A person who smokes, but fewer than 15 cigarettes per day.

lymph. A fluid that is collected from the tissues throughout the body, flows through the **lymphatic system**, and eventually enters the bloodstream. Lymph removes bacteria and certain proteins from the tissues, carries fat from the intestines, and supplies white blood cells to the blood.

lymph nodes. Enclosed masses of tissue that filter out foreign particles, such as bacteria, preventing them from entering the blood. **Lymph** nodes are spread throughout the body.

lymphatic system. The system of structures that carries **lymph** from body tissues to the bloodstream.

lymphogranuloma venereum. A **sexually transmitted disease** usually caused by *chlamydia trachomatis*. In men, symptoms include large dark lumps in the **groin** that open to drain **pus**, scar up, and open again. Women develop painful, oozing sores around the **anus**. Also called **buboes**.

menopause. The time in a woman's life when **menses** (**menstrual periods**) stop. Occurs when a woman's **ovaries** stop producing eggs and monthly bleeding from the **uterus** stops.

menses. Monthly flow of bloody fluid from the **uterus** through the **vagina** in adult women between **puberty** and **menopause**.

menstrual cycle. A repeating series of changes in the **ovaries** and **endometrium** that includes **ovulation** and about two weeks later the beginning of menstrual bleeding. In most women, cycles average about 28 days but may be shorter or longer. (See **menses, menstrual period**.)

menstrual period, menstruation. Periodic discharging of the **menses** in response to stimulation from **estrogen** and **progesterone**.

migraine. Severe, recurrent headache, usually accompanied by sensitivity to light and affecting only one side of the head, with sharp pain and sometimes nausea, vomiting, and trouble seeing. (See **focal neurologic symptoms**.)

minilaparotomy. A female sterilization technique performed by bringing the **fallopian tubes** through a small incision in the abdomen and then usually tying and cutting them.

mucous membrane. The membrane lining all passages and cavities of the body that communicate with the air. Cells or glands in the surface layer of the mucous membrane secrete **mucus**.

mucus. The fluid secreted by mucous membranes and **glands**. (See **mucous membrane**.)

nearly fully breastfeeding. See **fully breastfeeding**.

nephropathy. Any disease of the kidneys.

neuropathy. Any disease of the nerves.

orchitis. Inflammation of a testis. (See **testes**.)

ovarian cyst. A cyst is an abnormal sac or cavity containing a liquid or semisolid material and enclosed by a membrane. On the ovary, often arising from a **follicle**. When a cyst occurs on the **ovary**, it may cause some abdominal pain but rarely requires any treatment. Ovarian cysts usually disappear on their own.

ovary. Either of a pair of female sex **glands** that produce the reproductive egg cells, the ova (see **ovum**). The ovaries also produce the sex **hormones estrogen** and **progesterone**. These hormones contribute to the process of sexual development, regulation of the **menstrual cycle**, and the achievement and maintenance of pregnancy.

ovulation. The release of an egg cell from an **ovary**.

ovum. Egg cell, produced by the **ovaries**.

partially breastfeeding. Less than fully or nearly fully breastfeeding. (See **fully breastfeeding**.)

pelvic adhesions. Abnormal tough bands of tissue connecting internal body structures in the **pelvis**. Adhesions can interfere with movement of the egg and **implantation** of the **embryo** in the **uterus**.

pelvic infection. See **pelvic inflammatory disease**.

pelvic inflammatory disease (PID). Infection in the uterine lining, uterine wall, **fallopian tube**, **ovary**, uterine membrane, broad ligaments of the **uterus**, or membranes lining the pelvic wall. May be caused by a variety of infectious organisms including **gonorrhea** and **chlamydia**.

pelvis. The skeletal structure located in the lower part of the human torso, resting on the legs and supporting the spine. In females, also refers to the hollow portion of the pelvic bone structure through which the **fetus** passes during birth.

penis. The male organ for urination and sexual intercourse.

placenta. The organ that nourishes a growing **fetus**. The placenta (also known as "afterbirth") is expelled from the **uterus** within a few minutes after the birth of a baby.

postpartum. After childbirth; the first 6 weeks after childbirth.

preeclampsia. High **blood pressure** (**hypertension**) plus proteinuria (excess protein in the urine), or swelling, or both (but without convulsions) after 20 weeks of pregnancy. If not treated, may progress to **eclampsia**. Cause unknown.

progesterone. A **hormone** secreted chiefly by the corpus luteum, which develops in a ruptured ovarian follicle during the luteal phase of the **menstrual cycle** (after **ovulation**). Progesterone prepares the **endometrium** for possible implantation of a fertilized egg. It also protects the **embryo** and enhances development of the **placenta** and aids in preparing the breasts for nursing the new infant.

progestin. A word used to cover a large group of synthetic drugs that have an effect similar to that of **progesterone**. Progestins are used in oral contraceptives, injectables, and implants.

puberty. The time of life when the body begins making adult levels of sex **hormones** and the young person takes on adult body characteristics.

puerperal sepsis. Infection of the reproductive organs during the puerperium (first 42 days **postpartum**.)

pulmonary embolism. A blood clot formed elsewhere in the body that has traveled to the lung, causing shortness of breath and pain when taking a deep breath. Can be fatal.

purulent cervicitis. Inflammation of the **cervix** accompanied by a **pus**-like discharge.

pus. A yellowish-white fluid formed in infected tissue.

rectum. The lower part of the digestive tract (large intestine).

retinopathy. Any disorder of the retina (innermost part of the eye that receives images formed by the lens).

schistosomiasis. A parasitic disease caused by a flatworm that spends part of its life in a freshwater snail host. Schistosomiasis is widespread in Asia, Africa, and tropical America. People become infected while wading or bathing in water containing larvae of the infected snails.

scrotum. In the male, the pouch of skin behind the **penis** that contains the **testes**.

semen. The thick, white fluid produced by a man's reproductive organs and released through the penis during **ejaculation**. Contains **sperm**.

sepsis. The presence of various **pus**-forming and disease-causing organisms, or poisonous substances they produce, in the blood or body tissues.

septic abortion. Abortion involving infection.

sexually transmitted diseases (STDs). The term given to a group of diseases affecting both men and women and generally transmitted during sexual activity. These diseases usually cause discomfort, some may lead to infertility, and some may be life-threatening.

sickle cell anemia, sickle cell disease. Hereditary, chronic form of **anemia**. Blood cells take on abnormal sickle- or crescent-shape when deprived of oxygen. Sickle cell anemia can cause various problems, including impaired growth and development and decreased resistance to infections. (See **sickle cell crisis**.)

sickle cell crisis. Severe pain due to **sickle cell anemia**, particularly in the abdomen, chest, back, or joints. People with sickle cell disease are at risk of crises of unpredictable frequency and severity throughout their lives.

sperm. The male sex cell. Sperm are produced in the **testes** of an adult male and released into the **vagina** during **ejaculation**. If conditions allow, sperm swim through the opening of the **cervix**, through the **uterus**, and into the **fallopian tubes**. If **ovulation** has recently occurred, sperm may then penetrate and join with the female's egg. (See **conception**.)

spermatic cord. A cord consisting of the **vas deferens** and accompanying arteries, veins, nerves, and lymphatic vessels that passes from the **groin** down into the **scrotum** to the back of each **testicle**.

spotting. Light vaginal bleeding at any time other than during a woman's **menstrual period**. (See also **breakthrough bleeding**.)

sterilize (medical instruments). To destroy all microorganisms.

stroke. A stroke occurs when there is a sudden disruption in the flow of blood to an area of the brain. Deprived of blood, the affected brain cells either become damaged or die.

syndrome. A group of signs or symptoms that collectively indicate a particular disease or abnormal condition.

syphilis. **A sexually transmitted disease** caused by the microorganism (spirochete) *Treponema pallidum*. The spirochete usually enters the body through invisible breaks in the skin or through intact **mucous membranes** lining the mouth, rectum, or genital tract. About 3 weeks later, sores containing large numbers of spirochetes develop at the entry site. Typically, the sores heal, but the spirochetes spread throughout the body. If left untreated, syphilis may eventually progress to systemic infection and cause general paralysis.

testes, testicles. The two reproductive **glands**, in the **scrotum**, that produce **sperm** and the male **hormone** testosterone. ("Testis" if referring to one of the testes.)

thalassemia. An inherited type of **anemia**.

thromboembolic disorder (or disease). Abnormal clotting in the blood vessels.

thrombophlebitis. The formation of blood clots (thrombi) causing pain and swelling in the leg.

thrombophlebitis, superficial. Inflammation of a vein just beneath the skin.

thyroid gland. A gland located in the lower part of the front of the neck. The thyroid gland produces **hormones** that are essential for life and have many effects on body growth and development.

thyroid disease. Any disease of the thyroid **gland**. (See **goiter**, hyperthyroid, hypothyroid, thyroid gland.)

toxic shock syndrome. A rare condition associated with infections by varieties of the common bacterium *staphylococcus aureus*. Apparently caused when a bacterial **toxin** enters the bloodstream of persons lacking antibodies against the toxin. Symptoms include sudden onset of high fever, vomiting, diarrhea, low **blood pressure**, and a sunburn-like skin rash. Has been reported in women who forget to remove menstrual tampons or, in a few cases, who leave diaphragms in place for several days.

toxin. Poison; a poisonous substance of animal or plant origin.

trauma. A wound, especially one caused by sudden physical injury.

trichomoniasis. A sexually transmitted disease caused by *Trichomonas vaginalis*, a protozoan (microscopic organism). Symptoms in women include irritation, redness and swelling of the **vulva**, a bad-smelling vaginal discharge, and painful or difficult urination. Men often have no symptoms but may have a discharge from the **penis** and/or painful or difficult urination.

trophoblast. The outermost layer of cells of the developing **embryo** through which the embryo receives nourishment from the mother. The cells of the trophoblast contribute to the formation of the **placenta**.

trophoblast disease. Disease involving abnormal cell growth of the **trophoblast** during pregnancy.

tuberculosis. A contagious disease caused by the microorganism *Mycobacterium tuberculosis*. Most commonly affects the respiratory system but may also infect other parts of the body including the **pelvis**.

uterine fibroid. See **fibroid**.

uterus. The hollow, muscular organ that carries the **fetus** during pregnancy.

vagina. The passage leading from the external genital opening to the **uterus** in females. The vagina serves as a passage for discharge of **menses**, for reception of the **penis** during sexual intercourse, and for delivery of the **fetus** during childbirth.

vaginitis. Inflammation of the **vagina**. May be caused by microorganisms such as gonococci, staphylococci, streptococci, spirochetes; chemical irritation from use of too strong chemicals in douching; fungus infection caused by *Candida albicans*; protozoan infection; irritation from foreign bodies; vitamin deficiency as in pellagra; conditions involving the vulva and surrounding areas such as uncleanliness; or intestinal worms.

valvular heart disease. Health problems associated with improperly functioning heart valves.

varicocele. Enlargement of the veins of the **spermatic cord**. Symptoms include a dull ache along the cord and swollen tissue in the **scrotum** that feels like "a bag of worms."

varicose veins. Enlarged, twisted veins. Most commonly seen in the legs.

vas deferens (vas, vasa). One of the slim muscular tubes that transports **sperm** from the **testes**. These tubes are cut during a vasectomy.

vascular disease. Any disease of the blood vessels.

vulva. The exterior female genitals.

Index

A

abdominal cavity...A–16

abdominal pain...6–12, 6–18, 8–15, 9–17, 12–16, 12–20 to 12–21, 12–23, 16–12, A–17

abdominal skin infection...9–9, A–8

abdominal surgery...9–9

abdominal wall hernia...A–8

abnormal vaginal bleeding...5–16, 5–18, 6–13 to 6–14, 7–14, 7–17, 8–16, 8–18, 12–16 to 12–17, 12–20, 12–23, 16–12, A–3

abortion...2–1, 4–6, 5–8, 5–10, 5–26, 6–8, 6–10, 7–7, 7–9, 7–21, 8–9, 8–11, 9–7, 9–13, 9/10–2, 12–5, 12–9, 12–11, 12–20, 12–26, 13–8 to 13–9, 13–13 to 13–14, 14–8, A–8, A–21

abscess...8–15, 8–19, 9–18, 10–14 to 10–15, 16–15, A–13

abstinence...3–5, 11–14, 11–16, 14–1, 16–11

acetaminophen...9–16, 9–19, 10–12, 10–16. See also paracetamol.

acne...6–5, 7–5, 8–5

acquired immune deficiency syndrome...16–3, A–5, A–13, A–18. See also AIDS, HIV, HIV/AIDS.

acyclovir...16–20

adolescence...5–4

adolescent...5–8, 6–8, 7–7, 8–9

age...2–1, 4–14, 5–4, 5–6, 5–8, 5–26, 5–28, 7–4, 7–15, 7–20, 8–1, 8–22, 9–10, 9–12, 9–22, 10–9 to 10–10, 10–18, 11–5, 12–27, 16–6, 16–20

AIDS...4–10, 5–5, 5–10, 9–9, 10–9, 11–4, 11–16, 12–8, 13–19, 14–7, 14–17, 15–5 to 15–6, 15–15, 16–3, 16–10, 16–21, 16–22, A–5, A–13, A–18. See also acquired immune deficiency syndrome, HIV, HIV/AIDS.

allergic...11–6, 11–14, 13–8, 16–19

allergic reaction...9–5, 11–7, 11–11, 13–6, 13–13, 13–15

allergy to latex...11–6, 11–13 to 11–14, 13–8, A–7.

alligator forceps...12–13

amenorrhea...5–4, 5–17 to 5–18, 6–6, 6–12, 6–13 to 6–14, 7–1, 7–5, 7–9, 7–15, 7–18, 7–20, 8–1, 8–5, 8–14, 8–17, 12–23, 15–3, A–13

amoxicillin...16–18

ampicillin...13–15

anal fistula...16–15

anal intercourse...11–16, 11–18, 16–10

anatomical abnormalities...A–7

anemia...5–1, 5–4, 5–8, 5–27, 6–8, 6–14, 7–4, 7–7, 7–10, 7–15, 7–20, 8–5, 8–9, 8–14, 8–17 to 8–18, 9–9, 9–10, 10–9, 12–6, 12–9, 12–19, 12–23, 14–9, 15–7, A–3, A–6, A–13, A–18, A–21, A–22

anesthesia...8–5, 9–5, 9–6, 9–15, 9–20 to 9–21, 10–7, 10–10, A–1

anesthesia risk...9–5, 9–21

anesthetic...8–5, 8–12 to 8–14, 9–13 to 9–15, 9–20, 10–11

anti–anxiety therapies...14–9, A–7

anti–nausea medicine...5–23

antibiotics...8–19, 9–10, 9–18, 10–15, 12–9, 12–21, 12–27, 13–11, 13–15 to 13–16, 15–13, 16–13, 16–20, A–7

anticoagulants...15–6, A–3, A–7, A–8

anticonvulsants...12–9, A–7

antimetabolites...15–6, A–8

antiseptic...4–11, 7–12, 8–19, 9–18, 10–15, 12–12

anus...16–10, 16–14 to 16–16, A–13, A–14, A–17, A–18, A–19

aspirin...5–17, 7–16, 8–17 to 8–19, 9–16, 9–19, 10–12, 10–16, 12–14, 12–19

AVSC International...9–23, 10–19

azithromycin...16–17, 16–18, 16–20

Index　　　　　　　　　　　　　　　　　　　　　　　　　　　　　　　　　　I–1

B

baby oil...11–10

back-up method...7–8, 8–10, A–13. *See also* condoms as back-up method, spermicide as back-up method.

bacteria...4–10, 9–18, 10–15, 13–11, A–14, A–15, A–17, A–19, A–22

bacterial infection...A–13

bacterial vaginitis...A–5, A–13

bacterial vaginosis...A–5,16–13, 16–18

balanitis...A–8, A–13

barbiturates...5–7, 6–7, 8–8, 9–10, A–7

barrier methods...4–13, 4–15, 4–16, 4–17, 4–18, 4–22, 6–18, 11–1 to 11–18, 13–1 to 13–19, 14–1, 15–12, A–4, A–13, A–14

basal body temperature...14–3, 14–5, 14–8 to 14–9 14–10, 14–12 to 14–13, 14–17. *See also* BBT.

BBT...14–3, 14–18. *See also* basal body temperature.

benefits of breastfeeding...4–8, 15–5

benefits of family planning...1–4, 2–1

benign breast disease...5–4, 5–8, 6–5, 6–8, 7–7, 8–9, 12–9, 15–7, A–4, A–14

benzathine penicillin G...16–19

bile...A–14

bipolar electrocoagulation...9–21

birth defects...13–18

birth weight...7–21

bleeding...*See* breakthrough bleeding, heavy bleeding, irregular bleeding, menstrual bleeding, spotting, vaginal bleeding.

blisters...16–15, 16–20

blocked arteries...4–15, 5–6, 5–16, 6–13, 6–14, 7–6, 7–14, 8–16, 8–20, 9–8, A–3, A–17

blood circulation...A–14

blood clots, blood clotting...5–5, 5–6, 6–7, 7–6, 7–14, 8–7, 8–16, 8–20, 9–9, 9–16, 10–5, 10–9, 10–12, 10–15, 12–9, A–21 to A–22

blood pressure...4–14, 4–22, 5–6, 7–6, 9–8, A–2, A–14, A–18, A–22

breakthrough bleeding...*See* spotting.

breast cancer...4–8, 4–17, 5–6, 5–16, 6–7, 6–13, 7–6, 7–14, 7–21, 8–7, 8–16, 9–8, 12–9, 15–7, A–4

breast inflammation...*See* mastitis.

breast milk...4–1, 4–8 to 4–9, 6–3, 6–5, 7–4, 7–20, 8–5, 9–4, 11–5, 12–5, 13–5, 15–1, 15–3 to 15–9, 15–14 to 15–15, 16–10, A–5, A–16, A–17, A–18

breast surgery...A–8

breast tenderness...4–7, 5–4, 6–6, 7–5, 8–5, 9–17, 12–23, 15–13

breastfeeding...1–6 to 1–7, 4–1, 4–5, 4–6, 4–8 to 4–9, 4–13 to 4–14, 4–18, 4–19, 4–20, 4–22, 5–1, 5–5, 5–6, 5–9, 6–1, 6–3 to 6–9, 6–11 to 6–14, 6–16 to 6–17, 7–1, 7–6 to 7–9, 7–20, 8–1, 8–7, 8–9, 8–10 to 8–11, 9–11, 12–1, 12–9, 14–1, 14–8, 15–1 to 15–15, 16–3, 16–10, 16–17, 16–18, 16–20, 16–21, A–7, A–8, A–16, A–17, A–19, A–20

breasts, enlarged...4–7

breasts, sore...15–13

bromocriptine...15–6, A–8

bronchitis...9–9, A–8

buboes...A–14, A–19

butter...11–10, 11–15, 13–19

C

calendar calculation...14–3, 14–13, 14–17

calendar method...4–6, 14–3, 14–5, 14–7, 14–8, 14–10, 14–13 to 14–14, 14–17, A–4, A–6

Candida albicans...A–14, A–23

candidiasis...16–13, 16–18, A–14

carbamezapine...5–7, 6–7, 8–8, 9–10, A–7

cefixime...16–17

ceftriaxone...16–17, 16–20

cerebrovascular disease...A–3, A–14

cervical cancer...4–22, 5–26, 11–5, 12–8, 13–5, 13–18, 14–8, 16–16, A–4, A–18

cervical cap...4–5, 4–6, 4–13, 13–3 to 13–9, 13–12 to 13–13, 13–17 to 13–19, 16–8, A–2, A–8

cervical cap removal...13–13

cervical disease...12–18, A–4

cervical intraepithelial neoplasia...A–4

cervical lacerations...A–7

cervical mucus...5–3, 6–4, 7–3, 8–4, 14–7, 14–8, 14–9, 14–17, A–14

cervical secretions...14–3, 14–5, 14–6, 14–10, 14–11 to 14–12, 14–17

cervical stenosis...A–7

cervical tear...A–8

cervix...4–11, 12–3, 12–12, 12–13, 12–15, 12–16, 12–20, 12–22, 12–27, 12–28, 13–3, 13–8 to 13–13, 13–18, 16–21, A–13, A–14, A–17, A–21

chancroid...16–14, 16–20, A–14

checking the IUD...12–15

chest pain...5–6, 7–6

childbirth...4–8, 4–9, 4–14, 5–6, 5–9, 6–5, 6–8, 6–9, 6–17, 7–1, 7–4, 7–6 to 7–9, 8–1, 8–5, 8–7, 8–9 to 8–11, 9–13, 11–5, 12–1, 12–5 to 12–8, 12–10 to 12–12, 13–5, 13–7 to 13–9, 14–1, 14–7, 15–1, 15–4, 15–6, 15–7, 15–9, 15–12, 16–3, 16–10, 16–21, A–8, A–19, A–20, A–23

children...2–1, 2–2, 4–14, 5–1, 5–4, 5–8, 5–27, 6–8, 7–1, 7–7, 7–20, 8–1, 8–9, 8–22, 9–1, 9–3, 9–6, 9–11, 9–12, 9–19, 9–22 to 9/10–2, 10–1, 10–3, 10–6, 10–7, 10–9, 10–10, 10–11, 10–16, 10–17, 10–18, 11–10, 12–26, 13–4, 13–5, 14–9, 16–21, A–7

chills...9–18, 10–15

chlamydia...11–4, 12–21, 16–3, 16–12, 16–17, 16–18, A–14, A–19, A–20

cholestasis...A–5, A–14

cigarettes...5–5, 5–6, 5–8, 6–8, 7–7, 8–9, 12–9, 14–9, 15–7, A–2, A–17, A–19

ciprofloxacin...16–17, 16–20

circulatory system...A–14

cirrhosis...5–7, 6–7, 7–6, 8–7, 9–9, 9–10, A–5, A–15

clip...9–14, 9–22, 10–11

clotrimazole...16–18

coagulation disorders...9–9, 10–9, A–6

cocoa butter...11–10, 13–19

coconut oil...11–10

cold cream...11–10

combined oral contraceptives...1–5, 4–3, 4–9, 4–13 to 4–18, 4–20, 5–1 to 5–28, 6–3 to 6–6, 7–5, 7–18, 7–20, 8–6, 8–17, 8–18, 11–5, A–2 to A–8, A–15, A–16

community–based distributor...4–3, 5–8, 13–7

complications...3–5, 4–15, 5–15, 6–5, 6–12, 7–4, 7–11, 8–15, 9–1, 9–5, 9–7, 9–8, 9–18, 10–5, 10–14, 12–6, 12–16, A–3, A–15

conception...A–15, A–16

condom breaks...5–21, 11–11, 11–18

condoms...2–1, 3–5, 4–4, 4–7, 4–9, 4–13, 4–20, 4–22, 5–5 to 5–7, 5–9 to 5–11, 5–13, 5–14, 5–18, 5–19, 5–21 to 5–22, 5–24 to 5–25, 6–7, 6–9, 6–10, 6–12, 6–16, 6–17, 7–5, 7–6, 7–8 to 7–10, 7–19, 8–6, 8–8, 8–10, 8–11, 8–21, 9–5, 9–19, 10–1, 10–4 to 10–6, 10–11, 10–12, 10–16, 10–18, 11–1 to 11–18, 12–7, 12–8, 12–25, 13–4, 13–9, 13–17, 13–19, 14–17, 15–5, 15–11, 15–12, 15–14, 16–1, 16–5, 16–8, 16–9, 16–11, 16–20, 16–22, A–2 to A–8, A–13

condoms as backup method...5–7, 5–9, 5–10, 5–11, 5–13, 5–14, 5–18, 6–7, 6–10, 6–12, 6–17, 7–8, 7–10, 8–8, 8–10, 10–1, 10–4, 10–11, 10–12, 10–16, 14–4, 14–16, 14–17, 15–12

confidentiality...3–6, 12–8

congenital deformity, infant...A–8

cooking oil...11–10

copper T...12–3, 12–11

coronary artery disease...A–15

cortisone...15–6

counseling...3–1 to 3–8, 4–3, 4–21, 4–22, 5–5, 5–10, 5–17, 6–6, 6–15, 7–1, 7–5, 7–9, 7–15, 8–1, 8–6, 8–12, 8–15, 8–17, 8–20, 8–23, 9–6, 9–12, 9–21, 9–23, 9/10–1 to 9/10–2, 10–7, 10–10, 10–15, 10–18, 11–8, 11–13, 12–7, 12–11, 12–18, 12–24, 12–27, 13–7, 13–9, 13–15, 14–7, 14–15, 15–5, 15–8, 15–12, 16–6

cream, spermicidal...13–3

cryptorchidism...A–8, A–15

crystalline penicillin G...16–19

Cyclofem...7–3

Cycloprovera...7–3

cyclosporine...15–6, A–8

Index

I–3

D

decision table…1–4

Depo-Provera…7–3

depot–medroxyprogesterone acetate…7–3

depression…A–15

diabetes…4–16, 5–6, 5–8, 7–6, 7–18, 8–9, 9–8 to 9–10, 10–9, 12–9, 12–28, 15–7, A–2 to A–3, A–15, A–17

diaphragm…4–5, 4–13, 4–18, 4–20, 4–22, 13–1, 13–3 to 13–9, 13–11 to 13–19, 14–17, 16–8, A–2 to A–8, A–22

diaphragm insertion…*See* inserting a diaphragm.

diaphragm removal…13–6, 13–11, 13–16, 13–18

diaphragmatic hernia…9–10, A–8

diarrhea…4–8, 5–14, 5–18, 9–17, 13–11, 13–16, 15–5, 16–9, 16–10, A–22

diet…7–5, 15–3, 15–9, 15–15, A–18

discharge, vaginal…4–7, 5–24, 12–8, 12–14, 12–20, 12–22 to 12–23, 12–25, 13–15, 13–16, 16–7, 16–12, 16–13, A–14, A–23

disinfect…4–10 to 4–12, 7–12, 7–13, A–15

disposable needles…7–13

disposal…4–10, 7–13

dizziness…8–5, 9–17, 13–11, 13–16

DMPA injectable contraceptive…4–13 to 4–17, 4–20, 4–22, 5–6, 5–21, 7–1 to 7–21, 15–12, A–2 to A–8

doctor…1–3, 3–5, 5–15, 5–27, 6–12, 7–11, 8–14, 8–15, 9–16, 10–13, 11–11, 12–16, 12–22 to 12–23, 12–28

donovanosis…16–15, 16–21

douche, douching…13–10, 13–17, 16–13, A–23

doxycycline…16–18 to 16–21

Dramamine®…5–23

drug interactions…5–7, 5–16, 6–7, 6–13, 8–8, 8–16, A–7, A–8

dysmenorrhea…A–7, A–15

E

eclampsia…9–7, A–8, A–15, A–20

ectopic pregnancy…5–5, 5–8, 5–24, 6–6, 6–12, 6–14, 6–17, 7–4, 8–5, 8–15, 8–18, 8–22, 9–5, 9–11, 9–17, 9–21, 9–22, 10–5, 11–5, 12–5, 12–6, 12–9, 12–16, 12–18, 12–21, 12–23, 13–5, A–5, A–15, A–18

effectiveness…1–5, 3–4, 4–1, 4–19 to 4–20, 5–3, 5–4, 5–5, 5–23, 6–1, 6–4, 6–6, 6–11, 6–16, 7–1, 7–4, 7–18, 8–1, 8–4, 9–1, 9–4, 9–21, 10–1, 10–4, 10–5, 11–1, 11–4, 11–7, 12–1, 12–4, 12–16, 13–1, 13–4, 13–6, 14–1, 14–4, 14–5, 15–1, 15–4, 15–5, 16–17, 16–20

ejaculation…9–22, 10–1, 10–4, 10–5, 10–12, 10–16, 10–17, 11–5, 11–10, 11–17, 13–10, 13–11, 13–13, A–15, A–21, A–22

electrocoagulation…9–14, 9–21

elephantiasis…10–9, A–8, A–15, A–16

eligibility criteria…*See* medical eligibility criteria.

embryo…A–15, A–18, A–20, A–21, A–23

emergency oral contraception…5–1, 5–20 to 5–25, 5–28, 6–1, 6–18, 11–11, A–15

emphysema…A–8

endometrial cancer…1–6, 5–4, 5–26, 6–5, 7–4, 7–21, 8–5, 8–22, 12–8, 12–17, 12–22, A–4

endometriosis…5–8, 6–8, 8–9, 9–7, 14–9, A–7, A–16

endometritis…A–4

endometrium…A–15, A–19, A–21

engorgement…15–13, A–8, A–16

epididymis…A–16

epididymitis…A–8, A–16

epidural anesthesia…9–15

epilepsy…6–8, 7–4, 7–7, 8–9, 9–10, 12–9, A–6, A–7, A–16

erection…10–4, 10–17, 11–10, 11–14, 11–16

ergotamine…15–6, A–8

erythromycin…16–18 to 16–21

estrogen…4–9, 5–3, 5–5, 5–6, 5–7, 5–23, 6–1, 6–3, 6–5, 6–6, 7–3, 7–4, 7–5, 7–16, 8–3, 8–5, 8–6, 8–17, 8–18, A–14, A–16, A–19, A–20

ethinyl estradiol…5–23, 7–16

Eugynon 50…5–23

F

fainting, faintness...6–12, 6–16, 8–15, 8–21, 9–17, 9–19, 10–5, 10–11, 12–16, 12–23

fallopian tube...9–4, 9–13, 9–14, 9–22, 12–20, A–15 to A–16, A–19, A–20, A–22

family planning counseling...1–4, 3–1 to 3–8

family planning method...1–2 to 1–7, 4–1 to 4–5, 4–8 to 4–9, 4–19 to 4–22, A–13, A–19

family planning providers...1–2, 2–1, 3–3, 9–23, 10–11, 10–18, 12–12, 12–25, 13–6, 16–4, 16–6

fat...5–8, 6–8, 7–7, 8–9, 14–9, 15–7, A–19

fatigue...15–13

female condom...11–3, 11–7

female sterilization...1–5, 3–2, 3–5, 4–4, 4–9, 4–11, 4–13, 4–20, 4–22, 9–1 to 9–23, 10–5, 10–17, A–2 to A–8, A–19

Femenal...5–23

fertility...9–23, 10–18, 14–8 to 14–9. *See also* return of fertility.

fertility awareness...1–5, 4–5, 4–9, 4–13 to 4–18, 4–20, 4–22, 14–1 to 14–18, A–2 to A–8

fertilization...A–15, A–16

fetus...4–6, 5–26, 7–21, 8–22, 16–10, 16–14, A–15, A–16, A–18, A–20, A–23

fever...9–17, 9–18, 9–19, 10–13, 10–15, 10–16, 12–8, 12–16, 12–22, 12–23, 12–25, 13–11, 13–16, 14–1, 14–7, 15–13, 16–14, A–8, A–17, A–22

fibroid...A–16, A–23. *See also* uterine fibroids.

fibrosis...A–6, A–16. *See also* liver fibrosis.

filarial worms...A–16

filariasis...10–9, A–8, A–15 to A–16

film, spermicidal...13–10, 13–17

fixed uterus...9–7, A–8

foam, spermicidal...13–3, 13–10

foaming tablets, spermicidal...13–3, 13–6, 13–10, 13–17

focal neurologic symptoms...A–3, A–16

follicle...6–18, 8–18, A–16

follow-up...3–7, 4–22, 5–16 to 5–18, 6–13 to 6–15, 7–14 to 7–17, 8–16 to 8–20, 8–23, 9–16, 9–18, 10–7, 10–13 to 10–15, 11–12 to 11–14, 12–17 to 12–24, 13–14 to 13–16, 14–8, 14–15 to 14–16, 15–11 to 15–13

fungus infection...15–13, A–23

G

gallbladder disease...5–7, 5–16, 9–9, 12–9, 15–7, A–5

gastroenteritis...9–9, 10–9, A–8, A–17

genital exam...4–22

genital herpes...16–15, 16–20, 16–21, A–17. *See also* herpes.

genital tract infection...12–8, 16–12 to 16–22, A–8

genital warts...*See* human papillomavirus (HPV).

gestational diabetes...A–17

gloves...4–10, 4–11, 4–12, 7–12

glucose...7–18, A–15

glucose tests...4–22

goiter...A–6, A–17

gonorrhea...11–4, 12–20 to 12–21, 16–3, 16–12, 16–17, 16–18, A–17, A–20

granuloma inguinale...16–15, 16–21, A–17

griseofulvin...5–7, 5–16, 6–7, 6–13, 8–8, 8–16, 9–10, A–7

H

hair growth...8–5

hair loss...7–5, 8–5

hand lotion...13–19

hand washing...4–11

headache...4–16, 5–4, 5–7, 5–8, 5–14 to 5–17, 5–19, 6–6, 6–8, 6–12, 6–13, 6–15, 6–16, 7–5, 7–7, 7–11, 7–14, 7–17, 7–19, 8–5, 8–15, 8–16, 8–20, 8–21, 12–9, 14–9, 15–7, A–3, A–19. *See also* focal neurologic symptoms, migraine.

health care providers...1–1 to 1–2, 4–5 to 4–6, 4–22, 5–28, 8–5, 8–12 to 8–13, 8–22 to 8–23, 9–4, 9–12, 9–15, 9–18, 9–20 to 9–23, 9/10–2, 10–4, 10–11 to 10–12, 10–14 to 10–15, 10–18 to 10–19, 11–5, 11–15, 12–6, 12–12 to 12–15, 13–5, 14–6, 14–10, 15–6, 16–1, 16–4, 16–9

health risk...9–4, 10–5

heart attack...5–5, 5–6, 6–5, 7–4, 7–6, A–17. *See also* ischemic heart disease.

Index   I–5

heart disease...4–15, 5–6, 5–16, 6–13, 6–14, 7–6, 7–14, 8–16, 8–20, 9–8, 10–18, 12–9, 16–14, A–3

heavy bleeding...6–12, 7–5, 7–11, 7–16, 7–19, 8–18, 12–13, 12–18 to 12–19, 12–25, A–3

hematometra...A–8

hemoglobin...4–22, 9–9, 9–10, A–17

hemorrhage...9–7, A–8

hepatitis...4–10, 4–18, 16–3, A–5, A–17

hernia...9–7, 10–8, A–8, A–17 to A–18.
See also abdominal wall hernia, diaphragmatic hernia, inguinal hernia, umbilical hernia.

herpes...11–4, 16–3, 16–9, 16–15, 16–20.
See also genital herpes.

high blood pressure...4–14, 4–15, 5–5 to 5–6, 5–16, 7–6, 7–7, 7–14, 8–9, 9–8, 12–9, 14–9, 15–7, A–2, A–14, A–15, A–18, A–20

high–level disinfection...4–10 to 4–12, 7–12, 7–13, A–15

HIV...4–10, 4–17, 9–11, 10–9, 11–1, 11–4, 11–8, 11–16, 12–8, 13–6, 13–19, 15–5, 15–6, 15–15, 16–3, 16–8, 16–10, 16–11, 16–21, A–5, A–13, A–18. See also acquired immune deficiency syndrome, AIDS, HIV/AIDS.

HIV/AIDS...1–4, 2–1, 3–5, 5–19, 6–16, 7–5, 7–13, 7–19, 8–6, 8–21, 9–5, 9–19, 10–6, 10–16, 11–1, 11–4 to 11–8, 11–12, 11–14 to 11–17, 12–6, 12–16, 12–25, 13–4, 13–5, 13–19, 14–17, 15–5, 15–14, 16–1, 16–3, 16–8, 16–11 to 16–12, 16–22, A–5.
See also acquired immune deficiency syndrome, AIDS, HIV.

hormone...4–9, 5–3, 5–5 to 5–7, 5–12, 5–22, 6–3, 6–7, 6–14, 6–15, 6–17, 6–18, 7–3, 7–6, 7–14, 7–17, 8–3, 8–7, 8–8, 8–20, 10–17, 12–3, 12–5 to 12–6, 12–13, 13–5, 14–6, 15–4, A–18

HPV...See human papillomavirus (HPV).

Human Immunodeficiency Virus...See HIV.

human papillomavirus (HPV)...11–4, 16–16, 16–21, A–17, A–18

hydrocele...10–8, A–8, A–18

hypertension...See high blood pressure.

hyperthyroid...9–9, 14–8, A–6, A–18

hypothyroid...9–10, 14–8, A–6, A–18

I

ibuprofen...5–17, 7–16, 8–17, 9–16, 9–19, 10–12, 10–16, 12–12, 12–14, 12–19

immunities...4–8, 15–5, 15–15

implantation...A–16, A–18, A–20, A–21

impotence...10–15, 11–16

infection...4–10, 7–6, 7–13, 8–15, 8–19, 8–21, 9–5, 9–7, 9–9, 9–11, 9–17, 9–18, 10–5, 10–8, 10–9, 10–13 to 10–15, 11–4, 11–5, 11–8, 11–13, 12–5, 12–6, 12–8 to 12–11, 12–14, 12–18 to 12–19, 12–21 to 12–23, 12–26 to 12–28, 13–15, 14–9, 14–17, 15–13, 16–1 to 16–22, A–5, A–8, A–13, A–14, A–16, A–20 to A–22

infection–prevention...4–1, 4–4, 4–5, 4–10 to 4–12, 4–22, 9–3, 9–13, 9–14, 10–3, 10–11, 12–1, 12–12, 12–13, 16–5

infertility and sexually transmitted diseases (STDs)...11–5, 12–6, 12–8, 13–5, 16–3, 16–9, A–21

informed choice...1–6, 3–2 to 3–3, 3–7

informed consent...9–12, 9–23, 9/10–1, 10–10, 10–18

inguinal hernia...A–8, A–18

injectable contraceptives...See DMPA injectable contraceptives, NET EN.

injection...3–5, 4–3, 4–11, 5–21, 8–4, 8–12 to 8–13, 10–11, 16–17, 16–19, 16–20.
See also DMPA injectable contraceptives, NET EN.

inserting a cervical cap...13–1, 13–12, 13–16

inserting a diaphragm...13–1, 13–11, 13–16

inserting an IUD...12–7, 12–12, 16–4

inserting Norplant® capsules...8–12

insulin...A–3, A–15

interval procedure for female sterilization...9–13

intrauterine device...See IUD.

intrascrotal mass...A–8

intravenous antibiotics...9–18, 10–15, 16–19

iron deficiency anemia...See anemia.

irregular bleeding...5–8, 5–12, 5–14, 6–13 to 6–14, 7–16, 12–18 to 12–19, A–14 irregular menstrual cycles and fertility awareness-based methods...14–7, 14–8

irritation...11–11, 13–6, 13–13

ischemic heart disease...6–14, 8–20, A–3, A–18

itching...11–6, 11–11, 11–13 to 11–15, 13–13, 13–15, 16–7, 16–13

IUCD...12–3. *See also* IUD.

IUD...1–5, 3–5 to 3–6, 3–8, 4–3, 4–5, 4–6, 4–9, 4–11, 4–13, 4–15 to 4–18, 4–20, 4–22, 5–21, 9–20, 12–1 to 12–28, 15–12, 16–4, A–2 to A–8

IUD insertion...4–11, 12–1, 12–6, 12–7, 12–14, 12–27, 12–28, 16–4. *See also* inserting an IUD.

IUD removal...12–1, 12–3, 12–5, 12–6, 12–10 to 12–11, 12–13, 12–14, 12–16 to 12–19, 12–21, 12–22, 12–24 to 12–28

IUD strings...12–6, 12–13, 12–16, 12–22, 12–25

J

jaundice...5–7, 5–15, 5–19, 6–7, 7–6, 8–7, A–5, A–15, A–18

jelly, spermicidal...13–3, 13–11, 13–12, 13–17

JHPIEGO...4–10, 9–23, 10–19

Johns Hopkins Program for International Education in Reproductive Health...*See* JHPIEGO.

K

kanamycin...16–17

kidney disease...5–6, 5–8, 7–6, 9–10, A–8, A–20

L

lactational amenorrhea method...*See* LAM.

LAM...1–5, 1–7, 4–5, 4–8 to 4–9, 4–13, 4–15 to 4–20, 4–22, 15–1 to 15–15, A–2 to A–8, A–19

laparoscope, laparoscopy...4–4, 9–3, 9–6, 9–14, 9–16, 9–20, A–19

latex...11–3, 11–16, 11–18, 13–19. *See also* allergy to latex.

Lippes Loop...12–3

lithium...14–9, 15–6, A–7, A–8

liver disease...5–7, 5–16, 6–7, 6–13, 7–6, 7–14, 8–7, 8–16, A–5

liver fibrosis...9–9 to 9–10, A–6. *See also* fibrosis.

liver infection...5–7, 6–7, 7–6, 8–7

liver tumors...A–5

LNG-20...12–3

Lo-Femenal...5–23

Lo/Ovral...5–23

local anesthesia...4–22, 9–1, 9–3, 9–5, 9–15, 9–21

lubricant...11–3, 11–6, 11–10, 11–13 to 11–15, 11–18, 13–19

lung disease...9–9, A–8

lymph...A–19

lymph node...16–14 to 16–15, A–14, A–19

lymphogranulana venereum...16–15, 16–20

M

Mala-D...5–23

malaria...5–8, 6–8, 7–7, 8–9, 9–11, 12–9, 14–9, 15–7, 16–3, A–6

male sterilization...*See* vasectomy.

malignant trophoblast disease...9–7, 12–8, A–6

Marezine®...5–23

margarine...11–10, 13–19

mastitis...A–8

measles...4–8, 15–5

medical eligibility checklist...1–3, 1–6 to 1–7, 5–5, 6–6, 7–5, 8–6, 9–6 to 9–10, 10–7, 12–7, 13–7, 14–7, 15–5

medical eligibility criteria...1–4, 1–7, 3–7, 4–3, 4–13, 5–20, A–1 to A–8. *See also* medical eligibility checklist.

Megestron...7–3

menopause...5–4, 5–26, 7–15, 12–5, 12–13, 12–27, A–2, A–19

menses...4–22, 6–12, A–19

menstrual bleeding...4–8, 4–22, 5–9, 6–6, 6–10, 7–5, 7–8, 7–10, 7–15, 7–18, 7–20, 8–5, 8–10, 8–14 to 8–15, 9–20, 12–6, 12–10, 12–18, 14–8 to 14–9, 14–17, 15–3, 15–6, 15–9, A–2, A–19

menstrual blood...5–27

menstrual cramps...5–4, 12–6

menstrual cycle...5–9, 6–4, 6–9 to 6–10, 6–18, 7–7 to 7–8, 8–4, 8–10, 12–10, 12–13, 12–27, 14–1, 14–8, A–2, A–19

menstrual period...4–6 to 4–8, 5–4, 5–8, 5–9, 5–12, 5–18, 5–19, 5–26, 6–8 to 6–10, 6–14, 7–6 to 7–8, 7–16, 7–19, 8–5, 8–7, 8–9 to 8–11, 8–17, 9–4, 9–17, 9–20, 10–13, 12–1, 12–5, 12–6, 12–7, 12–10, 12–14 to 12–16, 12–20, 12–25, 12–27, 14–8, 15–1, 15–3 to 15–4, 15–6, 15–8 to 15–9, 15–11, 15–14, 15–15, A–19

menstruation...5–1, 9–11, 12–10, 12–13, 12–27, A–7, A–19

Mesigyna...7–3

mestranol...5–23

metabolic disorder, infant...15–6, A–8

metronidazole...16–18

miconazole...16–18

Microgynon...5–23

midwives...4–3 to 4–5

migraine...4–16, 5–7, 5–18, 6–15, 7–17, 8–20, A–3, A–16, A–19. *See also* focal neurologic symptoms, headache.

milk production...6–3, 6–5, 15–15

mineral oil...11–10, 13–19

minilap...9–3. *See also* minilaparotomy.

minilaparotomy...9–3, 9–5, 9–6, 9–13 to 9–14, 9–16, 9–20, A–19

minipill...6–3. *See also* progestin-only oral contraceptives.

miscarriage...4–6, 5–8, 5–10, 6–8, 6–10, 7–7, 7–9, 8–9, 8–11, 12–9, 12–11, 12–26, 13–9

missed pills...4–22, 5–11, 5–13, 5–19, 6–12, 6–17

MLCu-375...12–3, 12–4

mobile team...10–7

mood changes...4–7, 5–5, 5–14, 5–19, 7–5. *See also* depression.

mood–altering drugs...14–9, 15–6, A–7, A–8

mucous membrane...4–12, A–20

Multiload...12–3. *See also* MLCu-375.

muscle ache...13–11, 13–16

myocardial infarction...A–17

N

nausea...4–7, 5–4, 5–10, 5–14, 5–17, 5–19, 5–23, 7–5, 8–5, 9–17, 12–23, 16–18

needles...4–10 to 4–12, 7–12 to 7–13, 8–5, 9–14, 10–10, 16–10, 16–11, 16–12

Neisseria gonorrhea...A–17

neonatal intensive care...A–8

nephropathy...A–20. *See also* kidney disease.

nerve disease–5–8. *See also* neuropathy.

nervousness...8–5

NET EN...4–13 to 4–17, 4–20, 4–22, 5–6, 7–3, 7–18

neuropathy...A–20

noncancerous cervical lesions...A–4

nonmedical providers...5–8, 10–7, 13–7

nonpelvic tuberculosis...9–11, 12–9, A–7

nonsteroidal anti–inflammatory drugs...5–17, 7–16, 8–17 to 8–19, 12–19

Nordette...5–23

Nordiol...5–23

Noristerat...7–3

Norplant implants...1–5, 3–6, 3–8, 4–4, 4–9, 4–11 to 4–13, 4–15, 4–17, 4–20, 4–22, 8–1 to 8–24, 15–12, A–2 to A–8

no-scalpel vasectomy...10–10

no-touch IUD insertion technique...4–11, 12–12

Nova T...12–3

NSAID....*See* nonsteroidal anti-inflammatory drugs.

nulliparous...A–7

nurse...1–3, 3–5, 4–3 to 4–5, 5–15, 5–27, 6–12, 7–11, 8–14, 8–15, 9–16, 10–13, 11–11, 12–16, 12–22 to 12–23, 12–28

nurse–midwife...4–3 to 4–5

nurse–practitioners...4–3, 4–4

nutrition...4–8 to 4–9, 9–10, 15–9, A–8

nystatin...16–18

O

obese, obesity...9–10, A–5. *See also* fat.

ofloxacin...16–17

oral contraceptives...*See* combined oral contraceptives, progestin-only oral contraceptives.

oral intercourse...11–16, 11–18

orchitis...A–8, A–20

ovarian cancer...1–6, 5–4, 6–5, 7–4, 7–21, 9–5, 12–8, 12–17, 12–22, A–4

ovarian cysts...5–4, 6–18, 8–5, 8–18 to 8–19, 8–22, 14–9, A–4, A–20

ovarian tumor...5–8, 6–8, 8–9, 8–18, 9–11

ovary, ovaries...5–3, 5–20, 5–26, 6–4, 6–18, 7–3, 8–4, 8–5, 9–4, 12–20, 14–8, 15–4, A–20

overdose, anesthesia...9–5, 9–21

Ovral...5–23

ovulation...5–3, 5–20, 6–4, 7–3, 8–4, 14–3, 14–5, 14–11 to 14–13, 15–4, A–16, A–20

ovum...A–20

P

Panadol®...9–19, 10–16

paracetamol...5–17, 9–16, 9–19, 10–12, 10–15, 10–16, 12–14

parity...A–7

Pathfinder International...9–23

peak day (of cervical secretions)...14–11, 14–13, 14–17

pelvic adhesions...A–20

pelvic cancers...9–7

pelvic exam, pelvic examination...4–5, 4–11, 4–12, 4–22, 5–27, 8–22, 9–13, 9–14, 12–6, 12–7, 12–12, 12–14, 12–17, 12–18, 12–20, 12–23, 13–6 to 13–8

pelvic infection...12–10, 12–26, A–20

pelvic inflammatory disease...5–4, 5–8, 6–5, 6–8, 7–16, 8–9, 8–18, 9–7 to 9–8, 11–5, 12–1, 12–6, 12–8, 12–13, 12–16 to 12–18, 12–20, 12–21, 12–26, 12–27, 13–5, 14–9, 16–18, A–4, A–20

pelvic tuberculosis...9–9, 12–8, A–7

pelvis...A–20

penicillin...16–17, 16–19

penis...10–8, 11–3, 11–4, 11–6, 11–7, 11–9 to 11–11, 11–14, 11–15, 11–18, 14–4, 14–17, 16–7, 16–12 to 16–16, A–20

perforation...12–6, 12–13

petroleum jelly...11–10, 11–18, 13–19

pharmacist...4–3, 4–5

phenytoin...5–7, 6–7, 8–8, 9–10, A–7

physical exam, physical examination...4–1, 4–6, 4–7, 5–5, 5–7, 6–6, 6–7, 7–5, 7–6, 8–6, 8–7, 9–5, 9–13, 9–14, 12–21, 13–7, 15–5, 16–22

PID...*See* pelvic inflammatory disease.

placenta...12–10, 12–12, A–20

plastic condom...11–14

plugged milk ducts...15–13

pneumonia...9–9, 15–5, 16–10, A–8

postabortion...14–8, A–8

postabortion family planning...5–10, 6–10, 7–10, 8–11, 13–8, 14–8, 14–10, A–8. *See also* postabortion female sterilization, postabortion IUD insertion.

postabortion female sterilization...9–4, 9–7, 9–13, A–8

postabortion IUD insertion...12–5, 12–11

postcoital contraception...*See* emergency oral contraception.

Postinor-2...5–23, 6–18

postpartum...14–8, A–8, A–20

postpartum family planning...5–9, 6–9, 7–8, 7–9, 8–10, 8–11, 11–5, 13–8, 14–8, 14–10, 15–1 to 15–15, A–7 to A–8. *See also* postpartum female sterilization, postpartum IUD insertion.

postpartum female sterilization...9–7, 9–13, A–8

postpartum IUD insertion...12–5, 12–7 to 12–8, 12–12, 12–15, A–8

preeclampsia...9–7, 9–11, A–8, A–20

pregnancy...1–3, 1–5, 1–7, 2–1, 3–4, 4–1, 4–6 to 4–9, 4–13 to 4–20, 5–3 to 5–4, 5–10, 5–12 to 5–14, 5–16 to 5–18, 5–20 to 5–22, 5–24, 5–26 to 5–28, 6–3 to 6–4, 6–6, 6–9, 6–11 to 6–14, 6–18, 7–3 to 7–8, 7–14 to 7–15, 7–17, 7–18, 7–20, 7–21, 8–3 to 8–8, 8–10, 8–15, 8–16, 8–18, 8–22, 8–23, 9–4, 9–5, 9–7, 9–8, 9–17, 9–21 to 9–22, 9/10–2, 10–4, 10–5, 10–17, 11–1, 11–4 to 11–8, 11–11, 11–15, 11–17, 12–4 to 12–6, 12–10, 12–13, 12–17, 12–20, 12–22 to 12–23, 12–28, 13–4 to 13–5, 13–8, 13–14, 14–1, 14–4 to 14–5, 14–8, 14–16, 14–18, 15–1, 15–3, 15–4, 15–6 to 15–8, 15–12, 15–14, 16–3, 16–4, 16–10, 16–13, 16–14, 16–17 to 16–21, A–2, A–4, A–5, A–6, A–15

pregnancy rate...1–5, 3–4, 4–19, 5–3 to 5–4, 6–4, 7–4, 7–18, 8–4, 9–4, 10–4, 11–4, 12–4, 13–4, 14–4 to 14–5, 14–18, 15–4, 15–8

pregnancy test...4–1, 4–6 to 4–7, 6–17

premature birth...A–8

premature ejaculation...11–5

pressure on bladder, pain from...13–16

primidone...5–7, 6–7, 8–8, 9–10, A–7

procaine penicillin G...16–19

procedures...4–1, 4–4, 4–5, 4–21 to 4–22, A–1

    classification for providing family planning methods...4–22

    developing family planning policy...1–1

    infection prevention...4–10 to 4–12

    providing family planning methods...4–21 to 4–22, 5–10 to 5–11, 6–10, 7–9, 8–12 to 8–13, 9–13 to 9–15, 10–11, 11–8, 12–11 to 12–13, 13–9, 15–8

Progestasert...12–3

progesterone...12–3, A–21

progestin...5–3, 6–3, 7–3, 7–21, 8–3, 8–17, 8–24, 12–3

progestin-only injectables...1–6, 7–1 to 7–21

progestin-only methods...4–13 to 4–18. *See also* DMPA, Norplant implants, progestin-only oral contraceptives.

progestin-only oral contraceptives...1–5, 4–3, 4–6, 4–9, 4–13, 4–15, 4–17, 4–20, 4–22, 5–18, 5–21 to 5–23, 5–27, 6–1 to 6–18, 15–10, 15–12, A–2 to A–8

progestins...A–21

prophylactics...11–3. *See also* condoms.

prostate cancer...10–18

puberty...A–21

puerperal sepsis...12–8, A–8, A–21

pulmonary embolism...9–8, 14–9, A–21

purulent cervicitis...4–17, 9–11, 12–22, A–21

pus...8–15, 8–19, 9–17 to 9–19, 10–13 to 10–16, 12–22, 16–7, 16–12, 16–14, 16–15, A–21

R

radioactive drugs...15–6, A–8

rape...5–21

rash...8–5, 11–11, 11–13 to 11–14, 13–11, 13–13, 13–16, 16–9

rectum...13–16, 16–15, A–21

regret following sterilization...9/10–2

removing Norplant capsules...8–13

reserpine...15–6, A–8

retinopathy...A–21

return of fertility...5–4, 6–9, 7–1, 7–5, 7–8, 7–18, 7–20, 8–1, 8–5, 8–10

return visit...1–3, 3–5 to 3–7, 5–11, 5–16, 6–13, 6–17, 7–4, 7–9, 7–14, 8–16, 9–18, 10–14, 11–12, 12–14, 12–17, 13–9, 13–14, 15–11 to 15–12

reusable needles...4–11, 7–13

reversal, sterilization...9–5, 9–22, 10–6, 10–17

rhythm method...14–13 to 14–14, 14–17. *See also* calendar method.

rifampin, rifampicin...5–7, 5–8, 5–16, 5–18, 6–7, 6–8, 6–13, 8–8, 8–9, 8–16, 9–10, A–7

ring...9–14

risk...9/10–1

rupture of membranes...A–8

S

scalpel...4–12, 10–11

schistosomiasis...5–8, 6–8, 7–7, 8–9, 9–9 to 9–11, 12–9, A–6, A–21

scrotal injury...A–8

scrotal skin infection...10–8, A–8

scrotal surgery...A–8

scrotum...10–3 to 10–6, 10–8, 10–10 to 10–12, 10–15, 16–15, A–21

seizure...5–7, 5–16, 5–18, 6–7, 6–13, 7–4, 8–8, 8–16, 9–10

semen...4–10, 10–4, 10–8, 10–14, 10–17, 10–18, 16–10

sepsis...A–8. *See also* puerperal sepsis.

septic abortion...A–8, A–21

sexual ability...9–20, 10–3, 10–17

sexual behavior...16–8, 16–11

sexual contact...14–16, 14–17, 16–3, 16–10, 16–11

sexual desire...10–15

sexual enjoyment...5–4, 7–4, 8–4, 9–4, 10–5, 11–5, 11–6, 12–5

sexual intercourse...11–8, 11–17, 16–10, 16–11

sexual performance...10–1, 10–12, 10–15

sexual pleasure...10–15

sexual sensation...10–1, 11–1, 11–6, 11–14

sexually transmitted disease...2–1, 3–5, 3–7, 4–6, 4–17, 4–22, 5–5, 5–19, 5–20, 5–24, 5–25, 6–8, 6–16, 7–5, 7–16, 7–19, 7–21, 8–6, 8–9, 8–18, 8–21, 9–5, 9–7, 9–11, 9–19, 10–6, 10–8, 10–9, 10–16, 11–1, 11–4 to 11–9, 11–11 to 11–18, 12–1, 12–6, 12–8, 12–16, 12–17, 12–21, 12–22, 12–25, 12–26, 12–27, 12–28, 13–1, 13–4 to 13–6, 13–17, 13–19, 14–7, 14–9, 14–17, 15–5, 15–14, 16–1 to 16–22, A–4 to A–5, A–8, A–21

shopkeeper...4–3, 5–8, 16–5

shortness of breath...5–6, 7–6

sickle cell crisis...7–4, 8–5, A–21

sickle cell disease...6–8, 7–7, 8–9, 9–10, 10–9, 15–7, A–6, A–21

side effect...3–5, 5–1, 5–4, 5–14, 5–17 to 5–19, 6–5, 6–6, 7–4, 7–5, 7–10, 7–15, 8–5, 8–14 to 8–15, 8–17, 12–6, 12–13, 12–18, 13–6, 16–9

signs of pregnancy...4–7, 6–12, 6–17, 8–15, 9–17, 12–23

skin cream...11–18

skin lotion...11–10

skin rash...8–5, 11–11, 11–13 to 11–14, 13–11, 13–13, 13–16, 16–14. *See also* rash.

smoking...4–14, 4–15, 5–5, 5–6, 5–8, 5–26 to 5–28, 6–8, 7–7, 8–9, 12–9, 14–9, 15–7, A–2, A–17, A–19

soap and water...4–11, 7–12, 8–19, 9–18, 10–15, 11–11

social marketing programs...5–28, 16–5

sores...16–14, 16–15, 16–20

sore nipples...A–8

sore throat...16–14

spectinomycin...16–17

sperm...10–4, 10–5, 10–11, 10–14, 10–18, 11–4, 12–4, 13–4, A–22

sperm duct...10–8

spermatic cord...10–8, A–18, A–22

spermicide...4–5, 4–7, 4–20, 4–22, 5–6, 5–22, 5–24, 6–7, 6–9, 7–6, 7–9, 7–21, 8–8, 8–11, 11–3, 11–8, 11–10 to 11–13, 12–7, 13–1, 13–19, 14–17, 15–11, 16–1, 16–5, 16–6, 16–8, 16–9, A–2 to A–8

spermicide as back-up method–5–7, 5–9, 5–10, 5–11, 5–13, 5–14, 5–18, 6–10, 6–12, 6–17, 7–8, 7–10, 8–10, 15–12, A–13

spinal anesthesia...9–15

spontaneous abortion...*See* miscarriage.

spotting...5–4, 5–14, 5–18, 6–6, 6–12, 6–13 to 6–14, 7–1, 7–5, 7–16, 8–1, 8–5, 8–14, 8–17 to 8–18, 12–6, 12–25, A–22

spring clips...9–21

"standard-dose" oral contraceptives...5–22, 5–23

staphylococcus...4–10, A–22 to A–23

STD–*See* sexually transmitted disease.

STD risk assessment...16–1, 16–6 to 16–7

sterile...4–11, 5–26, 7–12, 7–13, 12–12

sterilize...4–10 to 4–12, 16–11, A–22

stitches...8–12, 8–13, 9–14, 9–16, 9–18, 10–13, 10–14

storing condoms, diaphragm...11–11, 11–15, 13–7

streptococcus...A–23

stroke...4–15, 5–5, 5–6, 5–16, 6–5, 6–14, 7–6, 7–14, 8–20, 9–8, 12–9, 14–8, A–3, A–22

subacute bacterial endocarditis...A–3

sulfamethoxazole...13–15, 16–17, 16–20, 16–21

superficial thrombophlebitis...A–3, A–22

suppository...13–3, 13–10, 13–17, 16–18

surgery...5–7, A–3, A–8

surgical procedure...8–6, 8–12 to 8–13, 9–13 to 9–14, 9/10–1, 10–11

syndrome...A–22

syphilis...4–17, 11–4, 16–3, 16–14, 16–19, A–22

syphilis test...16–22

syringe...4–10 to 4–12, 7–12 to 7–13

systemic infection...9–9, 10–9, A–8

T

TCu–380A...1–5, 4–20, 12–1, 12–3 to 12–5, 12–11, 12–14, 12–23, 12–25, 12–28, A–2 to A–8

tender breasts...*See* breast tenderness.

testes, testicles...10–3, 10–8, 10–17, 16–7, A–22

testis...A–22

tetracycline...16–17 to 16–21

thalassemia...A–6, A–22

thromboembolic disorder...A–3, A–22

thrombophlebitis...A–3, A–22

thrush...15–13

thyroid disease...5–8, 6–8, 7–7, 8–9, 12–9, 15–7, A–6, A–22

thyroid gland...A–22

toxic shock syndrome...13–8, 13–11, 13–13, 13–14, 13–16, 13–18, A–7, A–22

toxin...A–22

training...9–13, 9–23, 10–11, 10–19, 12–12, 12–26

trauma...A–8, A–23

Trichomonas vaginalis...A–23

trichomoniasis...16–13, 16–18, A–23

tricyclic anti-depressants...14–9, A–7

trimethoprim...16–17, 16–20, 16–21

trocar...4–12

trophoblast, trophoblast disease...A–6, A–23

tubal abscess...12–21

tubal ligation...9–3, 9–4

tuberculosis...4–18, 5–8, 6–8, 7–7, 8–9, 9–11, 12–9, 16–10, A–7, A–23

tying the tubes...9–3, A–19

Tylenol®...9–16, 9–19, 10–12, 10–16. *See also* acetaminophen, paracetamol.

U

umbilical hernia...A–8

uncircumcised...11–9, 16–13

undescended testes...10–8

unintended pregnancy...2–1, 4–19, A–2, A–4, A–6

United States Food and Drug Administration...7–21, 12–28

upset stomach...5–1, 5–19

urinary tract infection...13–6, 13–14, 13–15, 13–18, A–5

urination...12–8, 13–6, 13–15, 16–7, 16–12, 16–13

urine sugar...4–22

uterine cavity...A–5, A–7

uterine elevator...9–13

uterine evacuation...7–17, 8–18

uterine fibroids...5–8, 6–8, 7–4, 7–7, 8–9, 9–8, 14–9, 15–7, A–5, A–7, A–23

uterine involution...A–8

uterine perforation...9–7, A–8

uterine rupture...9–7, A–8

uterine sound...4–12, 12–13

uterus...9–13, 9–20, 12–1, 12–3, 12–4, 12–10, 12–12, 12–13, 12–26, 13–8, 13–9, A–4, A–8, A–23

V

vaginal abrasions...A–5

vaginal bleeding...3–8, 4–17, 5–1, 5–17 to 5–18, 6–1, 6–14, 6–16, 7–1, 7–7, 7–10, 7–17, 7–19, 8–1, 8–8, 8–18, 8–21, 9–7, 9–11, 9–17, 9–19, 12–7, 12–9, 12–20, 14–8, 16–12, A–3, A–4, A–6

vaginal discharge...*See* discharge, vaginal.

vaginal exam...4–11

vaginal infection...14–1, 14–7, 14–9, 14–17, A–5

vaginal intercourse...14–4, 14–12, 14–16, 14–17, 16–10

vaginal itching...*See* itching.

vaginal lesion...13–16

vaginal lubricant...13–19

vaginal lubrication...11–18, 13–5

vaginal method...4–6, 4–9, 5–25, 13–1 to 13–19

vaginal secretions...4–10

vaginal speculum...4–12, 12–12

vaginal tear...A–8

vaginal wetness...11–18, 14–17

vaginal yeast cream...13–19

vaginitis...4–17, 9–11, 13–16, A–5, A–23

valproic acid...5–18, A–7

valvular heart disease...4–15, 6–8, 7–7, 8–9, 9–8, 15–7, A–3, A–23

varicocele...10–8, A–8, A–23

varicose veins...5–8, 6–8, 7–7, 8–9, 9–11, 12–9, 14–9, 15–7, A–3, A–23

vas, vas deferens...10–11, A–16, A–23

vasa...A–23

vascular disease...4–15, 5–8, 7–18, 9–8, 9–10, A–2, A–3, A–23

vasectomy...3–2, 3–5, 4–4, 4–9, 4–13, 4–20, 4–22, 9–3, 9–5, 9–22, 10–1 to 10–19, A–2 to A–8, A–23

Vaseline®...11–10, 11–15, 13–19

vegetable oil...13–19

viral hepatitis...4–18, 5–7, 6–7, 7–6, 8–7, 9–9, 14–9, 15–6, 15–11, A–5

vitamin C...13–15

voluntary surgical contraception...9–3

vomiting...4–7, 5–10, 5–14, 5–18, 5–23, 13–16, 16–9, 16–18

vulva...13–15, A–23

W

wall chart...1–4

waste...4–10, 4–12

weakness...5–27, 9–20, 10–17, 11–16

weight...4–7, 8–23, 9–15

weight gain...5–4, 6–5, 7–1, 7–5, 7–10, 7–19, 8–5

WHO...*See* World Health Organization.

withdrawal...14–1, 14–4, 14–5, 14–10 to 14–14, 14–17

woman-controlled method...11–7, 13–1, 13–4, 13–5, 13–17, 13–19

World Health Organization...1–6, 1–7, 4–13, 7–20, 7–21, 9–6, 10–7, 15–15, A–1 to A–8

Y

yeast–like fungus...A–14

Illustration Credits

Page 6–5: Bolivia National Reproductive Health Program, IEC Subcommission

Page 7–12: Johns Hopkins Population Communication Services

Page 8–11: template: Wyeth-Ayerst; photo: JHPIEGO

Page 8–13: JHPIEGO

Page 9–15: Johns Hopkins Population Communication Services

Page 10–3: AVSC International

Page 10–6: Hatcher, R.A., et al. Family planning methods and practice: Africa. Atlanta, US DHHS, CDC, 1983.

Page 11–7: The Female Health Company

Page 11–9: Asociación Demográfica Salvadoréna

Page 11–10: left: Asociación Demográfica Salvadoréna; right: Asociación Hondureña de Planificación de Familia

Page 14–11: Georgetown University Institute for Reproductive Health

Page 15–10: left: WHO; right: World Bank

Production Credits

Supervision: Stephen M. Goldstein and Linda D. Sadler, Population Information Program, Center for Communication Programs, Johns Hopkins University School of Public Health

Design and typesetting: Greg Dayman, Christina Whittington, and Mary Pat Peabody, Prographics

Printing: Braceland Printing

How to Obtain More Copies of
The Essentials of Contraceptive Technology

The Essentials of Contraceptive Technology in English, Spanish, and French is available *free of charge* to health care professionals and programs in developing countries, USAID Collaborating Agencies, and other organizations working to promote reproductive health in developing countries. For developed-country orders, the price is US$5 per copy, postage and handling included. (Developed-country orders should be sent to the Population Information Program at the address below. Please pay with order.)

Only for those in the regions or countries listed, please send orders for 52 copies or fewer to one of the addresses listed under each country. (For orders of 52 copies, see below.)

If you want more than 52 copies, or you are unable to obtain copies from one of the distributors listed, please write to the Population Information Program (see below) or complete the Internet order form at http//:www.jhuccp.org/ect/ectorder.stm (With requests for multiple copies, please describe the intended users—for example, "auxiliary nurse-midwives in MOH clinics.")

Population Information Program
Johns Hopkins Center for Communication Programs
111 Market Place, Suite 310
Baltimore, Maryland 21202, USA
Fax: 1-410-659-6266
E-mail: orders@jhuccp.org